The Amateur's Mind

Other books by Jeremy Silman

The Exchange Variation of the Slav with John Donaldson (1994)
Gambits in the Slav with John Donaldson (1994)
Winning Chess Strategy with Yasser Seirawan (1994)
Winning with the Caro-kann Defense (1993)
Winning Chess Tactics with Yasser Seirawan (1993)
How To Reassess Your Chess, 3rd Edition (1993)*
Essential Chess Endings Explained Move by Move, Volume One (1992)
Winning With the Sicilian Defense (1991)
How To Get Better At Chess with Larry Evans and Betty Roberts (1991)*
The Accelerated Dragon Sicilian with John Donaldson (1991)
The Neo-Sveshnikov (1991)
The Classical Dragon with John Donaldson (1991)
Play Winning Chess with Yasser Seirawan (1990)
The Dynamic Caro-Kann (1989)*
The Dutch Defense with Larry Christiansen (1988)
The Semi-Slav, Non Meran Lines with John Donaldson (1988)*
A Complete Black Repertoire (1986)
The Endgame: Move by Move (1985)
Accelerated Dragon (1984)
Nimzo-Indian for Black (1984)
French Defense for Black (1984)
Caro-Kann for Black (1984)
1983 U.S. Championship with Larry Christiansen (1983)
Center Counter with John Grefe (1983)

*Pubished by Summit Publishing

The Amateur's Mind

Turning Chess Misconceptions Into Chess Mastery

IM Jeremy Silman

SUMMIT PUBLISHING
Los Angeles

First Summit Publishing Edition

ISBN: 0-945806-13-2

Cover design by Heidi Frieder

Printed and bound in the United States of America

SUMMIT PUBLISHING

Contents

Introduction

Every chess student dreams of finding the perfect teacher—someone who magically knows what's going on in the student's mind and is able to surgically remove the flaws contained there. Unfortunately, this doesn't happen in reality. The well-meaning master looks at the student's games, asks questions, and gives pat answers to the problems that appear before his eyes.

While this is a good technique, I often wondered what would happen if a teacher could really get inside the student's head. To accomplish this, I played games with my students (always starting them off with a good position), had them talk out loud before they made a move and after I made mine, and wrote down their thoughts. To my amazement, I was soon seeing problems that I never imagined they possessed.

To add to this, I also had them annotate a series of Grandmaster games. Their responses to the Grandmaster's moves and plans showed me which concepts they were able to understand and which ones were absent from their make-up.

The Amateur's Mind is the result of these sessions. It is a road map of typical thinking errors that turn out to be reflections of *your own* thoughts as much as they are the thoughts of the people that originally shared them with me.

Within these pages you will find much of interest: easy-to-understand rules and recommendations, new strategies, surprising insights; all designed to help you eradicate the "chessic" doubts and fears that reside within you. Study this information carefully and spend some time thinking about it. Hopefully, it will be your first step in turning the chess misconceptions that you've owned for so long into the chess mastery that you have always dreamed of attaining.

PART ONE

The Imbalances

The heart of my system of training is based on an understanding of imbalances. By recognizing the different imbalances (i.e. any type of difference) in a given position, a player of virtually any strength can understand what his responsibilities are towards that position with relative ease.

By way of illustration, let's take a look at the position in diagram #1.

Dzindzichashvili–Yermolinsky
U.S. Championship, Long Beach 1994

(1)

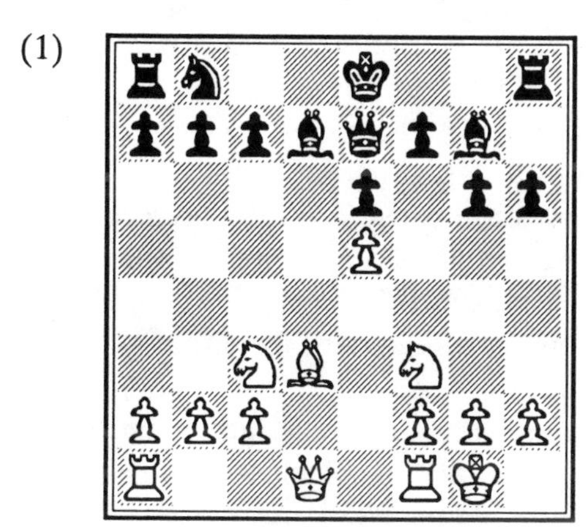

White to play.

What is going on here? Most players would either look at the position in a misty stupor or calculate move after move without really knowing what the respective plans are. However, an aquaintance with the list of imbalances would make things much easier:

List of Imbalances

1) *Superior Minor Piece* (the interplay between Bishops and Knights).
2) *Pawn Structure* (a broad subject that encompasses doubled pawns, isolated pawns, etc.).
3) *Space* (the annexation of territory on a chess board).
4) *Material* (owning pieces of greater value than the opponent's).
5) *Control of a key file or square* (files and diagonals act as pathways for your pieces, while squares act as homes).
6) *Lead in development* (more force in a specific area of the board).
7) *Initiative* (dictating the tempo of a game).

A complete explanation of these factors can be found in my book *How to Reassess Your Chess* (third edition). However, the basic idea of this system is to pick out these imbalances in a position and play to make the different aspects of your game triumph over his. With this in mind, let's take another look at diagram #1. Instead of just looking for a move (as we might have done previously), this time we will list all the imbalances that exist here: Material is even. White has a space advantage due to his advanced pawn on e5. However, this very pawn can also come under attack by ...Bc6, ...Nd7, and ...Qc5. There are no other weak pawns on the board for either side. White has a lead in development but the center is not completely open so it is hard to take advantage of this factor. Perhaps the most important thing to notice is Black's possession of the two Bishops. If White's pawn were not on e5 then the dark-squared Bishop would sweep across the board. This pawn advanced to curtail the Bishop's activity but in doing so it set itself up as a target.

These factors make the goals of both sides relatively easy to understand. White must defend his e5 pawn and find a way to advance his Knights and make them active. Black will play to keep the enemy Knights at bay (Steinitz said that the way to beat Knights is to take away all their advanced support points) and to tie White's pieces down to the defense of the e5 pawn. Since Black threatens to place his pieces on ideal squares with ...Bc6 (eyeing f3—one of the defenders of e5) followed by ...Nd7 (attacking e5), White lashes out in an effort to prevent Black from carrying out his ideas. **1.Nb5** Placing the Knight on an active square. Now Black must guard c7. How should he do this? 1...Na6 would show that Black has lost sight of his goal of putting pressure on e5—a Knight on a6 would no longer be able to go after the White pawn. Not wanting to be distracted from his desires against e5, Black simply takes the Knight and ends White's threats once and for all. **1...Bxb5! 2.Bxb5+ c6 3.Bc4 Nd7** So White was unable to make a dent in the Black position while the second player is still following his original idea of attacking e5. **4.Qd4 Qc5!** Many people don't like to trade Queens too early; they feel it is a wimpy thing to do. However, Black realizes that his goal is not to attack the enemy King. Nor does it have anything to do with other things that might require the retention of the Queens. By swapping the ladies, Black insures the safety of his own King and gets rid of a White piece that could defend e5. **5.Qxc5 Nxc5 6.Rad1 Rxd1 7.Rxd1 Ke7** and Black was better and tortured his opponent for a long time. Why is Black better? Because there are two big imbalances here: opposite colored Bishops and a target on e5. White has nothing to attack at all. There is no way he can put pressure on the Black position. However, Black can tie White down to the defense of the e-pawn. To add fuel to this fire, Black's Bishop is an active participant in the assault on this important pawn. White's Bishop is unable to defend this pawn and is not really doing much of anything else either. Thus the two imbalances are both in Black's favor. The following moves (played in the actual game) show that this assessment is valid: **8.h4 Rd8 9.Re1 a5 10.b3 a4 11.g4 Nd7 12.Kg2 Nb6 13.Ke3 Ra8 14.Nd2 axb3 15.Bxb3 Rd8 16.Nf3 Nd7 17.Kf4 Ra8 18.Re2 Ra5** and White was completely tied down to the defense of his e-pawn. Black went on to score a long, tough victory.

I would like to mention that I received a letter in April of

1993 from an irate subscriber of *Chess Life* magazine in which I was accused of offering inappropriate information to the readership. He complained that weak players in the 'E' through 'B' categories are not able to understand subtle things about minor pieces and weak pawns, adding that they can hardly see a mate in one! I think this is completely untrue. After giving a student the basic mating patterns and strategies you must begin feeding them advanced concepts. At first these ideas will not make sense, many players will have a vague idea of what you are talking about but nothing more. Even a fragmented understanding of these concepts will prove useful though, and eventually they will improve as these lessons are assimilated by repetition and example.

To prove this statement, I offer the following story. One of my students is a six-year-old girl with a rating of approximately 900. I would go through her tournament games, offer advice, and occasionally throw her concepts that would seem to be for much older and more sophisticated players. One day we were looking at a game she had played when I noticed that she had reached a complicated Rook and pawn endgame. To my delight, she moved her Rook to the seventh rank and began taking her opponent's pawns. "Rooks are strong on the seventh rank!" she said. A little while later she moved it away from the seventh. "Why did you retreat your Rook?" I asked. Looking at me like I was an idiot, she answered, "I'm putting it behind this passed pawn—Rooks should always be placed behind passed pawns!"

Let the gentleman who wrote me that letter take note. If a six-year-old girl can make use of such advanced concepts, then why can't adults with much higher ratings do the same?

PART TWO

The Battle Between Bishops and Knights

The seemingly insignificant difference between Bishops and Knights is actually one of the most important imbalances on the chessboard. What gives this even more weight is the fact that most players are not aware of this importance, thereby giving a student of the imbalances a huge advantage.

Rules concerning the war between minor pieces:

1) The point count system awards a net worth of three points to each piece, though the occasional book will give the nod to the Bishop with a whopping three and a half. Make no mistake about the respective values: they are completely equal. Either is fully capable of beating the other—it all depends on what you do with them, the pawn structure, and the other pieces.

(2)

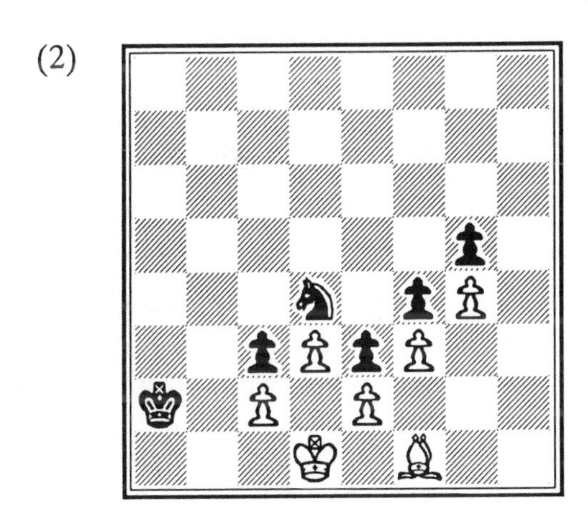

White to play.

A book can claim that a Bishop deserves a point count value

of three and a half all it wants—a simple glance at diagram #2 will show that the Black Knight is so superior to the entombed White piece that Black is virtually up material. After **1.Kc1 Ka1 2.Kd1 Kb2** Black wins easily. Bishops and Knights start out as equals. You are the one who makes them better than their counterparts.

2) Bishops are best in open positions where pawns don't block their diagonals. For example, the type of central situation that comes about after **1.e4 e5 2.d4 exd4 3.c3 dxc3 4.Bc4 cxb2 5.Bxb2** is just the sort of situation that Bishops thrive on since the the wide open diagonals allow the Bishops to reach their full potential.

3) Bishops are very strong in endgames where both sides have passed pawns that are dashing to their respective queening squares. The long-range capabilities of a Bishop make it much superior to the slow Knight in such situations.

(3)

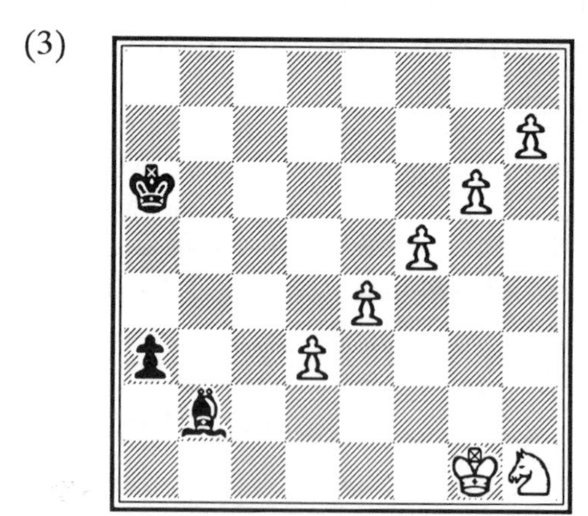

White to play.

This position is a bit over the top but illustrates point #3 extremely well. The Bishop sits on b2, far away from the queening square of the White h-pawn, and not only stops it from promoting but also prevents all the other White pawns from moving. In the meantime the lone Black pawn on a3 cannot be stopped because the ponderous Knight is unable to get over to the queenside in time.

4) The term "bad Bishop" means that your Bishop is situated on the same color as your center pawns. If you have

such a Bishop you usually want to do one of three things:

4.a) Trade it off for a piece of equal value.

4.b) Get the pawns off the color of your Bishop.

4.c) Get the Bishop outside the pawn chain. It will still be bad by definition, but it will also be active. A bad Bishop can be a strong piece!

(4)

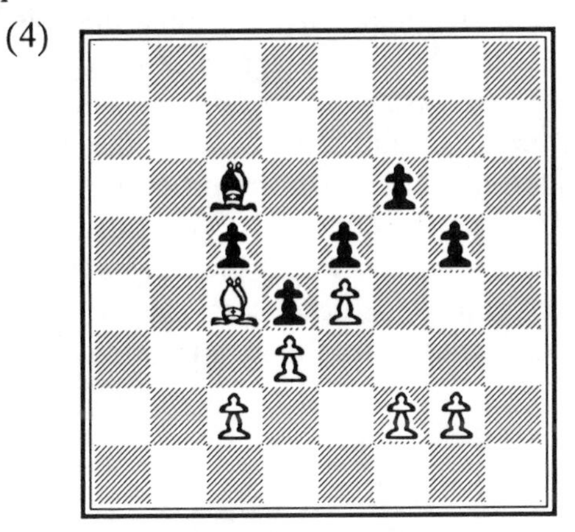

White to play.

White's Bishop on c4 is bad but active since it resides outside the pawn chain. Even though it has the stigma of "bad" assigned to it, it is still a very strong piece. If it stood on e2 it would be very inactive and fully deserving of the name "bad." The black Bishop on c6 is considered to be a good Bishop but

(5)

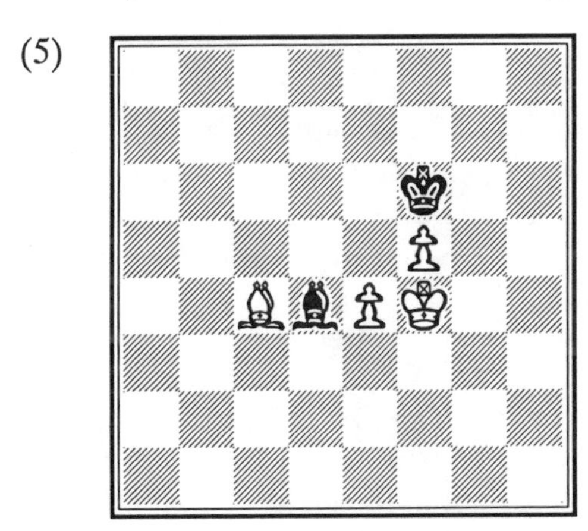

White to play.

it is not nearly as active as its White counterpart. This example shows us that the terms good and bad are useful for basic definition, but don't take them too literally!

5) A Bishop's weakness is that it is stuck on one color for the whole game. Anything resting on the other color is safe from its attention. Two Bishops work together very well since they control both colored diagonals, thereby negating this flaw.

White is two pawns ahead in diagram #5 but he can't win since his Bishop is useless—it is not able to chase the Black King away from e5 or f6 and it can't help the White pawns advance. Give White another Bishop on f2 and Black another on d7 and we will see a different result. Now both colors can be controlled and **1.Bh4+ Kg7 2.e5** sets the pawns in motion.

6) Knights love closed positions with locked pawns. Their ability to jump over other pieces makes them very valuable in such situations.

In diagram #6, Black's Knight is stongly posted on c5 where

(6)

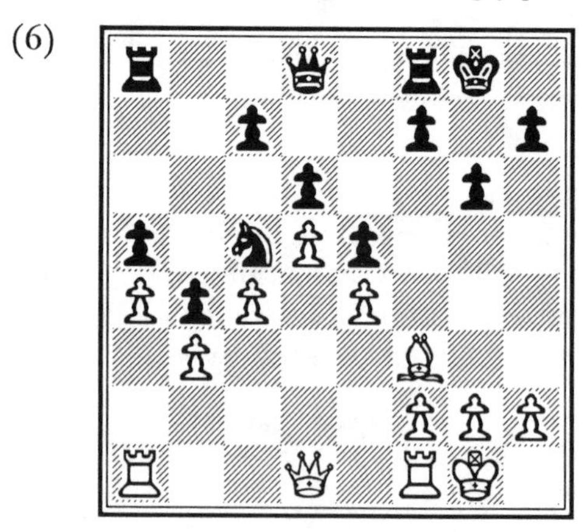

it is safe from attack and eyes the enemy pawns on b3 and e4. White's Bishop is hampered by all the center pawns which block it and make it a passive piece.

7) Knights usually stand better in the middle of the board. One old chess saying goes: A Knight on the rim is dim. There are two reasons for this: The first is that a Knight on one side's rim must make several moves to reach an endangered area on the other wing. A Knight in the middle can jump to either side at will. The other reason for this distrust of the rim is that a

(7)

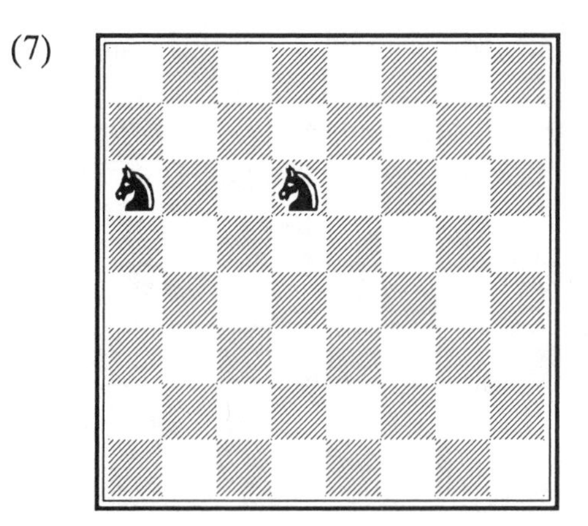

Knight simply controls fewer squares there.

In diagram #7, the Knight on a6 only controls four squares (b8, c7, c5, and b4) and must make three moves to reach the kingside. The Knight on d6 controls eight squares and can reach either wing in one hop.

8) Since Knights are not long-range pieces, they need to have secure, advanced homes to be effective. These homes are called <u>support points</u>. In the previous diagram the Black Knight rested on the c5 support point. Other possible support points (if he could reach them) would be c3 and d4. Note that a square like f4 is not a support point since White could easily chase an intruding Knight away by g2-g3. In general, a Knight would like to find itself as far up the board as possible:

8.a) Knights are not effective on the first rank. Here they act in a purely defensive role.

8.b) A Knight stuck on the second rank is also defensive, and is considered to be inferior to a Bishop.

8.c) A Knight on the third rank serves many defensive functions and is ready to jump further up the board at a moment's notice.

8.d) A Knight securely placed on the fourth rank is considered to be fully equal to a Bishop.

8.e) A Knight on the fifth is a powerful attacking unit and is usually stronger than a Bishop.

8.f) A Knight reaches its potential on the sixth rank. Here it eats most other pieces alive and the defender is often happy to sacrifice a Rook for the offending Knight and the pawn that protected it.

8.g) A Knight on the last two ranks offers diminishing returns since it does not control as many squares as it does on the sixth.

(8)

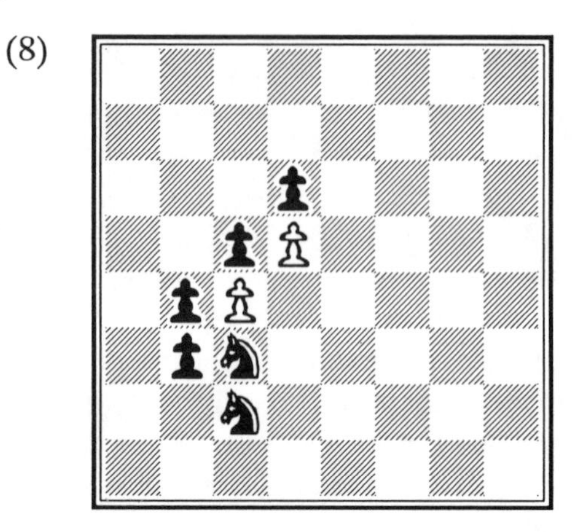

In diagram #8, the Knight on c3 attacks eight squares deep in the enemy camp. The Knight on c2 only controls six squares.

9) Knights are superior to Bishops in an endgame if all the pawns are on one side of the board. This is because the Bishop's long-range powers no longer have meaning while the Knight's ability to go to either color square means that there is no safe haven for the enemy King or pawns. This is illustrated

(9)

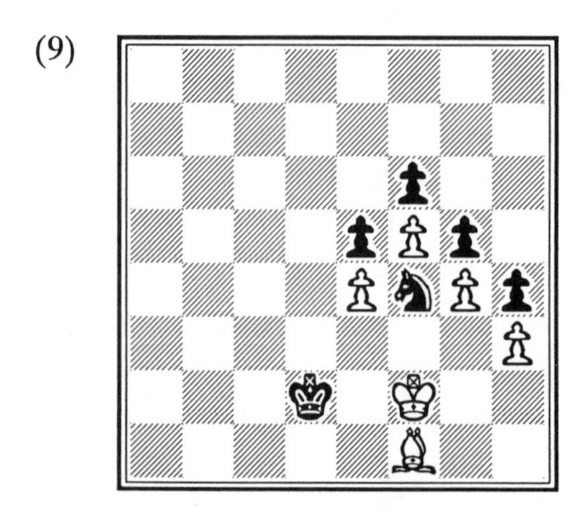

White to play.

in diagram #9.

The White Bishop cannot come into contact with the Black King, Knight, or pawns. In the meantime, the White pawns on e4 and h3 are vulnerable to the combined attack of the enemy King and Knight.

10) The first official World Chess Champion, Wilhelm Steinitz, pioneered work on the minor pieces. He stated that the way to beat enemy Knights was to deprive them of any advanced support points. Then they would be inactive and inferior to Bishops. The reverse, of course, is that if you possess Knights you must strive as hard as you can to create support points for them.

The Amateur's Mind

The first position that we will consider came about after the moves **1.d4 Nf6 2.c4 e6 3.g3 d5 4.Bg2 dxc4 5.Qa4+ Bd7 6.Qxc4 Bc6 7.Nf3 Bd5 8.Qd3 Be4 9.Qd1 c5 10.Nc3 Bc6 11.0-0 Nbd7 12.Qc2 cxd4 13.Nxd4 Bxg2 14.Kxg2 Bc5 15.Rd1 0-0 16.e4 Qe7 17.Qe2 Bxd4 18.Rxd4 e5 19.Rd1 Nb6.** This led to the position in diagram #10.

Silman-Gross, American Open 1992

(10)

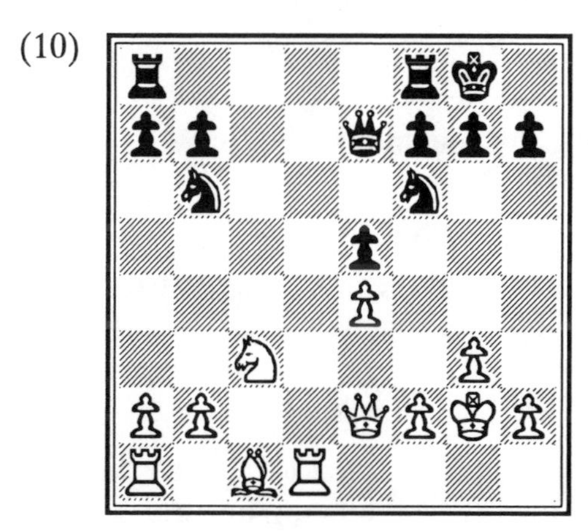

White to play.

What's going on in this seemingly boring position? The pawn structure is more or less symmetrical, nobody can lay claim to any space advantage, all the pieces are well defended and neither King is in any trouble. Aside from the fact that White's pieces are more aggressively posted since they are trying to take control of d5 while Black's Knights are trying to defend that square, the one major imbalance is a minor piece difference: White has a Bishop and Knight vs. two Knights.

In the game White will use Steinitz's rule (to make Knights ineffective you must take away all their advanced support points) and try to restrict the Knight on b6 by b3 and a4-a5. He will also place the Bishop on the flexible e3 square and move his Queen to b5 where it eyes the pawns on b7 and e5. All these things are small in themselves but together they add up to unpleasant pressure on the Black position.

20.Be3 Rfd8

On 20...Qb4 White would have played the bothersome 21.Bg5.

21.Qb5!

Making each of his pieces better than their Black counterparts. White's Queen is obviously superior to Black's lady on e7, his c3-Knight (ready to leap into d5 at a moment's notice) is more aggressively posted than either Black jumper, and his Bishop defends d4 and is constantly threatening to chop on b6.

21...Qe6 22.b3

Simply keeping the Knight out of c4.

22...h6

Black should have tried the more aggressive 22...h5! intending to advance to h4 with some kingside threats.

23.a4 Rxd1 24.Rxd1 Rc8 25.Rd3 Qc6?

Jack Peters recommended 25...Rc7 26.a5 Nc8. This holds onto his material for the time being but Black's position still remains quite unpleasant.

26.Qxe5 Re8 27.Qd6 Nxe4

Now Black loses by force.

28.Qxc6 bxc6 29.a5! Nxc3

Black would also lose a pawn after 29...Nd5 30.Nxd5. Even worse is 29...Nc8 30.Nxe4 Rxe4 31.Rd8+ picking up a piece.

30.axb6 Nd5 31.bxa7 1-0

Black's case is hopeless. For example, 31...Ra8 32.Rxd5! cxd5 33.b4 followed by b5-b6-b7.

How would an amateur handle White's position from the diagram? Would a student of mine, trained to recognize the imbalances that exist in this position, see and make use of them or would he miss everything and just look at random moves? This question interested me and so I asked some of my students to play me from the diagram in question. They were told to think out loud, which enabled me to write down their thoughts and see just what, if anything, was wrong with their methods of thinking.

Of course, I didn't expect my students to play as I did. White's play is rather subtle and is not something that a class player would ordinarily come up with. However, I did hope that they would notice the Bishop vs. Knight imbalance and try to make something of it. Instead, though, I found that my students (with one exception), after noting that this imbalance was present, refused to try to turn it into something significant. Why? Does the average class player think that a simple Bishop vs. Knight difference is very little to work with? Do they think that such things are unimportant (even though I constantly tell them that Bishop vs. Knight is extremely important)? Let's see if the following games can shed some light on these questions.

Wh: 1000 vs. Bl: J.S.

1000: White's King is a bit open so I prefer Black's position. Black's e-pawn is potentially weak, though. The main imbalance is Bishop vs. Knight and, at the moment, I have control of a file. I would now like to develop my pieces. I'd like to get

(11)

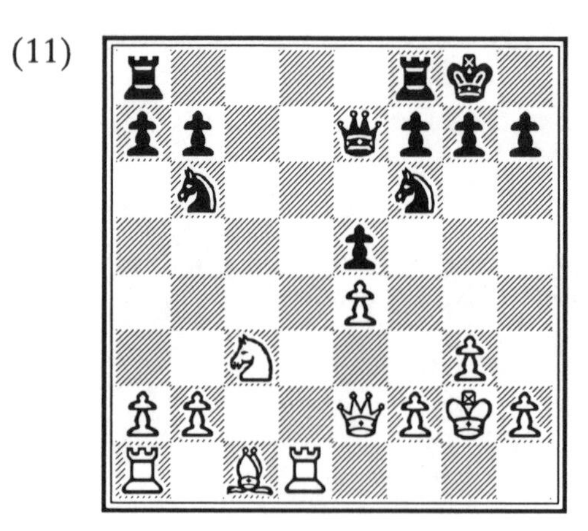

White to play.

my Knight to d5, so Bg5 gives me more control of that post. However, his b6 Knight also controls d5 and I don't know if I really want to give up my dark-squared Bishop. Maybe a3 followed by b4 and Bb2 is good since that adds new pressure to e5.

JS: In our next two games both White players will not question giving up their Bishop for the enemy Knight. 1000 deserves praise for thinking that his Bishop should be retained. Unfortunately, the plan he does come up with is bad because it fails to use the Steinitz rule (Take squares away from Knights). Instead he gives the inactive Black Knight on b6 a wonderful post on c4!

20.a3 Rfd8

1000: I'm not terribly worried about the trade so I'll keep going with my plan.

21.b4 Rxd1

1000: I don't want to move my Knight backwards so my move is forced.

22.Qxd1 Rc8

1000: With Qf3 I advance and eye e4 and c3.

JS: He hasn't noticed that Black is jumping on the c4 square. Avoid creating holes in your own position!

23.Qf3 Qc7

1000: I will guard the Knight and free my Rook.

JS: Poor 1000 doesn't realize it, but he is back to his old pattern of reacting to his opponent's moves. This is a bit unfair since he starts out with a good breakdown of the imbalances and looks for an aggressive way to continue. Why do things turn out so badly for him, then? He doesn't take his opponent's possibilities into serious consideration. In other words, he will create a weakness and not realize that it might be used against him.

24.Bd2 Nc4

1000: I can't let you take on d2.

JS: He tried 25.Qd3 but I pointed out it loses a piece after 25...Nxd2.

25.Be1 Rd8

1000: I can play 25.Nb5 to put pressure on his Queen and advance the Knight. It's dumb, though. He's much farther forward than me and I don't like his c4 Knight. I can go to c1 and get ready for a fork or skewer. Unfortunately that would hang my a3-pawn. I'll play h4 and hope to chase his Knight on f6 away with a later g4-g5. Then the d5-square might become available.

JS: Unable to find a solution to his problems on the queenside, he lashes out on the other side of the board.

26.h4 Qc6

1000: What is he up to? My e4-pawn is well defended. He's protecting f6 again, which means maybe he's intending g6. I can't move my Rook due to my a3 pawn so I'll play for more time.

JS: Note how White is coming up with all kinds of esoteric rubbish to explain his opponent's moves. He should be able to figure out their significance by working out how they relate to the positive imbalances in Black's position.

Here Black is simply defending the b5 and d5 squares and putting more pressure on the e4 pawn. He is also giving his Queen the option of going to e6 in some circumstances.

27.b5

JS: A one-move attack that simply chases the Queen to a good post on e6.

27...Qe6

1000: I'll get my a-pawn to safety by advancing it to a4.

28.a4 Rd4

1000: Guarding his c4 Knight. I'll play Ne2 and attack his Rook.

29.Ne2??

—and I stopped the game since White hung his e-pawn.

I hope the reader won't think me overly harsh for my comments in this game. I was not criticizing the man, just the player and his erroneous thinking processes. He does some things extremely well but if he wants to advance in the rating system he will have to accept my literary lashings and iron out these problems.

1600 vs. J.S.

(12)

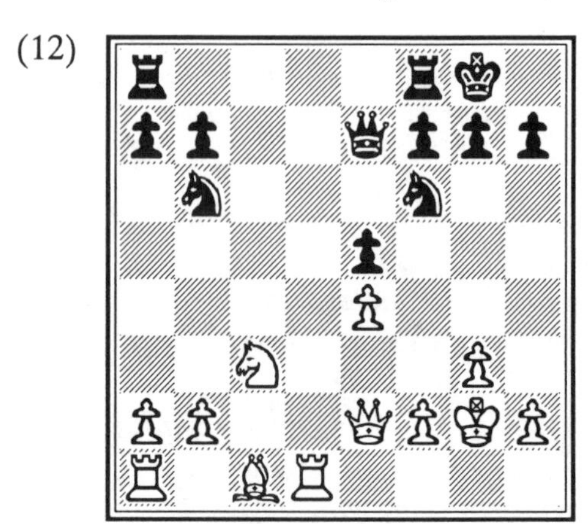

White to play.

1600: I like 20.Nd5. If he takes, I get a strong passed pawn. I have to get my Bishop into play. So f4 and if he takes I go Bxf4 is a possibility. However, my King would then be open. I could also play Qb5 to support the d5-square and the Nd5. I could also pin by Bg5 to control d5 more.

JS: I told him that he was not breaking the position down into imbalances. Instead he is just looking at a bunch of moves.

20.Bg5

1600: This also connects my Rooks and develops my Bishop.

JS: He never recognized his Bishop for Knight advantage so it's not possible for him to try to make use of it.

20...Rfd8 21.Rxd8+ Rxd8

1600: Now Rd1 to trade Rooks allows me to continue my fight for the d5 square.

JS: Though he has not done things in the way that I have suggested to him, to his credit he is following a reasonable idea (domination of d5 or the creation of a passed pawn) with admirable determination.

22.Rd1 h6 23.Rxd8+ Qxd8

1600: I will exchange so I can have d5 and the center.

24.Bxf6 Qxf6

1600: Now I will try to get a passed pawn.

25.Nd5 Qd6

1600: Now I will support my Knight and eye e8.

26.Qb5! Kf8 27.Nxb6

1600: This gives him doubled pawns.

JS: At the moment his Knight is superior to Black's, so why should he swap it without getting the passed pawn that he so desperately wanted? One must avoid dumping a plan for baubles lying on the side of the road.

27...axb6

1600: Now I will trade Queens since he has a doubled pawn and my King is closer to the center.

JS: I don't know why he thought that his King was closer to the center. It's clear that the opposite is true.

28.Qd5??

JS: White has played a reasonable game and the correct result would have been a draw. Instead he rushes into a lost King and pawn endgame. He didn't realize that a passed pawn can be a target if it doesn't have support.

28...Qxd5 29.exd5 Ke7 30.Kf3 f5 31.g4 g6

—and White lost the d5-pawn and the game.

1200 vs. J.S.

(13)

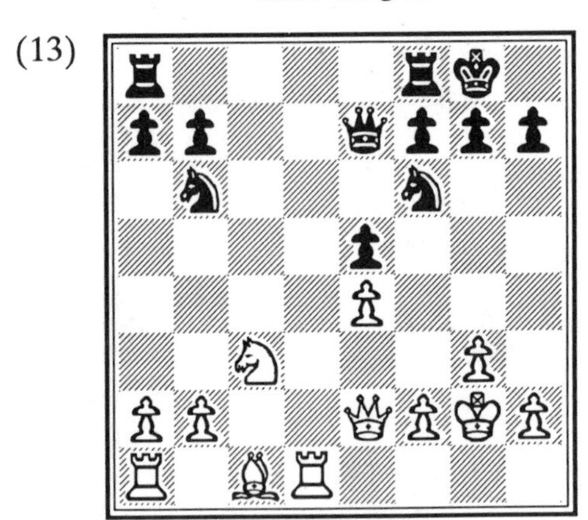

White to play.

1200: At first glance I see that Black's Queen is undefended. White has Bishop and Knight vs. two Knights. My Bishop has to move to complete development. So that would be one of my first considerations. I also control d5 so I could move my Knight to d5 attacking his Queen. This would also allow me to occupy both open files.

JS: 1200 noted the Bishop vs. Knight difference but made no attempt to use it.

20.Bg5

1200: I really like this move.

20...h6

1200: Putting the question to my Bishop. If I take his Knight and play Rac1 I could grab both files. I think this is a good idea. After Bxf6 if he takes with the pawn I've got a check.

21.Bxf6 Qxf6

1200: Now I'll advance to d5 and attack his Queen.

22.Nd5 Nxd5

1200: Now I'll take with the Rook and double up on the open d-file.

JS: Notice how he is jumping back and forth between a few ideas. One second he is trying to control d5. Then he is hoping to play on both open files. Finally he is going to double on the d-file. His thoughts are scattered and things only work out because he started with a solid position and trading a bunch of pieces did nothing to hurt him.

23.Rxd5 Qe6

1200: Black is piling up on my Rook. Now I can place all three of my pieces on that d-file.

JS: Black plays a planless, passive game (a really stupid way to play chess) and waits to see how White will react.

24.Rad1 f6

1200: Now he's lined up his Queen and King on the a2-g8 diagonal, which is alarming. If 25.Qc4 I don't have any threats. How can I get to that King? I can play Rd6 and chase him and if he leaves the diagonal I could check him on c4. However he has ...Qf7, when the diagonal is still defended. My original plan was to place all my pieces on the file. He could challenge me with ...Rd8 while I do this. I'm looking at Qh5 followed by Rd6 'cause he can't push the g-pawn so my Queen is safe. If 25.Qh5 Qf7 26.Qxf7+ Rxf7 is an even exchange, but it weakens his back rank.

JS: White should see that Black can't challenge on the d-file since White would chop anything that dared to step there. White is also unaware that any move of the Rook on d5 would hang the pawn on a2.

25.Qh5 Rac8

1200: Now he's threatening to bring his Rook down to the seventh rank and attack my pawn. So, 26.Rd6 Qf7 27.Qxf7+ Rxf7. If I could only get his Rook off of f8 and my Rook onto d7.

JS: We had just discussed double attacks so I was secretly creating a situation where the possibility for such an attack would exist.

26.Rd6 Qxa2

1200: I saw that but I didn't think he would take it. I guess I thought he had to defend with ...Qf7. Now I have to worry about my b2-pawn. If I move my Rook to d7 then ...Qxb2 is met by Qg6 and I may mate him.

27.Rd7

1200: This gives me a double attack on g7 and b7.

27...b6

1200: Protecting his pawns. I'll follow through with my plan.

28.Qg6?

JS: A quick move usually means a missed opportunity. He missed the winning 28.Qg4! with a double attack on g7 and c8. If 28...Rf7 29.Rxf7 picks up the c8-Rook. 28...g5 would also lose to 29.Qf5.

28...Rf7

1200: I'm in a bad endgame so Rxf7 is no help since his other Rook gets into play after 29.Rxf7 Qxf7 30.Qxf7+ Kxf7 31.Rd7+ Kg6 32.Rxa7 Rc2.

29.Rd8+ Rxd8 30.Rxd8+ Rf8

1200: If Rxf8+ Kxf8 is good for Black. I've got a lost

endgame but what can I do about it?

31.Rxf8+??

JS: What a strange move! He just said this was bad and then he does it anyway. I suspect this was due to too much respect for his opponent. Natural, obvious, and best is 31.Rd7 Rf7 32.Rd8+ Rf8 33.Rd7, leading to a draw.

If his opponent were lower rated then he would almost certainly look for a better move. If you suffer from this fear-of-the-opponent syndrome you should refrain from looking at your opponent's rating until after the game.

31...Kxf8

—and I stopped the game.

Lessons From These Games:

1) The imbalance of Bishop vs. Knight is of vital importance. If you have the Bishop you must strive to take away all the advanced posts from the enemy Knight. If you have the Knight you must fight to create a good home for the horse and to create situations where the Bishop is not particularly useful.

2) Bishop vs. Knight does not necessarily favor one piece or the other; you must plant the seeds which allow your piece to prosper. The same holds good for all the other imbalances. If you don't recognize and use it, you will find that this so-called advantage won't do you any good.

3) You must take your opponents' possibilities into account!

4) Don't ever play a quick, thoughtless move. That will usually turn out to be the move that ruins your game.

As interesting as I found the position that arose in Silman-Gross, I realize that some may find it dull. It *is* a quiet position and *does* require a subtle understanding to make anything of White's chances. Perhaps this type of chess does not allow us to fairly assess the average class player. Perhaps a more dynamic situation would show other aspects of the amateur's mind that we have not yet seen.

Fischer–Taimanov, Palma de Mallorca 1970

(14)

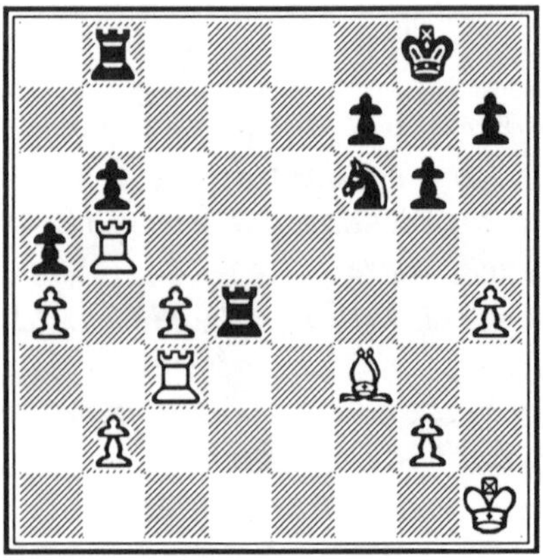

White to play.

True, the position in the diagram is an endgame. However, White must react sharply if he is to prevent Black from achieving an ideal set-up with his Knight on the wonderful c5 square.

What are the imbalances? White has a queenside pawn majority while Black has a majority on the kingside. The main imbalance is the active White Bishop vs. the rather unassuming Black Knight. Notice how White's two imbalances are working together; the Bishop's sphere of influence and the White pawn majority are both on the queenside.

All this seems nice for White but Black threatens to eat a free White pawn (on h4) with check. He also would like to play ...Ne4 when White can either give up his wonderful Bishop or allow the Black Knight to reach its dream square on c5—a post that would stop the White pawns dead in their tracks. How can White stop both these threats? The answer is that he can't! If White wants to make use of his differences he must give up the h4-pawn (not wasting time on its defense) and turn his queenside majority into a powerful passed pawn.

1.c5!

Making use of the pin on the b-file.

1...Rxh4+ 2.Kg1 Rb4 3.Rxb4!

Sharon Burtman pointed out the interesting possibility of

3.Rb3!? Rxb3 4.Rxb3 Nd7 5.c6 Nc5 6.Rxb6! Rxb6 7.c7 and Black cannot stop the pawn from queening. I found this most enlightening. Her rating at the time was 2175 but she saw the importance of time over material (i.e. giving up the h-pawn so that her majority could make itself felt) and even found a pretty alternative to Fischer's method of play. Does this mean that most experts would find all these moves? No, I think that the majority would not come close. Sharon, though, had been well versed in the imbalances (we had many sessions where I would yell, moan, and foam at the mouth—she quickly realized that the only way to shut me up was to learn these things!) and understood that her Bishop and majority had to take precedence over every other consideration.

3...axb4 4.Rc4 bxc5 5.Rxc5

The point of Fischer's play. The passed a-pawn is impossible to stop since the Bishop covers its queening square.

5...Kg7 6.a5 Re8 7.Rc1!

Rooks belong behind passed pawns so White hastens to place his Rook on a1. Note that Black wanted to do the same thing—he threatened to play ...Re1+ followed by ...Ra1.

7...Re5 8.Ra1 Re7 9.Kf2 Ne8 10.a6 Ra7 11.Ke3 Nc7 12.Bb7

Now the Black Rook is permanently locked out of the game.

12...Ne6 13.Ra5 Kf6 14.Kd3 Ke7 15.Kc4 Kd6 16.Rd5+ Kc7 17.Kb5! 1-0

So we have positional considerations (majority and Bishop vs. Knight) that need to be utilized by tactics. When I gave this position to a 1700 student of mine I hoped for nothing more from him than the realization that quiet play might allow my Knight to c5, when White's majority would be stopped and turned into a possible target (the c5 Knight would attack a4).

1700 vs. Silman

1700: My h4-pawn is hanging with check. The imbalances are 3 vs. 2 pawn majorities for both sides. The Bishop is better than the Knight. Black has a weakness on b6 while White has a

(15)

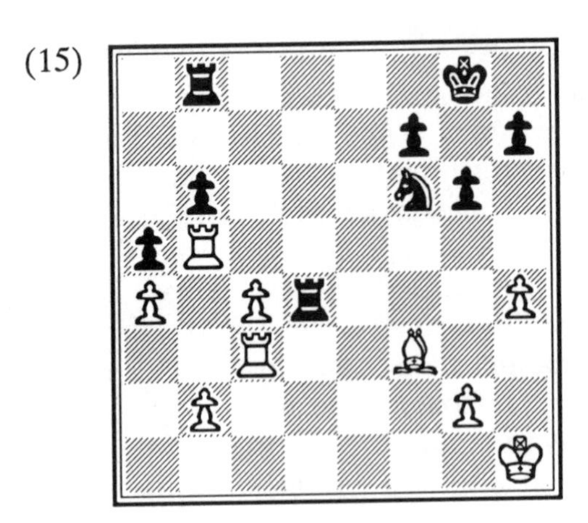

White to play.

hanging pawn on h4. What to do? What is my idea? King on g3, pawn on b3, and then the c5 advance. What is the ideal square for the Black Knight so I can stop it from getting there? Where would it like to be? c5 seems best, blocking my c-pawn and attacking a4. I have to prevent this. My Bishop stops ...Rd1+, my c3 Rook must stay put and defend c4. All this must wait, though, my h4 pawn needs to be attended to!

1.g3?

JS: He noted that the c4-c5 advance was important for him but he wanted to do it only after the preparatory moves g3 and b3. He also pointed out that Black wanted to place his Knight on c5, but then he didn't even bother to find a way to prevent this threat! Instead he became fixated on defending his h4-pawn, to the obvious exclusion of every other concept.

1...Nd7

1700: I will place my Bishop on d5 where it attacks f7 and defends c4. This frees my Rook.

JS: Black could have played ...Ne4 but I wanted to see if he would try to punish me with 2.c5 bxc5 3.Rxb8+ Nxb8 4.Rxc5—though 4...Rb4 allows Black to put up a fight. As it turned out, White never even considered it.

2.Bd5

JS: Played quickly.

2...Nc5

1700: He is attacking my a4 pawn. I will start a counterattack.

JS: Why did White feel that this was the moment to start a counterattack? Why not earlier, when he could have made use of his advantages?

3.Rf3 Nxa4

1700: I must take back on f7.

JS: Notice how White is just reacting to Black. First White defended his h4-pawn without regard to the other factors on the board (material takes precedence over positional considerations for most players). Then he allowed Black to place his Knight on c5. Only at this point, when Black had made his Knight the equal of the Bishop and the once active White Rook on b5 had been turned into an out-of-play piece, did White see the need for counterplay.

This shows us that you must make use of what you have before those differences turn into negatives!

4.Bxf7+

1700: I almost fell for 4.Rxf7?? Rxd5!

4...Kg7

1700: I will play Rf2 and guard b2 and my seventh rank.

JS: Black is still playing a game of reaction and defense. Now this poor attitude turns fatal.

5.Rf2 Rf8

—Stopped the game.

This game showed us that you must make use of your potential positive imbalances or they will turn into negatives. It also demonstrated what happens when you play a game of reaction: you end up playing defensive moves that do nothing but guard against the opponent's threats. Such tactics inevitably lead to a demise in your position that results in a slow and painful death or an eventual game-stopping blunder.

In our next example of an amateur's approach to a Bishop vs. a Knight, I showed the moves from a game Kaletski– (who had a rating in the high "C" range) –Samalii, Los Angeles 1993, to a student who had a rating of about 1100. He was required to comment on these moves and tell me what was going on.

It would be beneficial to the student to play through these moves without looking at the notes and make his own comments in a notebook. When he has completed this exercise he should go over the notes in the book and compare them to those in his notebook.

Kaletski–Samalii, Los Angeles 1993.
Notes by 1100 and J.S.

1.d4 Nf6 2.Nf3 e6 3.Bg5 c5 4.c3

1100: To keep a center pawn in the middle and let the Queen out.

JS: The other way to insure that White will retain a pawn on d4 is 4.e3, a move that frees the Bishop and, if Black captures on d4, allows White to recapture with exd4 and open the e-file.

4...Nc6 5.e4

1100: Grabbing the center but the pawn is not defended. It lets out the White Bishop. It looks all right. 5.e3 also lets the Bishop out but it defends the center better—though it doesn't grab as much territory. He could also have brought his Knight out with Nbd2.

JS: White grabs some space in the center but allows Black to grab the Bishop pair. What is better in this position, the Knights or Bishops? At the moment that question has no clear answer, it is up to both players to shape the pawn structure to suit their individual minor pieces.

5...d5

1100: Looks like a French Defense. This should be fine for

Black.

JS: A sharp but risky move. The simple 5...h6 forces White to give up his Bishop with 6.Bxf6 since 6.Bh4? g5 picks up the e4-pawn. After 5...h6 6.Bxf6 Qxf6 Black would attempt to show that his Bishops are superior to the White Knights. It is important to be on the lookout for ways to create imbalances right in the opening.

6.e5

1100: That was the problem! Though I must admit to not seeing it. How about ...Qb6? Or if you don't like that, then 6...h6 comes into consideration. If 7.Bh4 g5.

JS: Very interesting! 1100 was surprised by White's sixth move and panicked. Due to this panic, he was quite willing to give up a piece and hope that he gets enough after 6...Qb6 7.exf6 Qxb2 8.Nbd2. Instead of allowing this type of irrationality to consume him, a player must calm himself down after unexpected moves. Don't accept that you have made an error without a fight! An objective look at the position may show that you have a good reply.

6...h6

JS: The only good reply. Black destroys the pin and saves his piece.

7.Bxf6?

JS: And White makes an error. He should have played 7.Bh4 g5 8.Nxg5! with complications that are by no means bad for White. Notice how White played what he thought was a winning move (6.e5) but got flustered as soon as Black fought back (6...h6). Instead of looking for a way to keep the pressure on his opponent (7.Bh4 g5 8.Nxg5!) he meekly accepted his fate and made the lame capture in the game.

7...gxf6 8.Bb5

1100: White has knocked a hole in the kingside. Both are fighting for the center. Black can start taking in the center and at the moment Black's Bishops are locked in. I like White's position since he has Knights and more space. If 8...c4 the

(16)

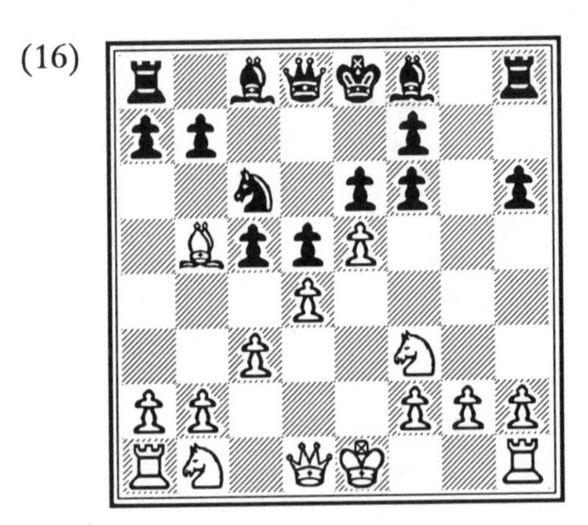

Black to play.

center gets locked and Black does not want this since White has the Knights. 8...a6 is good since the trade is no big deal. I like 8...Bd7 best.

JS: If both sides are fighting for the center then why consider passive moves like ...Bd7 or ...a6? Black should take the fight to the opponent with 8...Qb6! with an immediate attack on b5 and pressure on b2 and d4. After 8...Qb6 9.Bxc6+ bxc6 gives Black another center pawn (which he can use to hit the center with ...cxd4 followed by ...c6-c5) and allows Black's light-squared Bishop to come strongly into play via ...Ba6.

8...Bd7?

JS: This passive move gives White a free moment and allows him to consolidate his position. The pin was not really bothersome but many amateurs have a real fear of pins and try to break them as soon as possible.

9.Bxc6 Bxc6

1100: I think White did Black a favor and I like Black's position more and more. Black can take on d4 and play his Bishop to b4, or ...Rg8 puts pressure on the g-file.

JS: The Bishop does nothing here. I would still prefer ...bxc6 with an open b-file and one more pawn that can attack the White center and blow things open for the two Bishops.

To address 1100's previous comments, ...Rg8 put a Rook on

the file but such attacks need the support of several more pieces if they expect to draw success. Also lacking in sting is a later ...Bb4. What will the Bishop do on that square? Black's target should have been the White center (which restricts the Black Bishops) but he has not gone about this duty with sufficient energy.

10.0-0 Bg7

1100: Putting more pressure on e5, but I don't see the value of it since e5 is easily defended.

JS: Black has been floating for the last several moves and he continues to play without an active plan. Small wonder that the White Knights soon take over the game.

11.Re1

1100: Adds another defender and seems to be a good move.

11...h5 12.Nbd2 f5?

JS: Really horrible. Aside from hanging a pawn, this completely closes the center and makes the Knights much stronger than the Black Bishops. Black lost the thread of the game when he didn't notice that the battle was one of Bishops vs. Knights. As soon as that came about he should have tried to blast open the middle and activate those Bishops.

13.dxc5 Rg8 14.Nd4 Qg5 15.N2f3 Qg6

1100: I like Black's position. He has a lot of power on the g-file.

JS: 1100 likes the Black position because he has mating threats on the g-file. This is very attractive to the amateur. However, a realistic look at this position would show that White can easily defend the g2 point, when he would be left with an extra pawn and two strong Knights vs. two poor Bishops. These factors add up to a winning position for White. For example, White can now simply defend with 16.g3 or he can switch over to a counterattack with 16.Nxc6 bxc6 17.Qa4 when Black's only hope is the mate on g2—something White will never allow!

The game was stopped at this point.

Lessons From This Game:

1) If the integrity of your position is based on a one-mover like ...Qxg2 mate then you are dead meat since such an obvious threat is usually easy to parry. Instead you should nurture long-range plusses like material, superior minor pieces, etc.

When you find yourself crossing your fingers and hoping he won't see it you know that you are desperate!

2) Once a minor piece imbalance is established you must play with great energy to make that imbalance favor you.

Rosenthal–Steinitz, Vienna 1873

(17)

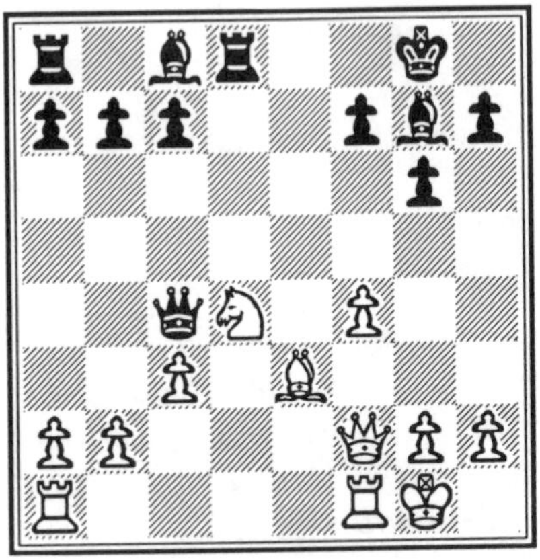

Black to play.

The position in diagram #17 is one of the first games where someone demonstrated how to defeat Knights. Here Steinitz shows us that if you take away all their advanced squares the horses become rather sickly creatures.

1...c5

Making the Knight move away from the fine post on d4.

2.Nf3 b6

Defending the very important c5-pawn. If this pawn were lost then the White Knight could return to d4.

3.Ne5

Trying to find another home.

3...Qe6 4.Qf3 Ba6

Defending the Rook and attacking White's Rook at the same time.

5.Rfe1 f6

The poor Knight is deprived of yet another square!

6.Ng4

The active 6.Nc6 Rde8 7.Bf2 Qd7 8.Rad1 Qc7 leaves the poor beast trapped. Black will eventually play ...Bb7 and snap it off.

6...h5

Forcing it back to permanent inactivity on the second rank.

7.Nf2 Qf7

A multi-purpose move. The Queen gets off the line of the Rook, defends g6, and covers b7, which allows the light-squared Bishop to rest on b7 and take control of the wonderful a8-h1 diagonal.

8.f5?

The pawn will be weak here.

8...g5 9.Rad1 Bb7

White has nothing to compare with the strength of this Bishop. The minor piece battle has clearly swung in Black's favor.

10.Qg3 Rd5!

Staying central and eyeing f5. 10...Qxa2 would give White counterplay after 11.Qc7.

11.Rxd5 Qxd5 12.Rd1 Qxf5

A pawn has been won and the central Black Queen will be able to deal with any temporary activity that White may get.

13.Qc7 Bd5 14.b3 Re8

Black doesn't worry about his a-pawn since he knows that White will never have the time to take it. Instead, the second player places all his pieces in the middle and starts his own counterattack.

15.c4 Bf7 16.Bc1 Re2 17.Rf1 Qc2

Threatening 18...Rxf2 19.Rxf2 Qxc1+ with two pieces for a Rook. Since two pieces are almost always better than a Rook (and usually superior to a Rook and pawn) White is compelled to retreat his Queen and accept the fact that he is doomed.

18.Qg3 Qxa2

—and Black went on to win the game.

Well, I am always talking about how a Knight must be deprived of advanced support points, so I was curious to see if two of my junior students (aged six with a 900 rating and nine with a 1200 rating) would catch on to this idea in the game we just looked at.

Rosenthal–Steinitz, Vienna 1873

(18)

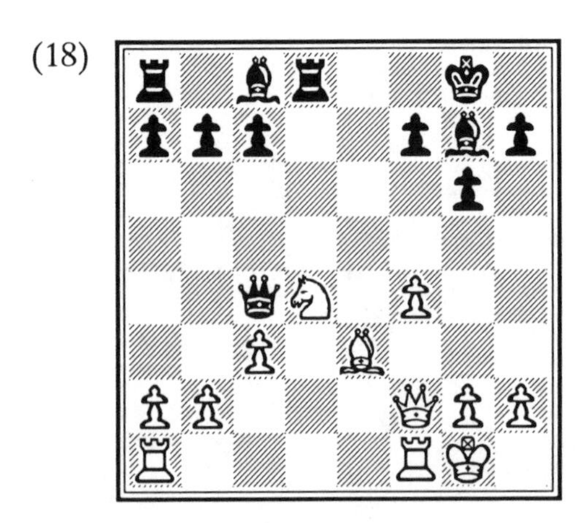

Black to play.

900: White is better.

1200: No, Black is better 'cause he has the two Bishops.

900: I still like White but I don't exactly know why.

1200: I'd go 1...c5 to attack the Knight and chase it to a bad place.

JS: I suppose 900 liked White since a glance gives the impression that White has the visually superior game; his Knight just looks better than everything else. However, a few pawn moves will show that this is just an illusion.

1...c5 2.Nf3

900: Nothing is hanging.

1200: No! The c5-pawn hangs, though f4 would hang too.

900: Let's play ...b6.

1200: If the a-pawn did not hang then Bxc5 Qxf4 would be good for Black.

JS: 1200 forgot that the c5-pawn was the only thing keeping White out of d4. There is no way that Black should allow the trade of his mighty c-pawn for the poor pawn on f4 (which just blocks White's Bishop).

2...b6 3.Ne5

1200 & 900: The Queen is attacked and we both like 3...Qe4.

3...Qe4

JS: The first deviation from the Steinitz game! So far the kids have played very well.

4.Rae1

1200 & 900: Now our Queen is indirectly attacked.

1200: I like ...Qd5.

900: That's good.

4...Qd5 5.Qf3

900: I like ...Bf5! with the idea of ...Be4.

1200: I like ...Be6 to recapture with the Bishop and threaten the a-pawn.

JS: 900 got her way on this one! Note how they are unconsciously trying to make their Bishops better than the Knight, though I would have been even happier if they had verbalized it for me.

5...Bf5 6.Nc6

1200 & 900: We both want to go ...Be4. If he goes Nxd8 then ...Bxf3 wins for us. It looks like White blundered!

JS: A very interesting moment, and one that shows us how many blunders are created. The attack on d8 made them focus their attention to that square. Thus the other threat, that of Ne7+, was completely missed. How does a player avoid this pitfall? One way is to write your move down first and then ask yourself, "After we play 6...Be4, can he take anything (yes, the Rook on d8. However, that is just what we want him to do!), does he have any checks?" At this point you would notice Ne7+ and, if such a move were really a threat, you would erase your move and look for something else.

6...Be4 7.Ne7+

1200 & 900: We didn't see this but it's still okay.

JS: I liked the fact that they didn't panic. Many older players would panic when this oversight hit them in the face and spin mentally out of control.

7...Kf8 8.Nxd5 Bxf3 9.Rxf3 Rxd5.

The game was stopped. The kids did excellently!

This example showed us how important it is to deprive enemy Knights of advanced support points. It also showed us how a fixation on one threat or square can lead to an unfortunate oversight.

I should point out that any kind of fixation in chess is bad, since it blinds you to other possibilities. No rule is correct all the time! For example, what if you have to make the following decision: You have two Bishops vs. Bishop and Knight. Should you take a square away from the Knight but close the position as you do so, or should you open the position and leave the Knight on its post? The following position (diagram #19) shows us such a quandary.

Longren–Silman, Santa Barbara 1989

(19)

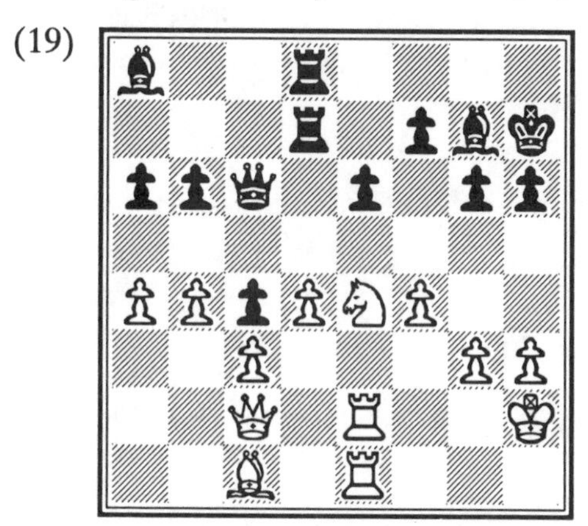

Black to play.

Black has the two Bishops, and there is little doubt concerning the strength of the one on a8 which, combining with the Queen on the a8-h1 diagonal, creates mating threats against the White King. Unfortunately, the White Knight is blocking this line on e4 and the only way to chase it away is by ...f7-f5. Is this the right idea for Black? The answer is a resounding no! This pawn advance does chase the Knight away but it leaves Black with a backward pawn on e6 and a permanently weakened square on e5 (which White could eventually reach by Nd2, Rf2, Nf3, and Ne5).

Another reason to avoid ...f5 is that it makes the central situation stiff—it would be very difficult to open things up; and Black *does* want to open the position up since that would benefit his two Bishops.

After considerable thought Black resisted the temptation to play the inflexible ...f7-f5 and instead played directly to rip open the middle of the board.

1...f6!

Now White cannot prevent the central rending ...e6-e5.

2.h4 e5 3.dxe5 fxe5 4.h5 Rd3

The game is already decided. The opening of the center has led to the activation of both Black Bishops and Rooks. It is true that the White Knight is still on e4, but the fact that it is stuck there and needs constant defense ties down all the White forces and gives Black a free hand everywhere else.

5.b5

Trying to draw the White Queen off the a8-h1 diagonal.

5...axb5 6.axb5 Qe6!

Heading for the kingside. Now ...Qg4 is a threat.

7.Nf2 Qd5 8.hxg6+ Kg8 9.Ne4 exf4 10.Bxf4 Qh5+ 11.Kg1 Qxg6

The combined action of the mighty Black Bishops and Rooks, plus the shaky state of the White King, make the result a foregone conclusion.

12.Qa2 Bd5

Black knows that the game is won so he defends his weak spots in an unhurried manner.

13.Qc2 Rf8!

This was the only Black piece that was not helping out. Now the threat is ...Rxf4.

14.Qc1 Bxc3!

Drawing the Knight away from its defensive location on e4. White resigned since 15.Rf1 hangs the Knight on e4 and 15.Nxc3 Rxg3+ 16.Kf1 Rg1+ 17.Kf2 Qg3 is mate.

Would an amateur be tempted by ...f7-f5? I thought he might, especially if he recalled my insisting that you must chase enemy Knights from advanced support points. Let's see what transpired when I handed the ball to a 1700 student.

1700: White has chances on the kingside since his Queen is pointing towards the Black King and White's pieces are all

(20)

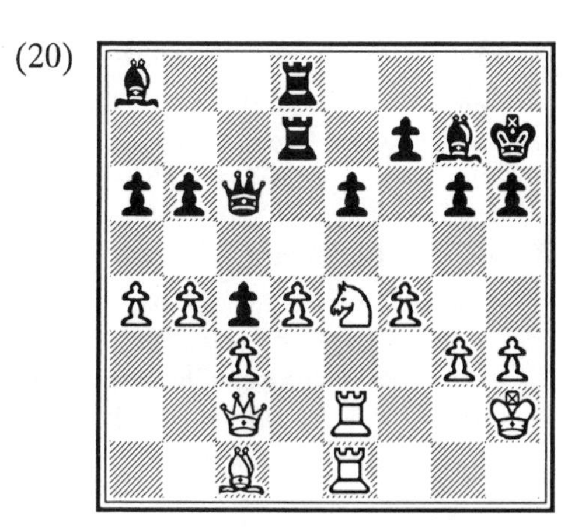

Black to play.

aiming at the kingside. White's King is exposed but well protected since the Queen and Rook defend the g2 square. What would Black's fantasy position be? He would like to make the Re1 move off the first rank and mate on h1 with his Queen via ...Qh1 mate. What would I like to do? He would like to get rid of his dark-squared Bishop and create weaknesses on that color complex. In terms of space, White is ahead. Since it is Black to move how can he achieve his fantasy mate? At the moment White's Bishop is better than Black's on g7—no doubt about it.

JS: What to make of this? He did not go into detail about Bishop vs. Knight and instead raved about a possible kingside attack for White and a possible Black mate on h1. He finally decided to chase the Knight away but his main concern seemed to be in White allowing a mate on g2 or h1. Of course, why would the opponent allow such a one move debacle? The answer is that a good opponent would not. This brings us to a very important rule: Always expect the opponent to see your threat. Always expect him to play the best move! When you find yourself crossing your fingers and hoping that he won't see it, you are making a big mental mistake and are embracing very bad mental habits.

1...f5 2.Nd2

1700: So I have forced the Knight back but now I must make an enemy Rook give up control of g2 or h1 . . . the White

Queen is no longer defending g2. I can't find a way to get his Rooks to move. Black controls f3. If I can make the Knight move to f1, it's still mate—or he could go to b1, but that would be horrible. How can I accomplish this? How about 2...Bxd4 3.cxd4 and now 3...Rxd4 or 3...c3 both give play but I can't see a clear continuation. It's interesting, though. I need to find some plan if there is no mate. I'll sacrifice with ...e5.

JS: Looking for a quick, violent conclusion (even though his Bishops originally gave him a long-range advantage), Black throws himself over the cliff. Why the hurry? Why the need to give up material? What is this guy doing?

2...e5?? 3.fxe5

1700: My idea is now to play ...Re7, ...Bxe5, and ...Rxe5 and if he takes my Rook it's mate on g2.

JS: Still living in the world of "He won't see it." I have tried hard to break 1700 of this habit but he clutches to it like life itself because he wins so many games against lower rated players who fail to see his threats.

3...Re7 4.Rf2

1700: This allows me to continue with my idea after 4...Bxe5 5.dxe5 Rxe5 and he can't take due to mate but aren't I down by a Bishop if he doesn't take? My Rook does get to d3 with pressure for the piece so it deserves consideration. Let's calculate. 4...Bxe5 5.dxe5 Rxe5 and now he just moves his Rook and I lose—it does not work. I don't see how I can get his Rooks out of the way. I can also consider a different idea, namely 4...h5 and 5...Bh6. However, it's very slow since his Knight will come to f3 and block everything. I can't mate him! White is well protected here. I think that White had the better position all along—there is no question about it. I gave up a pawn to try to open up the middle and fight it out but it was all in vain.

JS: Notice that when reality hit him he began to blame the position. His problem is that he wants instant gratification. Trying to make use of one's advantages in a slow, controlled manner is an alien concept to him. He only speaks of kingside attacks and mate.

—Stopped the game.

Lessons From This Game:

1) Always expect the best move from the opponent. That way you will make a move that accomplishes something positive even against the best reply.

2) If you have two Bishops open up the game. This takes precedence over chasing an enemy Knight from an advanced support point (something that can be done at a later time).

3) Rules and guidelines are useful, but every rule was made to be broken!

If you own the Bishop pair and they are already active (or the position is already open), then you must concentrate on limiting the range of the enemy Knight. Our next diagram shows a rather exaggerated case.

Hort–Ciocaltea, Budapest 1973

(21)

White to play.

Hort saw that Black's Knight had no future on the queenside so all he had to do was deprive it of any kingside squares and it would be just a useless slab of meat. Once he killed the Knight he could take his time and torture his opponent, secure in the knowledge that Black would be quite helpless.

1.g5! Bc8 2.g4!

Now the Knight can't go to f6, and on g7 it is deprived of the h5 and f5 squares. Grabbing my trusty old 1700 student, I set up the initial position (diagram #21) and had him give it a try.

1700 vs. J.S.

1700: First I must look for an imbalance for both sides. White has two Bishops but his pawns are doubled. However, g5 limits the Knight and h4 to follow up gets the pawns going. Black has a weak pawn on a6—it's not really passed since the White Bishop stops it, though White must keep his eye on it. Black has backward pawns on d6 and h7. White's Bishops are active. White also has more space. As White I must decide which side of the board to attack. I also want to limit his Knight and control f6. However, if he comes to f6 it's just a waste of time since e4 is not available. Black's plan is to get his Knight to c5 so I must prevent that.

JS: He saw that Black wanted to get his Knight to c5 but he evidently overlooked that the way to that square was from f6-d7-c5. He also mentioned that White has two Bishops and that the scope of the Black Knight should be limited. However, once he said this he promply forgot to do anything about it!

1.Ba5 Nf6

1700: He's going to d7 and c5 so I will attack d6 and slow him down.

JS: A purely reactionary move that just forces the Black King towards the center. Why play Bb4? Is the opponent going to hang the d6-pawn? I suspect not (especially when you are playing a master who is listening to your every thought!). Then why attack it in the first place?

2.Bb4 Ke7

1700: I must activate my King.

JS: In an endgame it is always a good idea to bring one's King towards the center. However, he doesn't seem to have any clear plan in mind. One reason for this is that he missed his chance to come up with an easy plan (dominate the Knight) and now the increased difficulty has left him completely confused. If you are lazy or careless early, the chances are that matters will become much worse later on.

3.Kf2 Nd7

1700: Black wants to go to b6 and attack c4. From there he can also jump into a4. If I play Bd3 I give up control of a4. I will bring my King closer.

JS: Black had no intention of playing ...Nb6. The amateur often thinks that a move with a threat is something to covet, when in reality a simple threat is usually easy to parry. The real quest is to find a square where the piece is happy, active, and secure on, not where it makes a one move threat and then gets chased away.

4.Ke3 Nc5

1700: This is a bad move. Now he has lots of weak points when I chop it off.

5.Bxc5 dxc5

JS: White has gained a passed pawn and Black's pawns on a6, c5, and e5 are all isolated. However, these factors don't carry any weight at all. Why? First, to accomplish these things White had to give up his Bishop pair. Now he is left with a bad Bishop (center pawns on the same color as the Bishop) vs. Black's good one. Though the pawns on a6, c5, and e5 are all isolated, none of them are in danger—Black's King will block White's passed pawn and defend both c5 and e5 on d6, while the White King will not be able to get close to the pawn on a6. We should also not forget that the pawns on e5 and a6 are also passed; that's two passed pawns for Black and only one for White.

6.g5

1700: This takes away f6 from his King and fixes his pawns on White.

JS: The best thing he has said all game! It is always good to fix enemy pawns on the same color as your Bishop since then they are vulnerable to the Bishop's later attentions.

6...Bc8 7.g4

1700: Defends h3 and keeps him out of f5.

7...Bd7

1700: I will bring my King to the queenside and win his weak pawns.

JS: White no longer has any advantage but he continues to speak as if I were lost! At least he has a positive attitude.

8.Kd3 Kd6 9.Kc3 e4??

1700: What's the meaning of that? What's going on? Does he want to resign?

JS: Black could have drawn the game by doing nothing since the White King cannot penetrate into the queenside. However, I decided to add some life to the game and see how he responded.

10.Bxe4 Ke5

1700: He is coming into f4 and hoping to use the passed a-pawn. I don't care if he wins my doubled pawn.

11.Bc2 Kf4 12.Kb3

1700: I'm going to trade Bishops with Ka3 and Ba4 and then Queen my d-pawn.

JS: Excellent! The way to make use of a passed pawn is to destroy the blockader (in this case my Bishop on d7 is the only thing blocking the White passer). White has suddenly begun to play good chess.

12...Ke3 13.Ka3 Kd4 14.Bb3

1700: I don't want to lose both pawns, which would happen after 14.Ba4 Kxc4 15.Bxd7 Kxd5.

14...a5

1700: Now I should have something good. 15.d6 is very tempting and it doesn't look like I can move anything else anyway. If I exchange too early I might even lose since he will get lots of pawns. After 15.d6 Ke5 16.Ba4 Kxd6 17.Bxd7 Kxd7

18.Ka4 and I think I win!

JS: Wow! He appears to be on a hot streak. To complete his variation, 18.Ka4 Kd6 19.Kxa5 Ke5 20.Kb6 Kd4 21.Kb5 is indeed a win for White.

15.d6 Kc3

1700: What is this? He's gone crazy again!

16.Ba4 Kxc4

1700: What did he do that for?

17.Bxd7 Kd5

1700: I'm up a Bishop for a pawn! This must be winning for me.

18.Kb3?

1700: The idea is to stop his queenside pawns. Then I can sacrifice my Bishop for a Kingside pawn and promote a pawn to a Queen over there.

JS: This turns out to be a waste of time. 18.Be8 Kxd6 19.Bf7 was the way to go.

18...Kxd6 19.Be8 Ke5

1700: He's lost.

20.Kc4 Kf4 21.Kxc5 Kxg5

1700: I thought he was going to g3. If 22.Bf7 Kh4 draws.

22.Kb5

1700: It looks like a draw.

Draw agreed.

Lesson From This Game:

Create a plan right away or you may float without a goal for the rest of the game.

So far we have seen Bishops and Knights dominate each other in different ways. However, how easy is it to make the decision concerning which piece to retain and which to give up? Could the reader recognize when a Bishop would beat a Knight or vice versa?

Kavalek–Kaplan, Solingen 1974

(22)

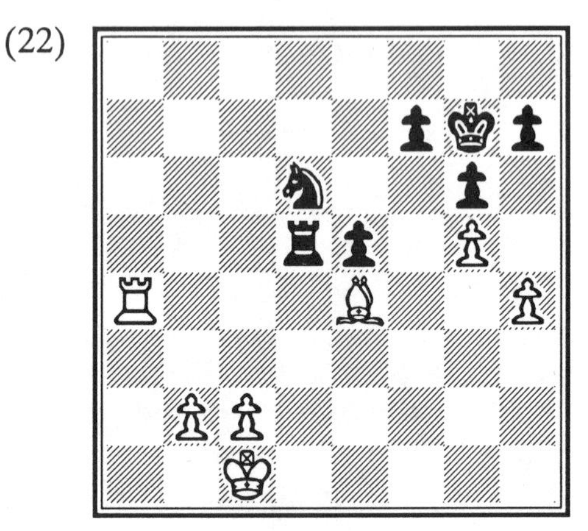

Black to play.

In this position Black has three possible scenarios: 1) He can play 1...Rc5 and play a Rook and Knight vs. Rook and Bishop endgame. 2) He can play 1...Nxe4 and transpose into a pure Rook endgame. 3) He can play 1...Rd4 and go into a Bishop vs. Knight endgame.

I asked a student with an A rating which choice he would make.

J.S. vs. 1850

1850: We have an endgame. I recall hearing that a Bishop is better than a Knight if passed pawns are on two sides. Here my King is in jail and my Rook is attacked. What would I like to do? What do I have? Where is his Bishop going? Do I exchange? What piece should I trade? I like 1...Rd4 because I can follow with ...f5 and get a passed pawn.

1...Rd4??

JS: I find it amazing that he would recite the rule that states, "A Bishop is better than a Knight if passed pawns are on both sides of the board" and then play directly into the inferior side of such a situation! It sounds to me like he had too many choices and he got hopelessly confused. However, when you have the luxury of knowing the previously stated rule then you might as well make use of it.

Instead of this, another rule (almost a joke rule actually, but there is a lot of truth in it) says, "All Rook endgames are drawn." Following this, we can accept that 1...Nxe4 2.Rxe4 f5 gives Black good chances to hold the game. The swap of Knight for Bishop also makes a lot of sense; Black should see a pawn race situation coming up and, knowing that Bishops are strong in such cases, he should hasten to hack the White Bishop off the board. Evidently, it is not enough to know the rules and guidelines. You must also make use of them!

2.Rxd4 exd4

JS: So we now have a situation where the Black Knight will not be able to cope with the White passed pawn. On the other hand, the White Bishop will easily stop any passed pawn that Black can create.

3.Bd5

1850: Why do this? He is losing the h-pawn!

3...Nf5

JS: I don't know why, but Kaplan also made the wrong decision in this game (and he was a very strong player who most definitely knew better!). That contest was decided after 3...h6 4.Kd2 hxg5 5.hxg5 f6 6.Kd3 Nf5 7.b4 fxg5 8.b5 Ne7 9.Bg2 Nc8 10.Kxd4 Kf6 11.Kc5 Ke5 12.c4, 1-0. Note how slow and ponderous the Knight was.

4.b4 Ne3

1850: Uh oh. If I take that pawn I won't be able to stop that guy on the b-file.

5.Bb3

1850: My Knight is dominated.

5...f5 6.b5 f4 7.Kd2 f3 8.Ke1

1850: He stopped my pawn but I can't stop his.

We ended the game here.

Lesson From This Game:

Bishops really *are* better than Knights in pawn race situations. It was demonstated to Kaplan and then 1850 found out also. Don't let it happen to you!

PART THREE

Acquisition of the Center, Territory, and Space

Every chess player is attracted to beautiful combinations and razor-sharp kingside attacks. This attraction makes us want to emulate the great attacking masters and, as a result, we study games by Kasparov, Alekhine, and Tal.

Though the ability to calculate is invaluable—and at least a basic understanding of the mechanics of attack imperative—the positional elements of chess tend to be ignored by the legions of amateurs that love the game. Why? Do amateur players think that subjects like territory and the center are boring? Or could it be that the literature on these things simply presents the information in a dull manner?

Whatever the reason for this relative ignorance may be, most amateurs don't have a clue about the proper use of a space advantage or a full pawn center. Instead they constantly look for forcing continuations aimed at the enemy King and, once they give themselves the green light, they will start a completely unjustified attack or, even worse, just sit tight and do nothing at all.

Personally, I like nothing better than to create a large pawn center and squeeze my opponent to death in its space gaining coils. After the game the poor victim often has a glazed look in his eyes; he knows he lost badly but he is not quite sure why.

The Center

Of the three areas of a chess board (kingside, center, and

queenside), the center is by far the most important. The reason for this is that your forces can move to either side with minimum effort and maximum speed. Due to this it is usually an excellent idea to play in the middle if you have the option to do so. Unfortunately, most amateurs seem to have "wing vision," they are always looking to play on one wing or the other.

The following rules concerning play in the center and on the wings may prove beneficial:

1) A full pawn center gives its owner territory and control over key central squares.

(23)

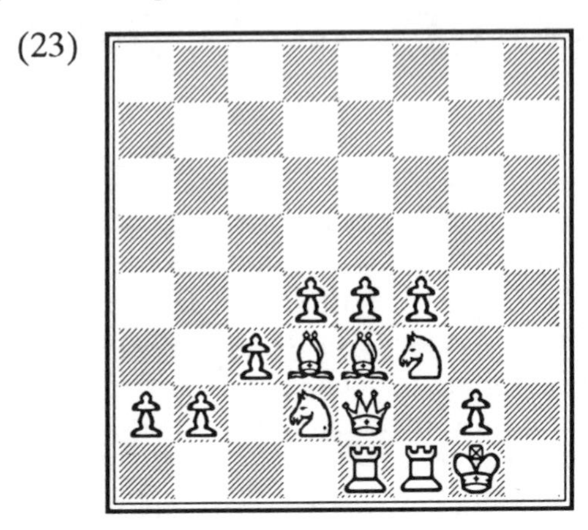

In diagram #23, White has a full pawn center that is well protected by other pawns and pieces. This center gives him strong control over c5, d5, e5, and f5.

2) Owning a full pawn center is a responsibility! Once you create it you must strive to make it indestructible. If you achieve this goal then your center will cramp and restrict your opponent for the whole game.

Note that in the previous diagram White placed his army behind his center, thereby making it very hard to tear down.

3) Don't advance the center too early! Every pawn advance leaves weak squares in its wake.

Notice in diagram #24 how the Black Knight cannot advance to the fourth rank due to the White center's influence. Even after ...Nc6 or ...Ng6 the Knight would still be unable to find an advanced central post. However, if White were to

(24)

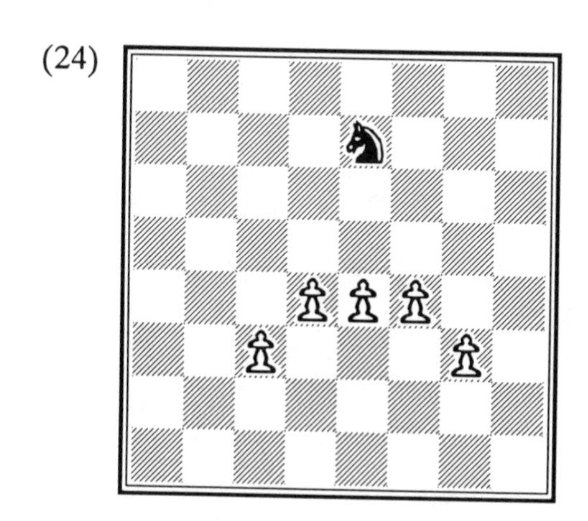

advance his center with e4-e5 then the d5 and f5 squares are suddenly available to the tormented horse.

4) If your opponent has created a full pawn center you must strive to attack it. He is telling you it is strong, you are telling him that it is a target. One of the most common cases of allowing a center in order to attack it comes about in the Grunfeld Defense. After **1.d4 Nf6 2.c4 g6 3.Nc3 d5 4.cxd5 Nxd5 5.e4 Nxc3 6.bxc3** White has possession of an impressive looking pawn center. If Black develops his pieces in a mindless manner then this center will eventually crush him. However, Black can attempt to show that the center is an object of attack: **6...Bg7** (aiming at d4) **7.Bc4 c5** (more pressure on d4) **8.Ne2 0-0 9.0-0 Nc6** (the heat increases on the d4 square) **10.Be3 Qc7 11.Rc1 Rd8** and it is still not clear if the center is strong or weak.

5) If the center pawns get traded then open files exist that make it easy to get one's Rooks into play.

After **1.e4 e6 2.d4 d5 3.exd5 exd5** it doesn't take a genius to see that the open e-file will be a nice place to stick a Rook (following the rule that Rooks belong on open files).

6) If the center becomes locked then the play switches to the wings. After **1.d4 Nf6 2.c4 c5 3.d5 e5 4.Nc3 d6 5.e4** it is easy to see that the center is a dead zone. All the play will have to come on the wings.

7) With a closed center, you know which wing to play on by going in the direction that your pawns point. The pawns point to the area where you have more space and that is the side that

you want to control.

(25)

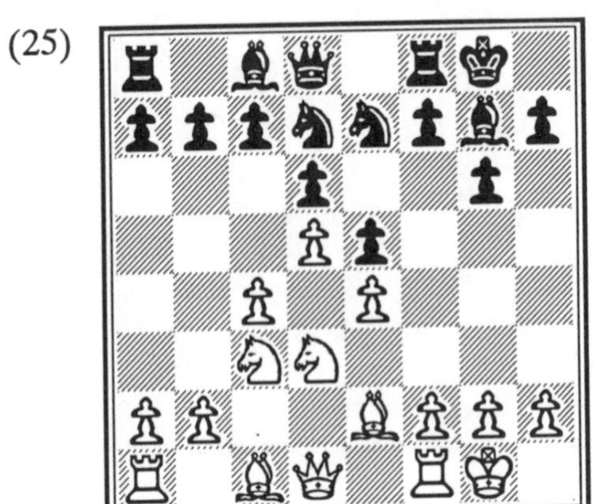

In diagram #25, Black's pawns point to the kingside while the White pawns flow to the queenside. Because of this, Black will play for a ...f7-f5 advance (gaining more kingside space and allowing his Rooks to enter the fight) while White will try for a c4-c5 advance (which leads to an open c-file for the White Rooks).

8) A wide open center allows you to attack with pieces. A closed center generally means that you must attack with pawns. This enables you to grab space and open files for your Rooks.

Space

In general, having more territory is a very positive thing. You get more room for movement and your pieces experience superior coordination. However, as your pawns advance (your extra territory is mapped out by your pawns in much the same way as a fence demonstates the land you own) certain squares may become weak, and it is possible—like ancient Rome—to expand too far too quickly. For this reason you must only annex extra space if you think you can control the territory behind your pawns. Also helpful are the following rules:

1) When you have more space it is usually a good idea to avoid exchanges.

Black can quietly resign in diagram #26 because his minor

(26)

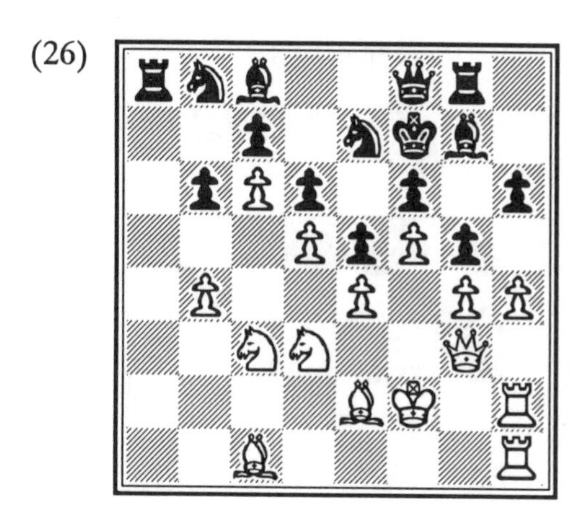

pieces are so cramped that none of them have useful moves. However, if we were to remove all the pieces and only leave the pawns and Kings Black would be fine, simply because the cramping effect of the White pawns no longer has anything to cramp!

2) If you have less space an exchange or two will give the rest of your pieces more room to move about in.

3) A space advantage is a permanent, long-term advantage. You don't have to be in any hurry to utilize it. Take your time and let the opponent stew in his own juices.

The Amateur's Mind

In our first game White comes out of the opening with an advantage in space but becomes worried about imaginary threats and ceases to think about an active plan for himself. Later, after some errors, White can still get some play in the center but he never even considers this and instead concentrates solely on the wings.

1750 vs. J.S.

1.c4 Nf6 2.Nc3 c5 3.Nf3 e6 4.g3 b6 5.Bg2 Bb7 6.0-0 Be7 7.d4 cxd4 8.Qxd4 d6

(27)

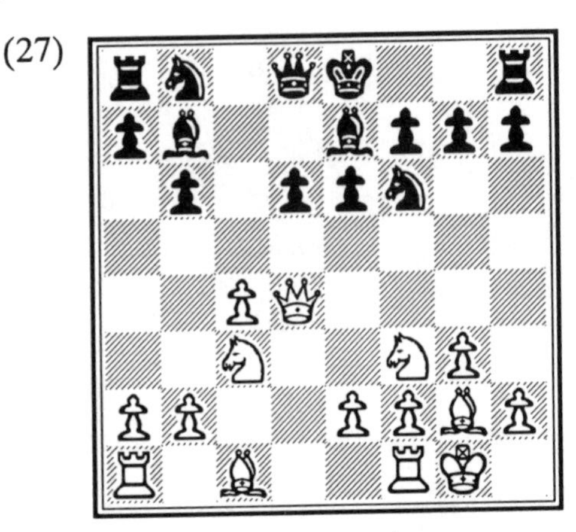

White to play.

JS: 1750 had never faced a hedgehog before (he is an e2-e4 player) and so he was completely unfamiliar with the positions that result.

1750: White has space and has more pieces out. The Black Bishop on e7 is temporarily bad but this is no big problem. Nobody has any real advantage. Since Black can attack my Queen by ...Nc6 I would be wise to retreat it to a safer square.

JS: I was happy that he noted the advantage in space and development but was disappointed that he didn't make any effort to use these plusses. A lead in development (especially if the enemy King is still in the center) is most useful if the game can be opened up. In this case Black can castle immediately so the development issue cannot be used in the traditional way (e.g. attacking the King). However, if White had noted Black's sole weakness on d6, he might have hit upon a plan that called for an immediate attack on this target by Rd1, b3, and Ba3. More fuel can be added to this fire by Ng5 and after the trade of light-squared Bishops White will play Nge4. In this case the better developed side's attack is difficult to parry since Black is not fully mobilized yet and his pieces are not ready to rush to the d-pawn's aid. Theory has shown that Black can defend against these ideas but I am always delighted to hear a student talk of "targets." Remember that one doesn't just attack a King—you must also attack squares and pawns. If you have such a target plus an advantage in development then you must make instant use of this weapon before it disappears (development leads are temporary since the opponent will eventually catch up!).

Another plan White has is to make use of his space edge by increasing it whenever possible and playing to stifle Black's counterplay (based on the ...b6-b5 or ...d6-d5 advances).

Instead of dealing with these issues, White cops out and starts to worry about his Queen being attacked. Keep in mind that an attack on your Queen is no big deal since you can simply move it to safety. The opponent doesn't gain points for screaming, "Check to your Queen!" The moral is: Don't fear checks or attacks. Just make sure that they are ineffective in the given position and go ahead with your own plans.

9.Qd3?

JS: This wastes a tempo and places the Queen on another vulnerable square since ...Nbd7-c5 will be uncomfortable. Since he did mention his edge in space, I would have been very happy if he tried to increase that advantage by 9.e4. Every move you make should do something positive. Fearing every possible threat that the opponent can throw at you is something that you must avoid at all costs.

9...0-0

1750: Since I have more space, I want to increase it by moving up in the center with e2-e4.

JS: That's more like it! To repeat: Every move you make should have a positive base and be geared to increasing the advantages that you already possess.

10.e4 Nbd7

1750: He threatens to put a Knight on c5. If I stop that by b4 then my c4 pawn is without potential support. So I'll stop it by Be3.

JS: This illustrates a typical problem with the amateur's thinking. Seeing a threat to win material, White notes that he can protect himself and develop a piece with 11.Be3. However, he fails to take into account the resultant position after he loses his dark-squared Bishop for the enemy Knight. Don't make positional concessions to prevent a threat unless you have no other means of defense.

11.Be3?

JS: Better was 11.Nd4 which allows the Bishop on g2 to help in the defense of the e-pawn. Then 11...Nc5 or 11...Ne5 can be met with 12.Qe2 followed by b2-b3, when White would still have a solid position with no weaknesses.

11...Nc5

1750: He's attacking e4 with three pieces so I have to capture him.

JS: The sins of his ninth move (9.Qd3?) plus the laziness of his eleventh (11.Be3) have come back to haunt him. Note how he keeps making concessions. First 9.Qd3 to stop a Knight from making a harmless attack on his Queen (this cost him a tempo and placed the Queen and an even more vulnerable square) and then 11.Be3, a move that gives up the two Bishops and the dark squares.

12.Bxc5 bxc5

1750: I was considering 13.h3 but I'm not worried about him going to g4 with his Knight. I'll move my Rook to e1 to give my pawn some added support.

JS: Since the player with less territory should strive to exchange pieces (and thus relieve his cramp), Black can be happy with his acquisition of Bishop for Knight.

White is still making a big error by not formulating an active plan. Instead he keeps guarding his e-pawn and worries about various harmless Knight jumps. Instead something like 13.e5 dxe5 14.Nxe5 Qxd3 15.Nxd3 Bxg2 16.Kxg2 is sensible since it gets rid of Black's two Bishops by swapping one off. By isolating Black's c-pawn, White can now entertain thoughts of pressuring it with a later Na4. I'm not saying that this plan is good for White, but it would have shown a good mental attitude in that White would have been actively attempting to devalue Black's two Bishops (by trading one off) and trying to create a target on c5.

13.Rfe1 Qb6

1750: He's attacking my b2 pawn. I'll simply defend it.

JS: White doesn't realize it, but he has allowed Black to take the initiative. This is shown by White's readiness to keep making defensive moves.

14.b3 Rfd8

1750: Defending d6 and perhaps threatening to play a ...d5 advance. If he pushes his pawn to d5 I'll go e4-e5 and attack his Knight. It's still basically even. I'll play Rad1 and strengthen my control of the center.

JS:White is playing sensible moves but he is slowly but surely running out of constructive ideas. By this I mean that he lacks a clear object of attack. It's not enough to just move your pieces into the center and hope that something good happens. It's your job to make that good thing happen. To accomplish this you must make all your pieces work towards a single goal. In our present game, White does not have a clear goal in mind. Note that the d6-pawn, though technically backward, is so solidly defended that White cannot hope to put any real pressure on it.

15.Rad1 Bc6

1750: He's preventing me from attacking his Queen by Na4. He's also preparing to play...Qb7 and increase the pressure in the center. If he does that I will play Nd2 and back that pawn up. Now I can play Qe3, which prepares to redirect it to the kingside via Qf4, etc.

JS: Every time your opponent moves you should ask, "Why did he do that?" It's very important to understand what the other side is trying to accomplish. Though White has paid attention to his opponent's plans throughout this game, he has not put enough energy into his own ideas. Now he seems to be leaning towards a kingside attack, but is this a realistic hope or a plan born out of the frustration caused by his earlier inactivity?

16.Qe3 a5

1750: Starting a wing attack via ...a5-a4. I can move my Knight to d2 and defend both e4 and b3 now or later. Another idea is to play Rb1. I'll first move my Queen to the kingside, defend on the queenside as I need to, and start an attack by g3-g4-g5.

JS: White finally realizes that he has to do something aggressive. However, a kingside attack is not a very realistic goal since Black has no weaknesses on that side of the board and White's army aims more at the center than at the kingside. White should have been playing for an e4-e5 advance.

Black intends to play ...a5-a4 and create an attackable target (in this case the proposed target is a weak pawn) on the queenside.

17.Qf4 a4

1750: Now I'll play Rb1, which makes his Queen a bit uncomfortable.

JS: The Black Queen is not a bit uncomfortable since if White ever plays bxa4 Black would simply move his Queen to safety and start to chew up the weak White pawns on a4, a2, and c4. Unlike White's earlier display, Black has no fear of one-move attacks.

18.Rb1 e5

1750: Forcing me to move my Queen. I can consider Qh4 but my Knight on c3 is undefended and my queen is in a risky place. I'll move it back to the safe e3 square.

JS: Black's last move (18...e5) fixes the center and takes away White's chances for central counterplay based on a e4-e5 advance. Though some players might be horrified by the apparent weaknesses on d6 (backward pawn) and d5 (weak square), these turn out to be illusions. The d6 pawn is firmly defended and if a Knight jumps into d5 then Black would capture it. This would lead to a White pawn going to d5, which would cover up the hole and the backward pawn (e.g. Nd5 ...Nxd5 cxd5 and the "weaknesses" no longer exist).

19.Qe3 axb3

1750: If I play Rxb3 he has to move his Queen. If he moves

...Qa6 he attacks my c4 pawn but I can defend. It's still even.

JS: White gets a surge of confidence by attacking the Black Queen. However, after the Queen moves to safety, White's pawns on a2 and c4 will be extremely weak.

20.Rxb3?

JS: An "active" move that worsens his position. Correct was 20.axb3 (leaving himself with only one target on b3 to worry about instead of two) followed by Nd2, when his position would still be very hard to crack.

White's statement claiming equality is way off the mark. He has no play and it's only a matter of time before White's two queenside targets (a2 and c4) lead to his demise.

20...Qa6

1750: Attacking c4. I can protect my pawn by Qe2, Qd3, or Nd2. The Knight move seems best since it also defends e4.

21.Nd2 Rd7

1750: He intends to double his Rooks. He can also play...Rb7 but since he could have played this right away (...Rdb8) he must intend to double on the a-file.

Now I could move my Knight to d5 when it's attacked by two pieces and defended by three. However, I need this Knight on c3 to defend my a2 pawn so I can't do that. I can attack his d7 Rook by playing Bh3.

JS: Still lacking a plan, White resorts to a series of one-move attacks (20.Rxb3 and 22.Bh3). This is a typical amateur mistake. A one-move attack is fine if it contributes to the overall improvement of your position. If it had no other point, then the move is simply a waste of time (your opponent will move his piece to safety!). In the present case White is just forcing Black to go where he wanted to.

22.Bh3 Rda7

1750: Tripling on the a-file, but who cares? It doesn't do him any good at all. Now I can continue to attack his kingside by g4-g5 and chase his Knight away.

(28)

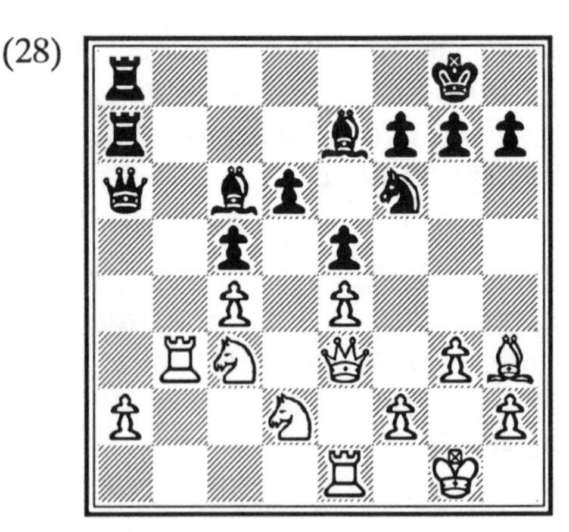

White to play.

JS: White is feeling pretty good right now but this is completely unjustified. However, many people go into depressions and play badly when they get such poor positions so his positive attitude may serve to keep him in the game. Actually, 1750 is quite a fighter and has saved many hopeless positions by refusing to acknowledge that all is lost. He always thinks there's a chance (this attitude is worth its weight in gold since even strong Grandmasters have been known to lose their vigilance and make bad errors in winning positions).

23.g4 Bd8

1750: Intending ...Ba5 attacking c3 and a2 in turn. I can push up my pawn to a3 after ...Ba5 so I'm not worried about that. I'll continue the attack on the kingside.

JS: The Knight on c3 eyes the d5 and b5 squares and defends the a2 and e4 pawns. Black would be happy to trade his bad Bishop for such a useful Knight.

24.g5?

JS: An unfortunate decision. White has weakened his King, the g-pawn, and the f4 square and now he allows the Black Knight to take up residence there. Don't create weak squares. If such squares are created then rush your Knights to them as fast as possible!

24...Nh5

1750: Heading for f4. Now I can move into d5 and protect the f4 point. Unfortunately he will capture and move into f4 anyway. If 25.Nd5 Bxd5 26.exd5 Nf4 27.Bf5 and Qe4 still gives me an attack on h7 and his king. Oops. I forgot that if I move my Knight I lose my pawn on a2. I must first guard my pawn and then Ne2 or Nd5 guards f4.

25.Rb2?

JS: Much too passive (though a good recommendation is hard to find). He should have accepted the loss of the a-pawn and tried to find some way to bring his Rook on b3 over to the kingside along the third rank. If you're getting positionally squashed and material loss is also looming, don't curl into a ball and wait to die. Give up some ballast (material) and attack the opponent for all you are worth. Put a scare into him and try to upset his equilibrium.

25...Nf4

1750: Now he threatens to win my g5 pawn. I have to guard it. On Qg3 the e2 and d3 squares are covered.

26.Qg3 Bxg5

1750: If 27.Qxg5 Nxh3+ wins my Queen by a fork. I better get my Bishop out of there.

JS: Now Black has won material, has a safe King, and he has retained the initiative. It's all over.

27.Bf1 Bd8

1750: I've lost a pawn but I'm not lost since I'm still firm on the queenside. I have to get rid of his Knight.

JS: He could admit he's lost and give up but instead he lies to himself and fights on. I can't criticize him for following the edict, "No one ever won a game by resigning."

28.Ne2 Ne6

1750: Heading for d4 so I must maintain my Knight on e2. I'll attack his pawn on d6.

29.Qd3 Bc7

1750: I'll head my passive d2 Knight to f3, h4, and f5. Also possible is Bh3 attacking the e6 Knight. Advancing f2-f4 can also be considered.

30.Bh3 Qc8

1750: Now his Knight is pinned, but he's threatening my pawn on a2.

31.Ra1 Ra3

Attacking my Queen. I'd like to play Nc3 and head for d5 but it would be pinned. It's still good, though. I'd just have to move my Queen out of the way first.

32.Nc3 Nf4

Here the game was stopped since 33.Bxc8 Nxd3 leads to a further loss of material for White.

Lessons From This Game:

1) Try to appraise your position honestly.

2) Never give up hope! A positive fighter's attitude will bring you points even from the most hopeless looking situations.

3) Look to the center for play. Chess is not just a bunch of battles on the wings.

4) Passive, planless play will lead to a loss every time.

5) Know what the opponent is planning at all times but don't allow yourself to become mesmerized by his ideas to the exclusion of your own.

6) Don't make pointless one-move attacks. If you are crossing your fingers and hoping he doesn't see it you are making the wrong move (you are also building bad mental habits). Always expect your opponent to see your threats! You want to play a move that improves your position no matter what he does. I tend to repeat this a lot but I find it's a mistake that the amateur makes over and over again.

In our next three games we see Black allowing White to build up a very imposing center. Would the amateurs with the

White pieces be able to make use of this central space advantage? Would they even notice that space was the advantage they possessed? These are important questions, since if you can't ascertain what kind of advantage you hold then you won't be able to make use of it.

2000 vs. J.S.

1.e4 d6 2.d4 g6 3.Nc3 Bg7 4.f4 e6 5.Nf3 Ne7

(29)

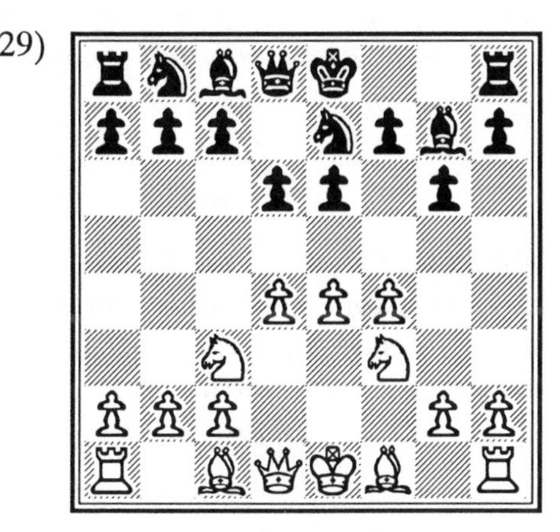

White to play.

JS: White reacted with scorn to Black's choice of opening. It's certainly ugly looking but it turns out to be a tough nut to crack!

2000: 6.Bd3 with the idea of eventually smashing him with f5 is the obvious move.

JS: His attitude shows some positive and negative features. The positive side is his confidence; he knows Black has played something fishy and he wants to punish his opponent for the insulting choice of opening. The negative part of White's reaction is the speed taken for his decision. <u>When someone does something unusual you must take extra time to measure its pluses and minuses.</u> This does not mean that there is anything wrong with 6.Bd3. I just expect the student to demonstrate a greater understanding of the position before a move is chosen!

6.Bd3 b6

2000: Wow...he really seems to be asking for it! How can I

take quick advantage of that move? Any targets? I'll just develop the rest of my army.

JS: White is still refusing to take a calm look at the imbalances. The main factor in White's favor is the advantage in space that his big pawn center gives him. With this in mind White should play to strengthen his center and prevent Black from undertaking any central counterattacking ideas (this is illustrated in the next game). By blindly developing his pieces he breaks one of my big rules: First develop a plan and then develop your pieces around that plan. If you develop your pieces before you attain an understanding of the situation you may ultimately find that your army is standing on the wrong squares!

7.0-0 0-0 8.Be3

2000: Strengthening my center.

JS: 8.Be3 is clearly a good move but that doesn't detract from the fact that White is exhibiting clear signs of laziness. Instead of taking a long think and becoming master of the position he sits back and hopes that positive things will just happen.

8...c5

2000: I can consider 9.dxc5 but 9...dxc5 looks boring. So my options are 9.d5, 9.e5, or 9.Ne2. 9.d5 seems bad because it leaves me with a weakness on d5. 9.Ne2 looks too passive for my tastes. Though 9.e5 gives up the f5 and d5 squares it opens things up and leads to a tactical battle that would suit my style.

9.e5?

JS: A very poor move. Black has just initiated a central counterattack and White goes along with his opponent's plans by allowing his center to be ripped apart. I would have preferred either to maintain the center with 9.Ne2 Bb7 10.c3 or to start a central tussle (after all—White is ahead in development!) with 9.dxc5 bxc5 (9...dxc5 leaves White with a space advantage, a solid pawn on e4, and a potential strongpoint on d6 after an e4-e5 advance) 10.e5!? (trying to leave Black with a weakness on c5 and also attempting to create a strongpoint on d6) 10...dxe5 11.fxe5 Nd7 12.Bf4 with Ne4 to follow.

9...cxd4 10.Bxd4

2000: Otherwise I lose a pawn.

10...Nbc6

2000: Now I'm considering Be4, which may be a tad slow. However, 11.exd6 is possible. Also 11.Nb5 is a serious thought. So it's a choice between these two moves. Since Nb5 misplaces the Knight on the side I'll go for exd6.

JS: White is still playing without any kind of plan. He is not reasoning things out and he is not analyzing any variations. This type of "move by move" existence is often employed by players from the beginning level right up to the revered ranking of master. No matter what your rating may be, it is the wrong way to play chess!

11.exd6 Nxd4 12.dxe7 Qxe7

2000: Now I have to make some decisions. I don't like his well placed Knight, so 12.Be4 Nxf3+ 13.Qxf3 Rb8 14.Rad1 playing on the file looks good.

JS: White has completely failed to evaluate the position. If he had taken some time to do so he might have realized that opening up the center and giving Black two Bishops is not a logical course of action. He should have realized this several moves ago (before he allowed it to happen) since now all the trumps rest in Black's hands and it is too late for White to do anything about it.

13.Be4 Ba6!!

2000: An active move that may not be sound. I have to be careful not to exchange a bunch of pieces and end up in an inferior Bishop vs. Knight endgame. Since 14.Nxd4 Rad8 runs into several pins (15.Nc6?? Qc5+ and 15.Nce2 Bxe2 are both bad for me) and 13.Rf2 Rad8 also looks terrible I must challenge his idea and chop off his material!

JS: Shocked into action, 2000 finally looks at a few variations and takes the correct mental stand: If you see a way to win material and don't see how your higher rated opponent can escape, you must go into the line and keep him honest.

I must point out that the variation he gave on his 12th move

(30)
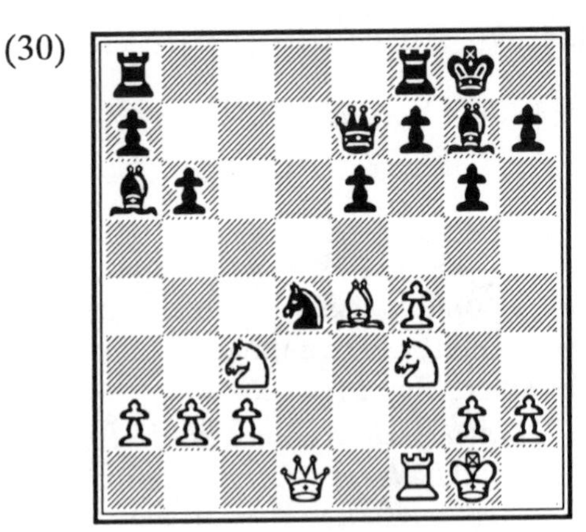

White to play.

via 13...Nxf3+ 14.Qxf3 Rb8 15.Rad1 also favors Black because the Bishop on g7 is better than any other minor piece on the board.

14.Bxa8 Rxa8?

JS: The most accurate order was 14...Bxf1 15.Nxd4 Rxa8. The text was played to see how White would react to a greater range of choice.

2000: I could keep the exchange with 15.Rf2 but 15...Rd8 gives him tempos and might be passive. The main move is 15.Nxd4, when 15...Bxf1 16.Kxf1 consolidates. So on 15.Nxd4 he will pin with ...Rd8 or ...Qc5 when 16.Ne2 Bxe2 17.Qxe2 Bxd4+ 18.Kh1 favors me.

JS: He had to play 15.Rf2 Rd8 16.Rd2, when 16...Nxf3+ 17.gxf3 leaves Black with compensation for the Exchange but nothing more. However, 2000 thought he was on a winning track and did the right thing by following his convictions.

15.Nxd4? Rd8?!

2000: Since 15.Rf3 Bxd4+ and ...Bxc3 wins for him I have to block with my c3-Knight.

JS: 15...Bxf1 was still more accurate.

16.Nce2 Bxd4+ 17.Nxd4 Bxf1

2000: Now 18.Nc6 still loses to 18...Qc5+. What's wrong

with the obvious 18.Kxf1? Am I falling for a trap . . . what am I missing? It looks like I'm winning.

18.Kxf1??

JS: He had to play 18.c3, when the strong Knight on d4 holds things together.

18...Qf6

2000: Oh! He intends e7-e5 . . . that's what he had in mind! Any smart ideas? If 18.Kg1 Rxd4 picks up my f4 pawn and 18.c3 e5 doesn't change anything. So I'll hold onto f4 with 18.g3.

JS: Notice how White never started any ideas of his own. Instead he just developed his pieces and reacted to Black's play. This type of descent into the opponent's world happens quickly and quietly and must be avoided at all costs. Naturally the only way to avoid this is to impose your will on the game before the opponent does!

19.g3 Rxd4

2000: 19.Qf3 allows ...Rd2.

20.Qe2 Qd8

JS: White's position is lost and we stopped the game at this point.

Lessons From This Game:

1) Even a seemingly bad opening will have some positive points. If you don't take what your opponent is doing seriously then these positive points will end up beating you.

2) A plan comes before development.

3) When you accept laziness into your mental processes it turns into a habit that's hard to break. Work hard from the very first moves!

4) If you think you see a win but are worried about falling into a trap you must be courageous and make him prove his point. Never let fear talk you out of a course of action.

Our next game arises from the identical opening. In this case a much lower rated player is able to come up with a reasonable antidote.

1600 vs. J.S.

1.e4 d6 2.d4 g6 3.Nc3 Bg7 4.f4 e6 5.Nf3 Ne7

1600: I have good central control and a kingside space advantage. I want to continue my development and keep an eye aimed at the kingside. I would also like to maintain the e7 Knight's lack of mobility. Though this position looks good for me Black is not just going to roll over . . . there is plenty of opportunity for him to get play in the center.

JS: Not at all bad! He's making a determined effort to break down the position. This effort was lacking in the previous game, even though this player is much the weaker of the two—evidently, attitude is not something that is measured by rating. What nobody mentions is that a kingside attack can only succeed if you control the center or if the center is locked. Because of this and his extra central territory White should play to make his center indestructible and to restrict Black's counterplay. Once this is achieved White can turn his attention towards a wing.

6.Be2

1600: Develops the Bishop and prepares to castle and activate the Rook.

JS: Is the Bishop better on d3 or e2? Though d3 enables White to envision an eventual f4-f5 break I must ask how real this possibility is. If it turns out to be just a pipe dream, then e2 makes sense since it enables White to place a Rook on the d-file and discourage Black's ...c5 break.

6...b6

1600: He's going to play ...Bb7 and put pressure on the e4 pawn.

7.0-0

1600: Looking at it afterwards I think my 0-0 was a poor move. If the center closes up, my White Bishop would be good and his is a bad one which he could exchange with ...Ba6. With my Rook on f1 this exchange would be forced.

JS: This type of thinking just takes up time and makes a player paranoid. At the moment the center is not closed and Black's light-squared Bishop is far from being bad. Besides, he can't really stop ...Ba6 anyway and if Black wants to take three moves (...b6, ...Ba6, and ...Bxe2) to trade a piece that's moved only once then White should rejoice. Don't allow yourself to get in a state of mind where everything your opponent does has some lurking threat behind it.

7...0-0

1600: I'm looking at the center and whether it makes sense to close it up with 8.e5 when Black can take or play ...d5. If 8.e5 dxe5 9.fxe5 my f-file is opened and my dark-squared Bishop is freed but my d-pawn is weak. If he closes with d5 then a later c5 makes it like a French type of opening. It also gives him use of the f5 square. So I don't like the e5 advance. I'm also looking at a fantasy plan of Knight on g5 and Rook on h3 with a kingside attack but that's easily defended against. His threat is to attack d4 with ...c5 and ...Nbc6 with pressure so Be3 looks good.

JS: It must be kept in mind that pawns on e4 and d4 control all the critical central squares. As soon as you push one of them you give up some of this control! After 8.e5? Black would not activate White's f1 Rook and c1 Bishop with 8...dxe5? Instead he would simply play 8...Bb7 when White has given up control of the f5 and d5 squares and an eventual ...c7-c5 would blast the once proud center apart. Don't think that moving forward means that you are automatically improving your position!

8.Be3

The game was stopped here because the student's time had expired.

Black's position is not easy. White intends to play Qd2 and Rad1 and a ...c7-c5 advance would allow White the opportunity to rip open the d-file whenever it was favorable (White would only play dxc5 in answer to ...c7-c5 after he got his heavy pieces on the d-file). Also note that ...c7-c5 followed by ...cxd4 leaves Black with a backward pawn on d6. Because of this potential weakness along the d-file Black's plan of ...c7-c5 is not very effective. Unfortunately, Black does not have any other methods of counterplay and White can lay claim to an advantage. All this comes from White's advantage in space and Black's lack of counterplay.

Lessons From This Game:

1) If you're going to worry about something make sure it is worth worrying about!

2) Games are often won by simply taking space and restricting the opponent's options. You don't have to attack like a wild man to score a point.

In our final example with this favorable White opening, the first player (a man with a solid "A" rating) tries hard to defend his center right from the start.

1950 vs. J.S.

1.d4 g6 2.e4 Bg7 3.Nc3 d6 4.f4 e6 5.Nf3 Ne7

1950: White has a broad center and the Silman school says that White has an obligation to maintain the center and once this is done White can switch to a wing action. So how to develop and maintain the center? I can find moves just to protect my center but is that enough? I'm looking at Bc4. 6.Bd3 does not seem bad either. Also reasonable is 6.e5, gaining space, but I can do that at any time. That's why Bd3 is all right since e5 frees it. Black must attack the center. He can do this with any one of four pawns but the most likely is the c-pawn. There is something to be said for placing the c3 Knight on e2 and bolstering my center with c3. I'll go for Bd3.

JS: I was very happy that he seemed to remember the content of our lesson on the center. I looked forward to him defending his center with everything he had.

6.Bd3 b6

1950: Preparing to fianchetto.

7.Ne2

1950: The troubling thing about my move is that I am moving a piece twice in the opening but since it's a semi-closed game this is not terribly important. At least, I hope it's not!

7...Bb7

1950: c2-c3 is coming but there is not any reason to play it at this point. There are more important moves to play. Ordinarily you don't want to castle where a fianchettoed Bishop is bearing down but in this case he has fianchettoes on both sides! However, my pawn center is blunting both of them. I can't help but be tempted to play g4 with the idea of Ng3 but it leaves my King open. 8.0-0 also looks natural since it placed the Rook on the someday to be opened f-file. I'll go for the restrained approach.

8.0-0 0-0

1950: Now I feel that his King is stuck on the kingside and I'd like to play there. I'll either play c3 or Be3. By defending d4 with c2-c3, my e2 Knight is free to move to g3 and threaten f4-f5. To stop this Black will be tempted to play ...f7-f5. Then exf5 gxf5 opens his King... however, if he answers 9.c3 f5 10.exf5 with 10...exf5 then I feel that I have given up my good central pawn. So perhaps the immediate 9.g4 is the right way to go.

JS: He was so careful to defend his center and then he suddenly abandoned the idea and went charging the kingside. Why? The simple 9.c3 would give him a fine game with no weaknesses. Only after making his center indestructible should he entertain ideas concerning attacks against my King.

9.g4 f5

—Stopped the game.

Lessons From This Game:

1) Once you start a plan make sure you finish it; don't allow

yourself to get sidetracked.

2) If you own the center and are killing all the opponent's counterplay, there is no hurry to start an attack on the wing. Continue to take your time, gain more space, and take away the enemy's options.

The next example is a fine game played by Fischer against the Romanian GM Gheorghiu. I showed this to a student who owned a 1600 rating (though he was 1900 in postal) and asked him to annotate it as we went.

Fischer–Gheorghiu, Buenos Aires 1970

1.e4 e5 2.Nf3 Nf6 3.Nxe5 d6 4.Nf3 Nxe4 5.d4 Be7

1600: I like 6.Bc4. It attacks f7 and threatens Ng5 and it allows me to castle. He could push to d5 but then I play Bb3 followed by Nc3 when it is equal. Another interesting move is 6.c4 when 6...d5 7.cxd5 Nxd5 8.Bc4 Be6 9.Nc3 is promising.

JS: This incoherent litany really shows why he doesn't do so well in tournaments. He never tried to figure out what he had that his opponent didn't. Due to this, he began to look at moves in a complete state of ignorance. Not seeing (or caring) that he had a slight advantage in space, he first looked at 6.Bc4, saying that 7.Ng5 would then be a threat. Why? Would Black just sit around and allow White to capture on f7? Even after the impossible 6.Bc4 pass 7.Ng5 0-0 (though 7...d5 makes 7.Ng5 look really useless) we have to ask what White has accomplished. Since 8.Nxf7 Rxf7 9.Bxf7+ Kxf7 is good for Black (two minor pieces is usually superior to a Rook and pawn), the Knight move to g5 will turn out to be just a waste of time.

He also mentioned 6.Bc4 d5 7.Nc3 but then 7...c6 leaves the Bishop on b3 hitting granite while the c3 Knight would also find itself doing nothing (can't go to e4 and is putting no pressure on the well defended d5 square).

Finally, his claim that 6.c4 d5 7.cxd5 Nxd5 8.Bc4 Be6 9.Nc3 is promising falls on its face after 9...Nxc3 when Black has won a piece!

It's clear that he is just trying to develop his pieces, but you must only develop pieces to posts where they do something, preferably in relation to the imbalance (in this case, space).

6.Bd3

1600: Logical, but it does not seem very aggressive to me. It's solid but rather boring. Black should play ...Nf6.

JS: Why allow the Black Knight to remain on the active e4 square? With 6.Bd3 White develops the Bishop to a safe but important post and gains time by hitting the enemy Knight.

6...Nf6

1600: White is slightly better because he has space and his dark-squared Bishop is better. White should gain more space. How to do this? 7.c4 and 7.0-0 and 7.Bg5 are all good. Even 7.h3 is possible which keeps Black's Bishop back. I'd go for 7.h3.

JS: He got one right because he finally began to take note of the space edge! 7.h3 is an excellent move because it restricts the enemy pieces and the player with an edge in space should be choking the opponent's army at every opportunity.

7.h3! 0-0 8.0-0 Re8

1600: White can play 9.Bf4, 9.Bg5, 9.Re1, 9.Nc3, and 9.c4. I'd probably play 9.Re1.

9.c4

JS: White continues his plan of adding to his advantage in space and, at the same time, taking away squares from the enemy pieces.

9...Nc6

1600: Simply 10.Nc3 to fight for d5 and e4 is correct. This also keeps a flexible position.

JS: This is very natural and good. Some players try 10.a3 so as to prevent ...Nb4. However, this Knight sally is nothing to fear since Bb1 saves the Bishop when White, by a2-a3, could chase the Knight back to where it came from. Don't go out of your way to prevent things that cause no real harm!

10.Nc3 h6

1600: I like Qc2 when a later Bxh6 may be possible or Ne4 getting rid of a kingside defender. I don't like Bf4 but Re1 looks good.

JS: White's pieces do aim at the kingside but I don't see how Qc2 helps make Bxh6 a threat.

11.Re1 Bf8

1600: 12.Be3!? is best, since I don't like exchanges.

JS: While I don't like his 12.Be3 (which just clogs up the White army), I do like his statement that exchanges are not what White wants. It appears that 1600 is well aware that the side with more territory should avoid unnecessary exchanges since that just helps to relieve Black's cramp.

12.Rxe8

JS: The trade of one Rook won't do any harm to White's cause.

12...Qxe8

1600: Now 13.Bd2 followed by Qc2 and Re1 is indicated. It's still just a bit better for White 'cause Black is very solid; White can't get him anywhere.

13.Bf4

JS: The Bishop is obviously more active here than it would be on d2.

13...Bd7

JS: Note how the lack of space prevents Black from posting his pieces on active squares.

1600: I don't like Qc2 anymore. 14.Qd2 gives potential for sacrifices and a kingside attack.

JS: So he finally realizes that his Qc2 had no real point (aside from allowing potential forks by ...Nb4). This is why one should make the Queen one of the last pieces to be moved—you often don't know where it belongs till most of the other pieces are out.

14.Qd2

(31)

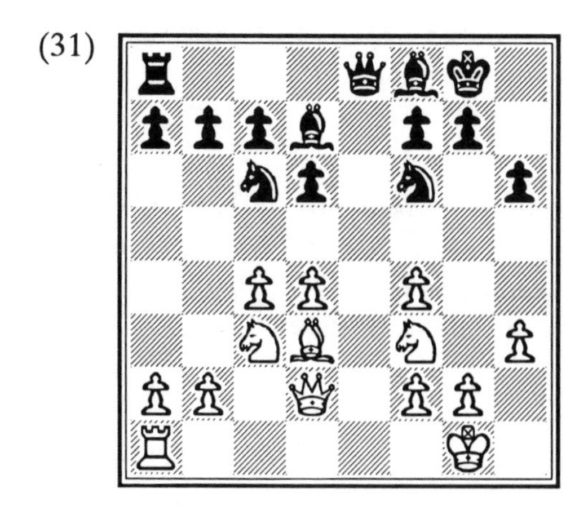

1600: Black can't attack White in the center. 14...Ne7 with the idea of ...Ng6 makes sense.

14...Qc8

1600: Does this threaten to sacrifice? Looks scary since 15...Bxh3 16.gxh3 Qxh3 and, if Black can get rid of the Bishop on f4, ...Ng4 would create a strong threat of ...Qh2+. Perhaps 15.Nd5!? which threatens Nxf6 and ties his Queen to the defense of c7 is worth trying. Re1 is what I would like to do if ...Bxh3 were not a threat.

JS: When someone makes a seeming threat it is very important to determine if this threat is real or imagined. If his sacrifice ultimately fails then why would you go out of your way to prevent it? In this case White sees that ...Bxh3 is nothing to worry about so he happily continues with his space-eating ways.

15.d5

1600: This cramps Blacks game more and forces him back. White is attacking on the kingside while Black should play ...Ne7 and play for a queenside attack.

JS: How does ...Ne7 help Black with a queenside attack?

15...Nb4

1600: White could play 16.Be4 when 16...Nxe4 17.Nxe4 is

OK for White.

JS: White does not wish to give up the two Bishops here. He also sees that 16.Bb1 allows soothing exchanges after 16...Bf5.

16.Ne4!

1600: Black must play ...Nxd3 but then 17.Nxf6+ is strong.

JS: Black does not wish to allow his kingside pawns to be shattered so he captures on e4, though this allows the White Bishop to step out of the way of the b4 Knight.

16...Nxe4 17.Bxe4 Na6

1600: Where is the killer? 18.Bxh6 fails. White probably has to start a pawn attack via 18.Kh2, g4, and g5. Another way is 18.h4-h5, Kh2, Rg1, g4-g5. Here Black would have big problems. Another idea is Nh2 and Ng4.

JS: Why the crazed wing attack? It seems that most amateurs suffer from a lack of patience. They probably think that if you don't do something forcing then your advantage will disappear. In this case White sees that ...Bf5 is still a threat so he centralizes his Knight and prevents this move once and for all.

18.Nd4 Nc5 19.Bc2 a5

1600: White is still better but has no big attack. White must get his Rook into the attack. 20.Kh2 with the idea of g4 still looks good. White must play for a kingside attack. 20.a3 and b4 doesn't work and 20.a4 is horrible. 20.Re1 is not as strong as a g4, Rg1 idea.

JS: 1600's pawn storm idea is not so bad (he is trying to do something positive) but why weaken one's King when you can play quietly in the middle with no risk?

20.Re1

1600: Going to e3 and g3.

20...Qd8 21.Re3 b6 22.Rg3

JS: This threatens the simple Bxh6.

22...Kh8

1600: White should have something crushing since he has too much over on the kingside. 23.Qc3 Qf6 24.Rf3 Re8 is not so clear but I know that something good is hiding from me.

23.Nf3!

JS: White does not want to allow Black to defend with ...Qf6. Now Qd4 is a huge threat and 23...Qf6 is met by 24.Be3! followed by Bd4.

23...Qe7 24.Qd4

Here we ran out of time and stopped the game. White threatens Bxh6 and the only way to stop this is by 24...f6 (which weakens the light-squares and allows Nh4 followed by Ng6) or by **24...Qf6** (this was played in the game) with the follow-up: **25.Qxf6 gxf6 26.Nd4** (heading for the hole on f5) **26...Re8 27.Re3** (White feels that his superior pawn structure is enough to win so he carefully prevents Black from gaining any counterplay) **27...Rb8 28.b3 b5 29.cxb5 Bxb5 30.Nf5 Bd7 31.Nxh6** with material gain and a win on the 35th move.

Lessons From This Game:

1) You can win games just by increasing your edge in territory bit by bit.

2) If you own a space advantage, play to restrict the enemy pieces.

3) The side with more space should not trade too many pieces.

4) The side with less space should strive to exchange whenever possible.

5) Don't be in a rush to force things. A slow squeeze is quite enough to torture the opponent and force his eventual capitulation.

Our next example shows a position where the center is dead and the space advantage lies on the kingside.

Reti–Carls, Baden-Baden 1925

(32)

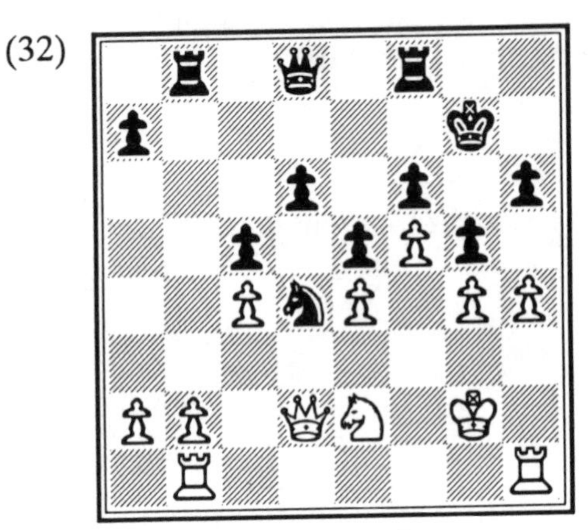

White to play.

Reti won this position in instructive fashion. He first avoided unnecessary exchanges and then made use of the h-file—a file that can be opened whenever White wants it to be opened.

1.Nc3!

Avoiding exchanges and bringing the Knight to the active d5 post.

1...Rh8 2.Rh3!

Of course, since White has a space advantage on the kingside, that is where he directs his play. The text follows an instructive but common idea. White will play on the h-file but, seeing that 2.hxg5 hxg5 allows exchanges, he will only open it when he triples by Rh3, Rbh1, and Qh2. Since Black has far less territory on that file, he will be unable to copy White's movements there.

2...Rbg8 3.Rbh1 Qd8 4.Nd5!

Threatening Kg3, Qh2, hxg5 and Rh7+.

4...gxh4 5.Rxh4 Kf7 6.Kf2 Qf8 7.Rxh6 Rxh6 8.Rxh6 Qg7 9.Qa5! 1-0

Mate follows 10.Qc7+. Reti made this look easy, but good

things just happen if you play where your favorable imbalances reside.

Could an amateur with a 1700 rating handle things so well? Would he recognize his chances on the h-file? I decided to allow my student the chance to walk in Reti's shadow.

1700 vs. J.S.

(33)

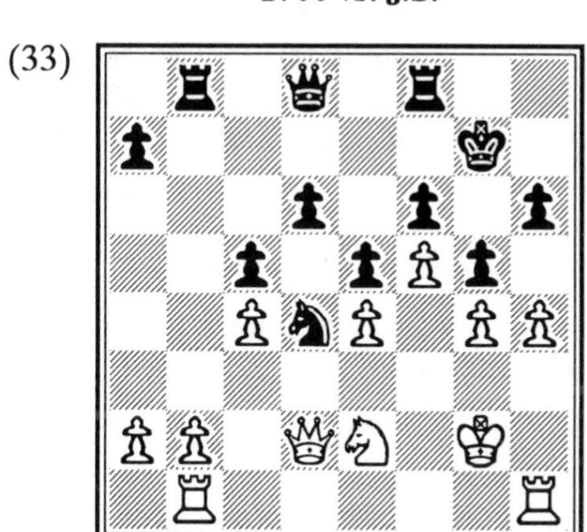

White to play.

1700: First we must look at the imbalances. Black has an imbalance on the queenside and on d5, e6, g6, h5. Black's position is a big hole...it's bad. For White: White has no imbalances. He has one on f4 (though it is guarded by the Knight). White has space everywhere while the open file for Black means nothing. The best place for the White Knight is e6. White does not want to trade Knights 'cause his is more mobile than the Black one. White can also cramp Black some more by h5.

1.h5??

JS: I almost had a heart attack when he played this lemon, and it was only the fact that my student was a doctor that saved me.

First, he seemed to think that imbalances meant weaknesses. An imbalance is <u>not</u> a weakness! It is any difference in the position. Thus it can be positive, negative, or neutral. Here he *saw that he possessed an advantage in territory on the kingside and then he willingly closed that side up completely!*

It only took one move for him to destroy his advantage, since Black is the one who has all the play on the queenside.

1...Rb4 2.b3 Rfb8

JS: Since Black no longer has to worry about attacks down the h-file, he is free to devote his full attention to the other wing.

1700: Black is trying to pile up on the queenside—he is hoping to exchange the pawn on c4 (by ...R8b6, ...Qb7, and ...Rxc4) and pick off the Rook on b1. This is permanently prevented by Nc3.

3.Nc3 Qb7

1700: He is pinning my e-pawn to my King. What happens if I play Nd5 and attack his Rook?

4.Nd5 Qc6

1700: Why does he want to give me a Rook for a Knight? I don't understand this. Do I take his Rook or do I double on the b-file? Ahhh . . . if 5.Nxb4 Qxe4+. What does that do? It does not look so bad for me. 5.Nxb4 Qxe4+ 6.Kh3. White is not winning but Black might have a draw. Actually he might get my Knight and two pawns for that Rook. This is good for him so I can't do that. I'm also worried about 5...Nxb3 6.axb3 Rxb3 7.Rxb3 but that is not so dangerous. I better protect my e-pawn.

5.Re1 R4b7

1700: Black has queenside space but his pieces are inactive. How good is space if your pieces are not active? So I must take the fight to him even if I lose a pawn: 6.b4 cxb4 7.Nxb4. However, then 7...Qxc4 is possible. I'm not worried 'cause I will take with the Rook.

JS: 1700 is a frisky guy, but if you have less space than the opponent you should not go out of your way to open things up. 1700's desire to win at all costs often clouds his judgement.

6.b4??

JS: Opening the b-file for the Black Rooks and creating a weak c-pawn.

6...cxb4 7.Rxb4 Rxb4 8.Nxb4 Qxc4

1700: If 9.Rc1 Qxb4 10.Rc7+ Kg8 11.Rc8+ wins his Queen! The other move is 9.a3 but what do I do about 9...a5? So 9.Rc1 looks very good.

JS: He is tricky, but unfortunately (for him) this simply does not work.

9.Rc1 Qxb4 10.Rc7+ Kf8 11.Rc8+ Ke7

1700: So my sacrifice did not work.

We stopped the game, discussed his horrible 1.h4-h5?? and took my blood pressure.

Lessons From This Game:

1) A space advantage means little if there is no way to penetrate into the enemy position.

2) Open files are precious things. Don't close off the very files that you can make inroads on!

Silman–Barkan, U.S. Open 1981

(34)

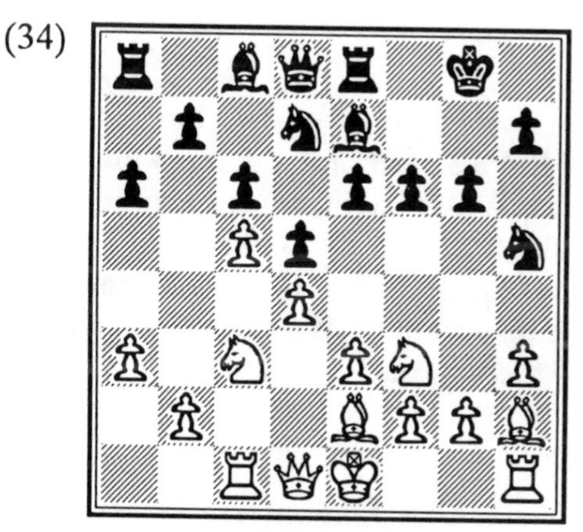

White to play.

In the position in diagram #34, it is not hard to see that White enjoys a clear space advantage on the queenside. Normally the first player might try to add to this by b2-b4 and a3-a4, followed by an eventual b4-b5.

However, it is not enough to look at your own plans to the exclusion of the opponent's. Just what *is* Black going to do? Apparently, he will attempt to advance in the center with ...Bf8 and ...e6-e5 (thus annexing territory of his own). Why should White allow this? Why not take space everywhere and leave Black with little or no counterplay? This is the reasoning White employed when deciding on his next move.

1.e4!

Grabbing a spatial plus in the center also. Now White would welcome 1...dxe4 since 2.Nxe4 would allow him to make use of the d6 square and, once White castles and places a Rook on e1, the backward pawn on e6. This move shows us that it is not enough to be able to simply recognize a space advantage. You must also be able to *create* extra territory—don't expect it to just magically happen.

1...Bf8 2.0-0 Bh6 3.Rc2 Kh8 4.Re1 Nf4 5.Bf1 Rg8 6.b4

White's last few moves are easy to understand. He has gotten his King to safety, placed a Rook on the e-file (which can be opened whenever White decides to play exd5), and solidified his position on the queenside.

6...Nf8 7.a4 g5

Since Black is clearly worse on the queenside and in the center, he goes for his last shot on the kingside. Normally central play (which White has) will prove to be more valuable than this type of deperado attack on the wing. However, White comes up with a very greedy idea: He decides to take control of the kingside also! If successful, White will gain an advantage in all three areas of the board.

8.Bxf4 gxf4 9.Nh2!

Preparing to bring the Queen over to h5. Black can't prevent this by 9...Qe8? since 10.exd5 cxd5 11.Nxd5 would prove to be more than bothersome.

9...Ng6 10.Qh5 Bf8 11.exd5 cxd5 12.Bd3

White has an enormous advantage. His pieces aim at the kingside and dominate the center. White also has a powerful queenside pawn majority that gives him excellent chances in any endgame.

12...f5 13.Nf3 Be7 14.Rce2 Bf6

Trying to cover the weakened e5 and g5 squares.

15.Rxe6!

Decisive. The White army bursts into the Black position, picking up pawns as it goes.

15...Bxe6 16.Rxe6 Be7

Stopping Rd6.

17.Bxf5 Nf8 18.Ne5! Qe8 19.Nf7+ Kg7 20.Nxd5!

(35)

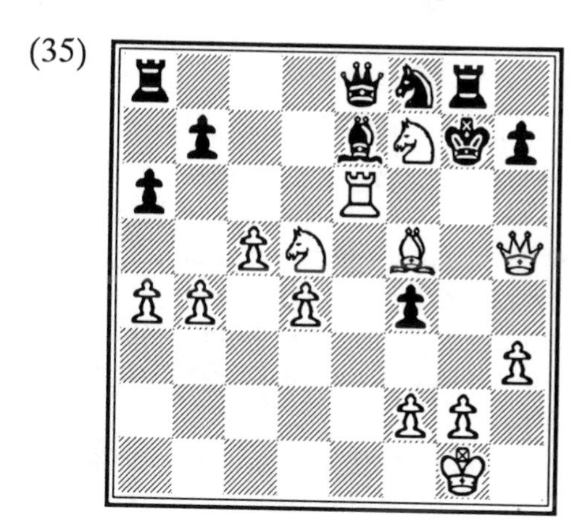

Black to play.

Note that the centrally located White pieces also control critical squares on both wings.

20...Nxe6

Or 20...Qxf7 21.Rxe7.

21.Qh6+ Kxf7 22.Bxe6 mate

Though White started with his space advantage on the queenside, he went out of his way to create the territory in the other areas. Can the amateur also create a space advantage where none seems to initially exist? This is the problem that I set before a couple of my students.

1500 vs. J.S.

(36)

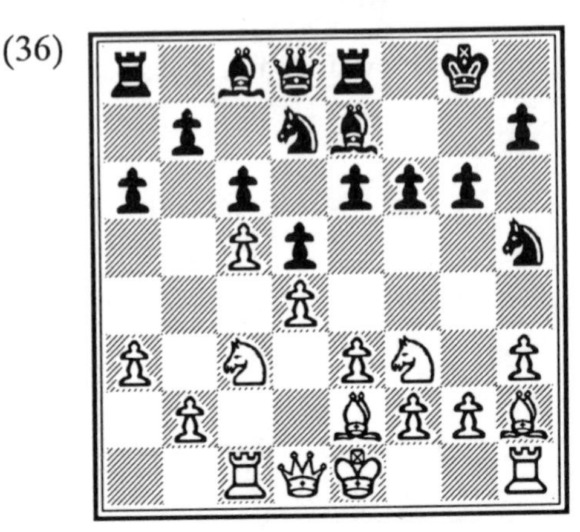

White to play.

1500: Material is even. White's pawn structure is better than Black's. His pawns are aiming at the queenside and he has a space advantage there. My Bishops are superior. The h2 Bishop is bad but it's outside the pawn chain. Black has a slight space edge on the kingside. Black's d6 square is weak. White definitely has the better game here. Due to the nature of the position (closed center) I can get more space on the queenside with b4.

JS: He did a good job in recognizing what White had. Unfortunately, he did not pay much attention to his opponent's plans.

1.b4 Bf8

1500: Black's trying to get his Bishop active by playing it to h6. Another possibility is to play it to g7 and go for a push in the center. I would like to get to his backward pawn on b7 if I can. I am debating whether to castle or not to castle right now.

JS: He is doing a really good job. He saw that Black might begin some central play but it never occurred to him to strike there first. Why make it a battle between one person's queenside vs. another's center or queenside when you can have it all?

2.0-0 e5

1500: He's playing to open up the center and activate his Bishops. His two options are to take or push. I eventually need to play a4 and b5 but I'm not quite sure where to place my pieces on that side. I'll forge ahead.

3.a4 e4

1500: Grabbing more space in the center. I'll move my Knight over to the queenside.

JS: All of a sudden Black has a space advantage in the center that aims at the kingside. This translates to active kingside play for Black, compared to the passive stance that Black was forced to endure in the Silman–Barkan game.

4.Nd2 Ng7

1500: Black is playing for a kingside pawn storm by pushing his pawns there. So I should push on with what I want to do since it's now a race.

JS: He keeps showing excellent powers of reasoning and wisely states that you should play quickly on your respective side in a race situation. The only flaw is this: If you can keep the enemy tied up and inactive, why let him in a race in the first place?

5.b5 f5

1500: He is continuing to put pressure over there. I don't think Black has any immediate threat so I must make my attack faster.

6.bxc6 bxc6 7.Rb1 Ne6

1500: Black's trying to get his pieces over to the queenside. I will push my a-pawn so I can sink something into b6.

JS: I played ...Qxa5 so he took it back.

1500: I will play Na2-b4 and put pressure on c6 and a6.

8.Na2 a5

1500: I'm starting to panic. Every entry point is defended by his minor pieces and pawns.

9.Qc2 Bh6 10.Bd6

1500: The point of Qc2 was to play Bd6 even if his Bishop was on f8. Then if he took I could open the c-file with cxd6. Unfortunately, with my wandering your attack has gotten more serious.

10...f4 11.Rb3 Qh4

1500: My Bishops are still better but I think Black's position is now superior since it's easier for his pieces to get through to me.

—Stopped the game.

1650 vs. J.S.

(37)

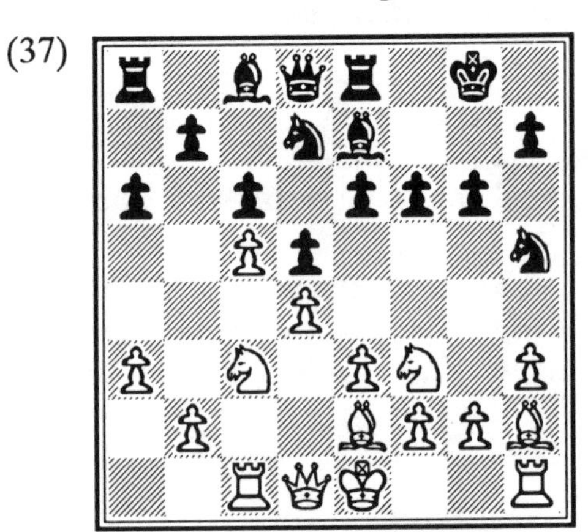

White to play.

1650: White has more space on the queenside. He also has two developed Bishops. White's Knights have better central positions. Black should be breaking in the center with ...e5 which frees his Bishops and other pieces. White should prevent Black from attacking the center.

JS: Excellent! White not only notes his own queenside play but also sees that he should prevent Black from getting his own stuff in the middle.

1.e4 Bf8

1650: I don't want to capture since it opens the e-file. I will build pressure on e4 with Qc2.

2.Qc2

JS: Not a terrible move but pretty much unnecessary. The e4-pawn was already well defended so an extra defender is sort of pointless. Instead, he should have castled, since you don't want your King sitting in the middle when the center is opening up.

2...Bh6 3.Rb1

1650: Bring it to b1 so I can play b4 and gain more space on the queenside.

3...Bf4

1650: I have a space advantage so I don't want to trade since that will give him more room. Instead I will force him to retreat.

4.g3?

JS: Absolutely terrible. It is good that he knew that exchanges should be avoided if you have a space advantage, but don't prevent trades if it results in an entombed, useless piece.

4...Bc7

1650: Now I will try to gain an attack on the kingside since his pawns are kind of weak. First I will activate my e2-Bishop by getting my Knight out of the way.

5.Nh4

JS: 1650 has sort of lost his mind around here. First he plays the excellent e3-e4, but then he kills off one of his own pieces with g2-g3 and next he sticks his Knight away from the center on h4.

5...Ng7

1650: Now I will gain more space.

6.f4

JS: It is wonderful that he wants to gain more space, but why weaken his kingside and leave the poor King stuck in the center?

6...dxe4 7.Nxe4 Nf5

1650: I don't want to trade since I have the space edge.

JS: He is stuck on that rule. In this case he does not want to trade since it allows Black to open the e-file to the White centralized King.

8.Nf3 Ne3

1650: My Queen is being attacked but I want to keep her as close to the center as possible by Qd3. If he checks me on g2 his Knight is trapped.

9.Qd3 Nd5

1650: Now your Knight is in the center on a strong square. I will continue to eye his kingside and activate my Bishop.

JS: I don't know why White wants to avoid castling so badly (not to even mention the fact that he keeps sticking his Knight on the rim). Evidently he does not realize that a centralized King stops the Rooks from connecting and will come under attack if the enemy can open up the center.

10.Nh4 f5

JS: Threatening ...Nxf4.

1650: I will bring my Knight to the nice g5 square.

11.Ng5 e5!

JS: Taking advantage of the fact that White's Knight on g5 is only defended by the pawn on f4.

1650: He is trying to open up the file for the Rook. I have to capture it.

12.dxe5 Nxe5

1650: He is giving up a piece to get an attack on my King with his Rook.

13.fxe5

1650: Oh . . . he's getting a piece back! I've really blown it.

13...Qxg5

1650: Black is now better. I must attack the Queen and protect the pawn.

—Stopped the game.

Lessons From These Games:

1) If you can grab space and prevent the opponent from laying to it then by all means do so!
2) Don't allow a race if you don't have to.
3) It is rarely good to leave your King in the middle.

PART FOUR

The Confusing Subject of Pawn Structure

If you ask an amateur player what he thinks of when you say hanging, doubled, backward, or isolated pawns, the most likely response will be, a weakness. Funnily enough, though, most amateurs don't really care or know how to go after pawn weaknesses, much preferring the thrill of a King-hunt. The other side of the story follows the same pattern. If the amateur gets these so called weaknesses, he will usually panic since he is not aware of the dynamic potential inherent in all these structures. The simple truth is, it is impossible to label anything in chess as always being weak. The list that follows shows when to punish the existence of these pawns, and when to welcome them into your own position.

(38)

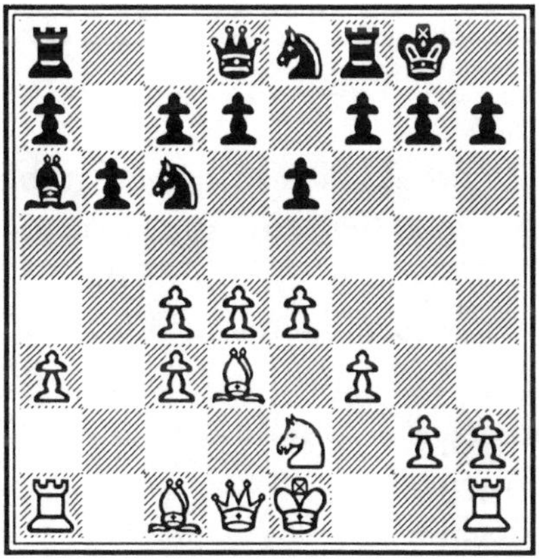

White to play.

1) NEGATIVE: The doubling of pawns reduces the

flexibility of these pawns and, at times, leaves one or both of them vulnerable to attack (though it's usually the lead-off pawn that is the weakest).

White's c-pawns are doubled in diagram #38. Though the pawn on c3 is very safe, the guy on c4 is further advanced and thus vulnerable to attack by the enemy pieces. Black will torment this pawn by ...Nc6-a5 (when his Bishop and Knight both attack it) followed by ...c7-c5 and ...Rc8 and, if necessary, ...Ne8-d6.

2) POSITIVE: The doubling of pawns leads to extra open files for your Rooks and increased square control.

After **1.e4 e5 2.Nf3 Nc6 3.Nc3 Nf6 4.Bc4 Bc5 5.0-0 0-0 6.d3 d6** White can play the silly looking **7.Be3**.

(39)

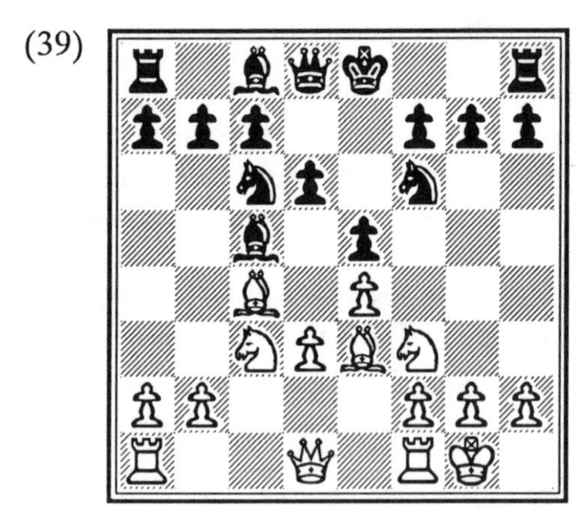

White to play.

Is it wise for White to allow his pawns to be doubled? Actually, White would love Black to capture on e3! After 7...Bxe3 8.fxe3 White gets increased control of the d4 and f4 squares and immediately creates a fine open f-file for his Rooks. Since e4 is solidly guarded by a pawn, and since the e3-pawn is quite safe (Qe2 defends it), White suffers no negative consequences at all from this doubling.

Funnily enough, Black would do well to answer 7.Be3 with either 7...Bb6 (when 8.Bxb6 axb6 gives Black the open a-file) or 7...Bg4, when 8.Bxc5 dxc5 gives Black the use of a half open d-file and powerful control of d4. Note that the doubled pawn on c5 is easily defended by ...b7-b6.

3) NEGATIVE: An isolated pawn cannot be defended by another pawn and is very vulnerable to attack if it stands on an open file.

(40)

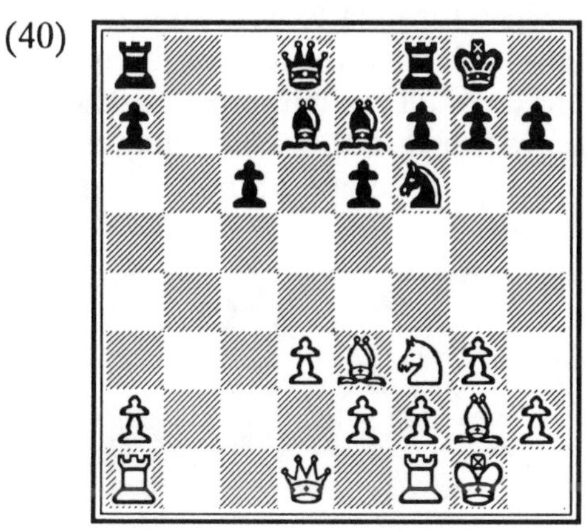

White to play.

In diagram #40, White can bring a whole army to bear on the poor c6-pawn by Rac1, Nd4 or Ne5, and, if necessary, Qa4 or Qc2.

4) POSITIVE: The creation of an isolated pawn may bestow upon its owner the use of a half-open file.

(41)

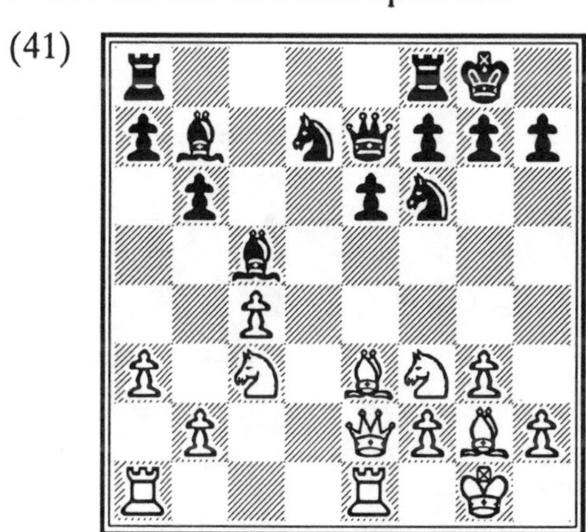

White to play.

After **1.Bxc5** (in diagram #41) Black could safely play

1...Qxc5 or 1...Nxc5. However, **1...bxc5!?** also deserves serious consideration. True, this pawn is now isolated. However, it is not very weak since it doesn't stand on an open file, it keeps the White pieces out of d4, and Black is able to generate pressure down the newly opened b-file against White's pawn on b2.

5) NEGATIVE: The formula to beat an isolated pawn calls for control of the weak square in front of the pawn (so that it can't move), the trade of all the minor pieces, the retention of a Queen and one or two Rooks, the doubling of these pieces against the pawn, and the use of a friendly pawn to attack and pin the isolated target.

(42)

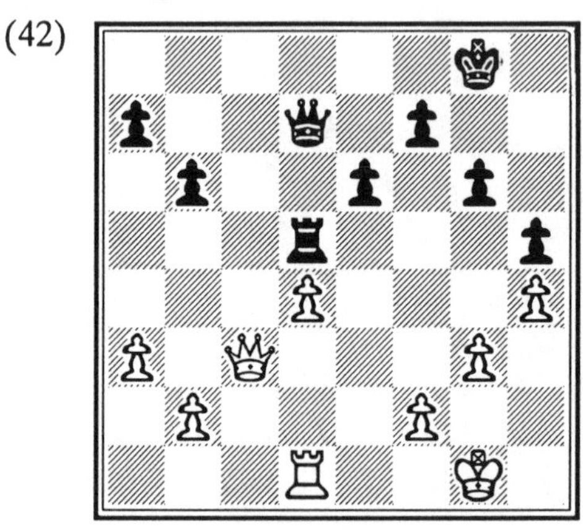

White to play.

In diagram #42, Black wins the fixed, isolated d-pawn by playing **1...e5**.

(43)

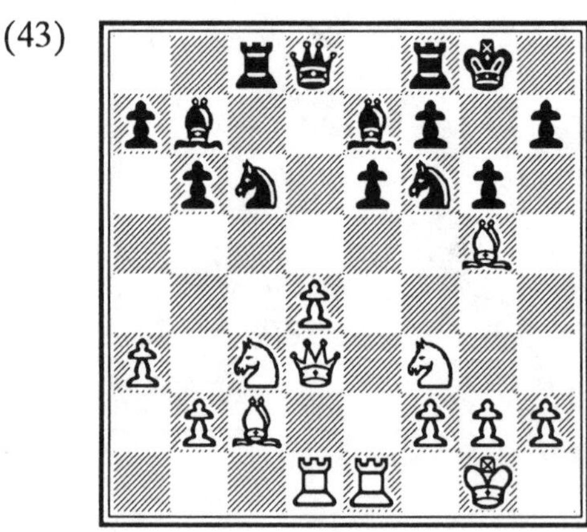

6) POSITIVE: An isolated d-pawn at Q4 gives its owner plenty of space for his pieces and open files for his Rooks. The person that possesses this pawn should play for dynamic play with his pieces.

White's d-pawn (in diagram #43) gives him extra space, use of the e5 square (a nice home for a Knight), and possibilities of a kingside attack or a central advance with d4-d5.

7) FINAL LINE OF DEFENSE: If the isolated d-pawn becomes weak and minor pieces get traded off, the exchange of the rooks makes the isolated d-pawn a negligible disadvantage.

(44)

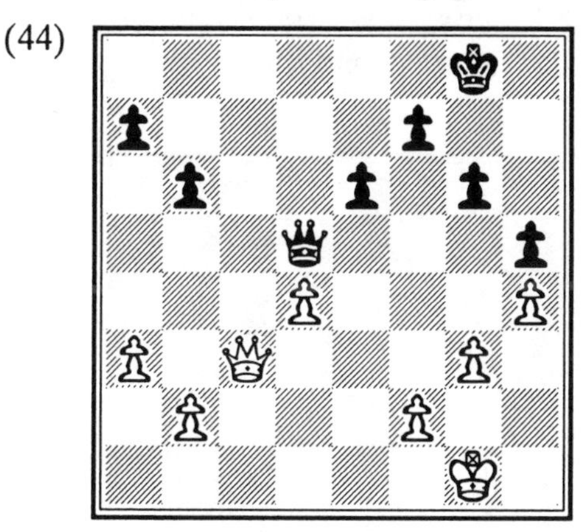

In diagram #44, Black is unable to apply more pressure to the pawn and White can easily hold the position.

8) NEGATIVE: A backward pawn is only weak if it is sitting

(45)

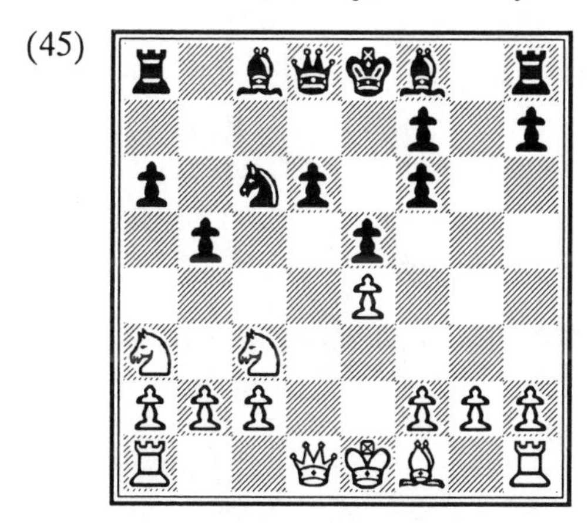

White to play.

on an open file and it is unable to advance. The side playing against the backward pawn should strive to control the square directly in front of it, since this square cannot be defended by a pawn.

In diagram #45, White will play to increase his control of the d5 square by Nd5, c2-c3, Na3-c2-e3, and if necessary, g2-g3 followed by Bg2.

9) POSITIVE: A backward pawn acts as a guard to a more advanced pawn to the side of it. This advanced pawn can block enemy pieces and control important squares. The backward pawn cannot be considered a bad thing if the square in front of it is well defended.

(46)

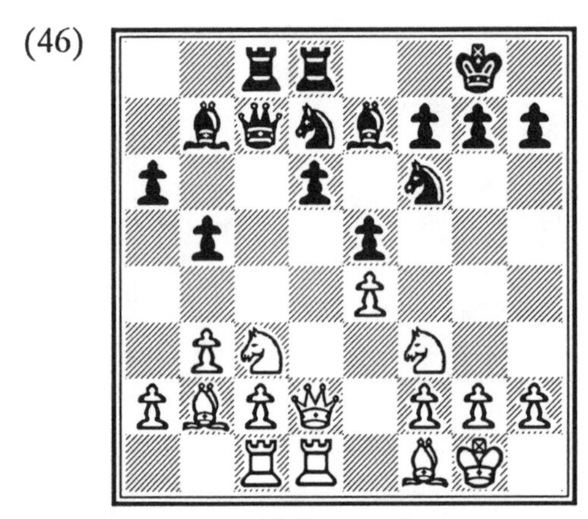

White to play.

In diagram #46, White can play 1.Nd5 but after 1...Nxd5 2.exd5 the d5-square is covered up by a pawn. In this position the d6-pawn is well defended and is not really a weakness at all. In fact, Black's active pieces and pressure on e4 gives the second player the advantage.

10) NEGATIVE: "Hanging pawns" can be weak if the other side is able to direct his forces onto them and avoid their dynamic potential.

White has created strong pressure (in diagram #47) on the d5-pawn and there is nothing Black can do to save it. **1...Ne4** fails to **2.Nxd5! Bxd5 3.Bxe4.**

(47)

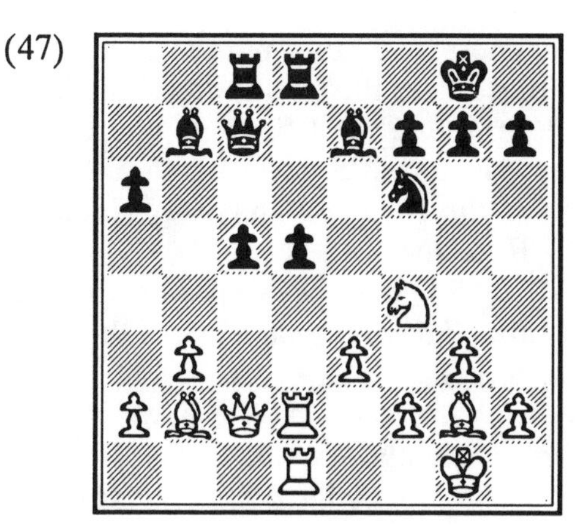

Black to play.

11) POSITIVE: The traditional hanging pawns on c5 and d5 (or c4 and d4 if White has them) control many important central squares, give their owner an advantage in territory, and also offer play on the half open b-file and e-file.

In diagram #48, Black's "hanging pawns" are well defended and give him extra space, control of the center, and strong play down the b-file. Since Black threatens to play 1...Qb4, White takes steps to prevent this. **1.Nd3** Covers b4, threatens the

(48)

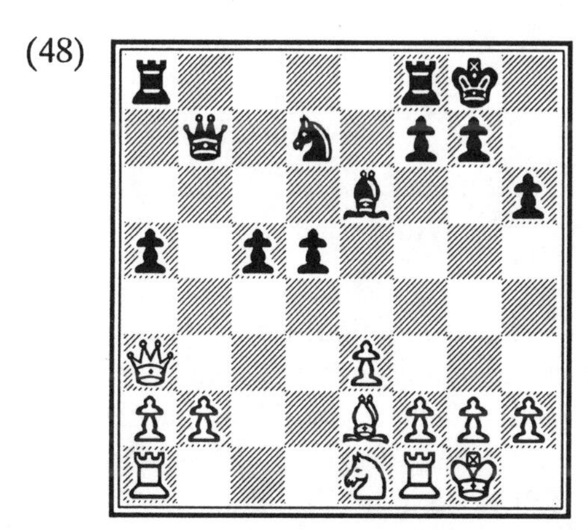

Bertok–Fischer, Stockholm 1962
White to play.

pawn on c5, and prepares for Nf4 with pressure on d5. **1...c4!**

This creates a weakness on d4 that White will not have time to use. With 1...c4! Black fixes the enemy pawn on b2 and turns it into an immobile target. 2.Nf4 Rfb8 and White was in grave difficulties. After **3.Rab1? Bf5 4.Rad1 Nf6 5.Rd2 g5!** White gave up a piece and the game with **6.Nxd5? Nxd5** rather than face 6.Nh5 Ne4 7.Rc2 Qb4.

12) REMEMBER: So-called weak pawns are only weak if you can seriously attack them or make use of the weak squares that may come with them.

13) NEGATIVE: A protected passed pawn is *not* always an advantage, though most players think it is. If the square in front of it can be controlled by the other side, then the pawn is stopped in its tracks and becomes a non-factor for a long time to come. Even worse, if this square falls into the hands of a Knight, then the horse will radiate power on neighboring squares and pawns.

(49)

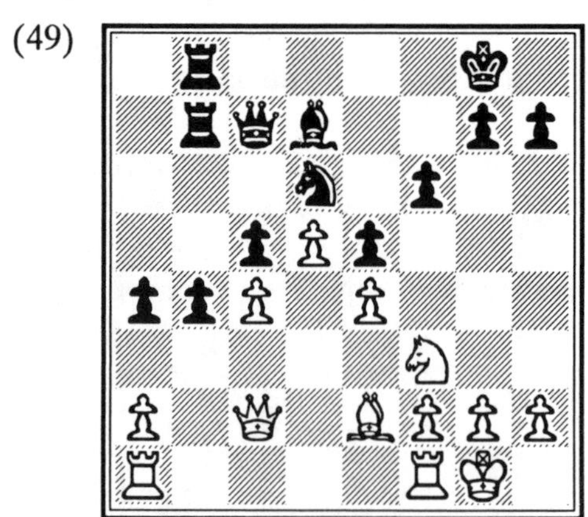

White to play.

In diagram #49, Black's Knight on d6 prevents the enemy passed pawn from going anywhere. It also eyes b5, b7, c8, e8, f7, and f5, aside from attacking the White pawns on c4 and e4.

With White's pawn stopped, the active Black queenside majority shows itself to be more valuable.

14) POSITIVE: A passed pawn is very strong if its owner has play elsewhere and can use it as endgame insurance or if the square in front of it is in his hands.

In diagram #50, Black is in big trouble since he does not

(50)

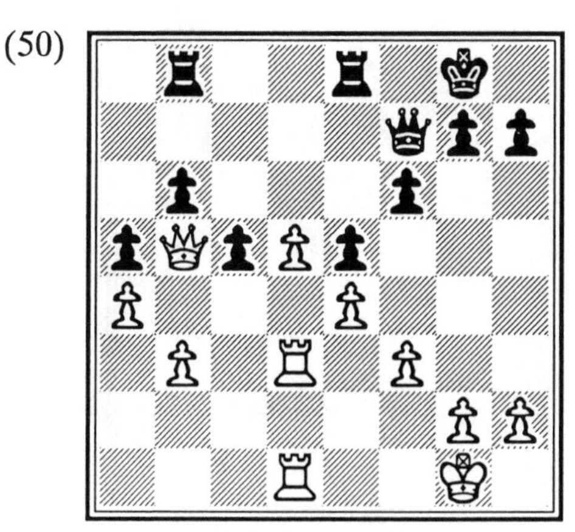

White to play.

have control of the square in front of the passed pawn. White plays 1.d6 followed by 2.d7 and the whole Black army will be forced to run before the pawn's might.

The Amateur's Mind

After giving my students several lessons concerning strong and weak pawns, I usually wait a few weeks and then give them the chance to show me what they remember about our discussions. The first game revolves around the proper use of hanging pawns.

1600 vs. J.S.

1.d4 Nf6 2.c4 e6 3.Nf3 b6 4.e3 Bb7 5.Bd3 d5 6.b3 Nbd7 7.0-0 Be7 8.Nbd2 0-0 9.Bb2 c5 10.Qe2 cxd4 11.exd4 dxc4 12.bxc4 Rc8

1600: I will back up my pawns with Rooks.

JS: Not delving deeply into the position at all but still coming up with a reasonable method of development. White must realize

(51)

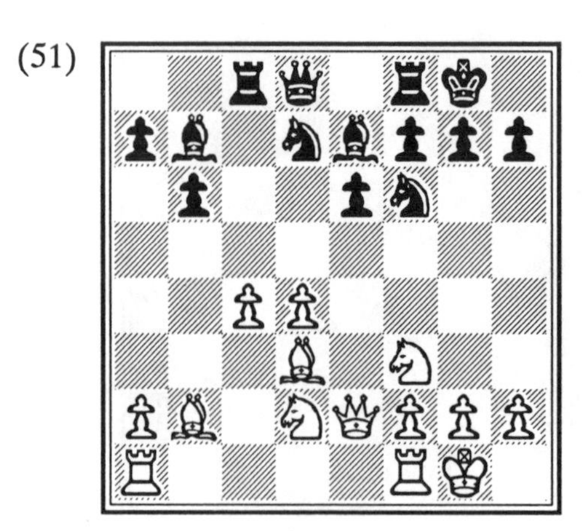

White to play.

that, aside from the well known potential weakness of his pawns, this structure also has its good sides. The pawns on d4 and c4 control all the important central squares (e5, d5, c5) and give White more space. If White can make his pawns safe from attack (putting his Rooks behind them strives to do this) then this advantage in territory will give him a promising position. He will then have tactical chances based on a timely d5 advance, or, if this should never prove effective, the simple Ne5 followed by Nd2-f3 will enable White to annex even more squares.

13.Rac1 Re8

1600: There is a possible discovered attack on my Queen on the e-file. But there are two pieces in the way at the moment so I will continue to back up my pawns with my Rooks, which also gives my Queen more room to move.

JS: There is an old saying that goes: "When in doubt, place your Rook opposite the opponent's Queen, it's bound to prove useful." Though this is partly said in jest, the truth is that such a Rook-Queen faceoff can be beneficial. In this case thoughts of a quick d4-d5 advance can now be thrown out the window since it opens up the e-file and brings the dormant Rook to life. However, even if Black's Rook did not stand on e8 this advance, which does activate the b2 Bishop, also gives Black's Knight access to c5 and is usually only played if there is some sort of tactical justification to back it up.

It turns out, however, that ...Re8 has a more substantial purpose than some hazy hope of a future attack against White's Queen. That purpose will become clear after Black's next move.

14.Rfd1 Bf8

1600: If I go back to f1 with my Queen then ...Bb4 might be good for him. There is also a possibility that he will play an ...e5 advance. I don't need to worry about ...Bb4 because I can defend by Bc3.

JS: White was showing signs of early laziness in placing his Rooks opposite the pawns without a detailed plan of action. Now that he has moved his Rooks he becomes hopelessly passive and doesn't even try to find further ways to improve his position.

The problem White is facing is the very common fear of ghosts—a fear of things that may or may not be real. It is the job of the player to decide whether a threat is real or not, but you can't ever decide one way or the other without proof. This means you must analyze and come to a final and clear assessment of the situation. Is the White Queen really in enough danger to warrant its retreat to the passive f1 square? No, of course it isn't. Is ...e6-e5 a threat? No again. So it seems that White went out of his way to place his Queen on a bad square for absolutely no reason at all.

If you find yourself in this kind of mind-set you will never come up with dynamic ways to put pressure on your adversary. More aggressive (and constructive) ideas are 15.Ne5 Nxe5 (if Black does not do this then White will follow up with 16.Ndf3 with a very nice game) 16.dxe5 Nd7 17.Ne4 and though White has a weak pawn on c4 his control of d6, pressure down the newly opened d-file, and chances of attack against the Black King give him many attractive possibilities.

15.Qf1?

1600: So my Queen is safe if he plays ...e5.

JS: Black never came close to threatening ...e6-e5 so White has found himself in a frame of mind that will come up often in this book—the overwhelming desire to respond to every possible threat; real or imagined. This is the bane of most amateurs and must be avoided at all costs. In this case, White has used a precious tempo to move his Queen from a fine square to a poor one.

15...g6

1600: He's going to put his Bishop on g7. I can move my Bishop back to b1, then swing my Knight over to b3.

JS: This shows the main idea behind Black's 13th move. The Bishop will go to g7 where it will defend the King and eye the target on d4. Notice how Black is improving his position with every move while White is floundering about in a panic.

16.Bb1 Bg7

1600: I can now swing over to b3 . . . wait! He'll go ...Bxf3 and open me up on the kingside. I can move my Queen to d3 before I play Nb3, then f3 is defended.

JS: White is still reacting to every Black possibility. At least he realizes that his Queen was not participating in the game on f1, but the original e2 square is where it really belongs.

17.Qd3 Qc7

1600: Putting more pressure on c4. I can put pressure on the e-file by Re1 followed by Ne5. At the moment my Knight is not doing much.

JS: White continues to flit about from one idea to another but at least his ideas are becoming more aggressive! The intended 18.Nb3 would have been well met by 18...Ba6.

18.Re1 Red8

1600: Now he's putting pressure on d4. I'll play Nb3 and guard it.

19.Nb3 Qf4

JS: Tempting was 19...Ba6 while 19...Ng4! with the threat of 20...Bxf3 was extremely strong. However, I wanted to give him more room to come up with his own ideas and not just react to what I was doing.

1600: Now he's attacking my f3 Knight and also threatening to move his Bishop to e4. If I move my Knight to e5 he still can play ...Be4. It's better to move my Knight back to d2.

20.Nfd2?

JS: He is so sure that everything is going to be bad for him that he miscalculates. Black does not threaten 20...Be4 because 21.Rxe4 would win two pieces for a Rook. Also 20...Bxf3 21.Qxf3 Qxf3 22.gxf3 is not necessarily the end of the world for White. Finally, 20.Ne5?? would have lost to 20...Nxe5 21.Rxe5 Ng4. A bad or lazy attitude will always lead to the worst possible results. Never give up hope and even if things have not been going well you must fight to the bitter end. You will be surprised how often you can turn a game around!

Instead of this passive and useless retreat (remember: 20...Be4 didn't work. Don't take time out to stop your opponent from blundering!), White should have remained calm and played the simple 20.Qe3.

20...Ng4

1600: Threatens to check me. I have to move my Queen to g3.

21.Qg3 Qxg3

1600: I will capture towards the center.

JS: Still defending and following the basic rules. This is simply not good enough! You must strive to come up with creative ideas that challenge your opponent!

22.hxg3 Nb8

JS: This Knight is coming to c6 where it will chew on the d4-pawn.

1600: He has two pieces against d4 and one Rook against c4. I must chase his Knight away.

23.f3 Nf6

1600: I want to keep his Knight from moving to h5.

JS: Why? A Black Knight on h5 would not have helped the second player in his battle against the weak pawns on d4 and c4. Since ...Nh5 could always be calmly answered by Kf2, White should have taken the opportunity to play a more useful move. Superior was either 24.Kf2 or the more assertive 24.a4! (intending to create a weakness on b6 by a4-a5xb6) 24...a5 25.c5! when the Black pawns are also turning out to be in need of defense.

Remember: Be assertive—create pawn weaknesses, fight for squares and space, do something positive! Just because you have some weak pawns doesn't mean you can't create some in the opponent's camp also.

24.g4?! Ne8

JS: Eyeing d4 with the g7 Bishop and giving himself the possibility of ...Nd6 with more pressure against c4.

1600: c4 is adequately guarded by the c1 Rook so I'll centralize my Knight.

25.Ne4 a5

1600: He's threatening ...a4 and a capture on d4 so I have to guard d4.

26.Red1

JS: Black would now meet 26.a4 with 26...Bc6 27.c5 Bxa4 and the Knight on b3 is no longer defended by its twin.

26...a4 27.Na1 Nc6

1600: Putting another piece on d4. I have to defend it.

28.Nc2 Na5

1600: Now he has two attacking c4. I can still defend, though.

29.Ne3

The game was stopped here since both 29...Bh6 30.g5 Bxe4 and 29...Bxe4 followed by 30...Bh6 would win material.

So the pawns eventually fell (a case of use 'em or lose 'em). This occurred, however, due to inactivity on White's part. If he had made use of his advantages in space and piece activity then the hanging pawns might well have been heroes instead of goats.

Lessons From This Game:

1) Always play to improve your position, don't panic and retreat from good squares.

2) Owning hanging pawns means that you must play dynamically. Passive play will lead to your hanging pawns turning into weaknesses.

3) If you are playing against hanging pawns you must attack them with everything you've got.

In the next example we see hanging pawns in a better light; Black is able to advance them and demonstrate their dynamic potential.

1800 vs. J.S.

The starting moves were **1.d4 d5 2.c4 e6 3.Nc3 c5 4.cxd5 exd5 5.Nf3 Nc6 6.g3 Nf6 7.Bg2 Be7 8.0-0 0-0 9.Bg5 cxd4 10.Nxd4 h6 11.Be3 Re8 12.Rc1 Bf8 13.Nxc6 bxc6**

(52)

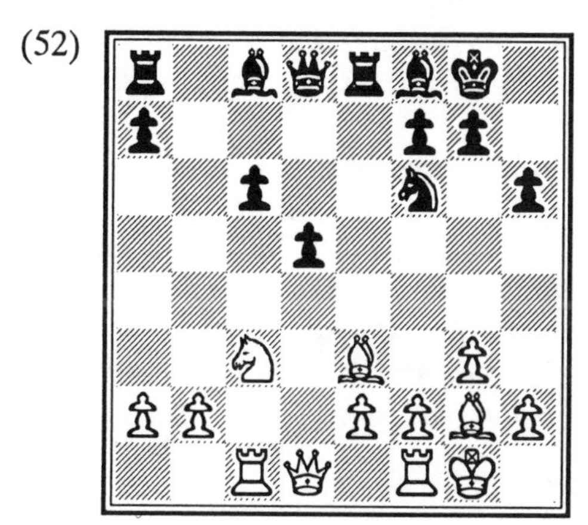

White to play.

1800: My center pawns are gone and my Bishop is blocking my e-pawn. His c-pawn is weak. He can't move it because his d-pawn would fall. He has more pawn islands and his a-pawn is isolated and weak and my Bishop on e3 ties his pieces down to its defense. I could attack his c6-pawn by Qa4 but this pawn is easily defended. His pieces are passive right now and are sitting on the back rank. What's the nastiest move to attack his pawns? Wait a minute . . . 14.Qa4 almost wins a pawn outright! If 14...Qc7 then 15.Nb5! is very strong.

JS: White is looking at Black's pawns as weaknesses without any good points whatsoever. This is not a correct view. The trick to battling potentially weak pawns is to first contain them (fix them on vulnerable squares) and only then to attack them (14.Na4 is the best move). Instead, White goes right for the throat but forgets that they can move forward and annex some space.

14.Qa4

JS: Note that 14...Qc7 is bad but White's idea of 15.Nb5?? is not the reason because 15...cxb5 wins a piece! Instead 14...Qc7 fails to 15.Nxd5.

14...c5

1800: Now his d-pawn is extremely weak. I don't see how he can defend everything.

JS: He has a positive attitude but it is somewhat lacking in realism. Note that White did not fall for 15.Nxd5 Nxd5 16.Bxd5 Qxd5 17.Qxe8 Bb7.

Now the question is raised: Are Black's pawns wimpy targets or towers of strength? They do control the e4, d4, c4, and b4 squares so they can't be all bad! The battle lines are drawn: White will try to either win a pawn or force one to advance which will (hopefully) create a weak square on c4 or d4. Black will defend his dynamic duo and try to create counterplay on the half-open b- and e-files.

15.Rfd1 Be6 16.Nb5?

1800: Attacking a7 and c5 simultaneously.

JS: This move does uncover an attack on c5 but White seems unaware that Black is allowed to play a move too! Don't get so full of your own plans that you forget that you have an opponent. Much better was 16.Bf4 which takes away the b8 square from Black's Rook, theatens Be5 in many situations, and creates the possibility of e2-e4.

16...Qb6

1800: Now both his pawns are pinned. There must be a way to pounce on them!

JS: Black was easily able to defend his c-pawn and now threatens something that White misses entirely. However, Black's position was already very good since the White Knight can be chased back, the hanging pawns can be solidly defended by ...Red8 and ...Rac8, and White must constantly worry about threats along the b-file and pawn advances like ...d5-d4.

17.b4?? Bd7

1800: My Knight's in a little trouble.

The game was ended at this point. We went back to the starting position in the previous diagram and made him play the correct 14.Na4 (instead of the previously tried 14.Qa4).

(53)

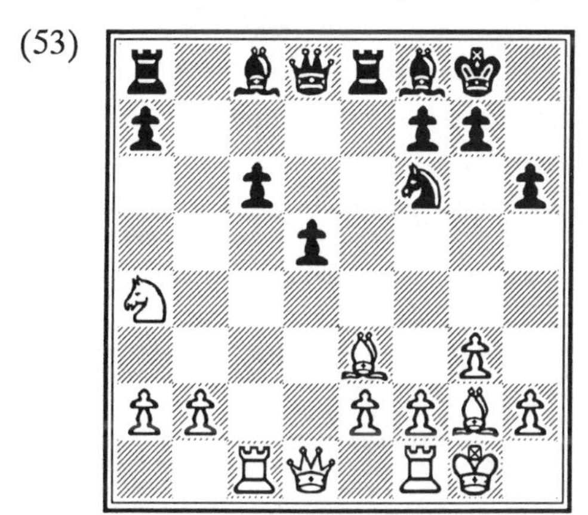

Black to play.

14...Qa5

1800: If my Rook eats on c6 then ...Bd7 wins, so I'll play Bd2 and attack his Queen, which also gets it off the poor post on e3.

JS: White shows that he still doesn't understand the position. The Bishop on e3 was not badly placed at all. Indeed, it helped control the critical c5 point in an effort to fix the pawns on squares where they can't do much good. Black's 14...Qa5 is an active attempt to counter White's control of c5 and put pressure on the a2 and e2 pawns. If Black did not do this White would have gotten a fine game by Bc5 followed by the exchange of dark-squared Bishops and Nc5 with a bind on the d4 and c5 squares. In that case the Black hanging pawns would serve no active part in the game.

As it turns out, 15.Rxc6! was correct after all, since the complications that follow 15...Bd7 16.Rxf6! have been shown to favor White. I could not expect 1800 to know this but I did have hopes that he would understand the need to block the Black pawns. Something like 15.Bc5 would have made me happy (though 15...Ba6 is a good reply) because his heart would have been in the right place. Even 15.a3 followed by 16.b4 would have shown that he wanted to control c5. After this game, I hit him on the head with my nurf bat several times, whereupon he became well aware of the correct plan in these positions.

15.Bd2? Qb5

1800: He's attacking e2 but this is no big deal . . . I can push it or guard it with my Rook.

JS: White is looking at direct threats and moves but is not looking at a long-range plan. Because of this he soon ends up in a passive position.

16.e3

JS: Black also gets active play after 16.Re1 Bg4!

16...Bf5

Here we stopped the game due to lack of time. Black's well placed pieces clearly outgun their passive counterparts.

Lessons From This Game:

1) Any kind of weak pawn must first be contained (blocked) before it is attacked.

2) No pawn structure is always good or always bad. Look for the potential plusses in any given pawn structure and make sure the opponent doesn't achieve them.

3) Though I repeat this in every chapter, I will take the

time to do so again: Don't just react to the opponent's plans. Find an active idea and follow it with as much energy as you can muster. On the other hand, don't get carried away with your own ideas and forget you have an opponent. Take his plans into account also and make adjustments when necessary.

The game that follows, played in a weekend tournament by a student of mine, made a deep impression on me. It takes one of the most maligned of structures, the dreaded tripled pawns, and shows that they are not necessarily bad—even in an endgame!

Harold Valerie (1650) vs. an opponent in the 1900 range.

(54)

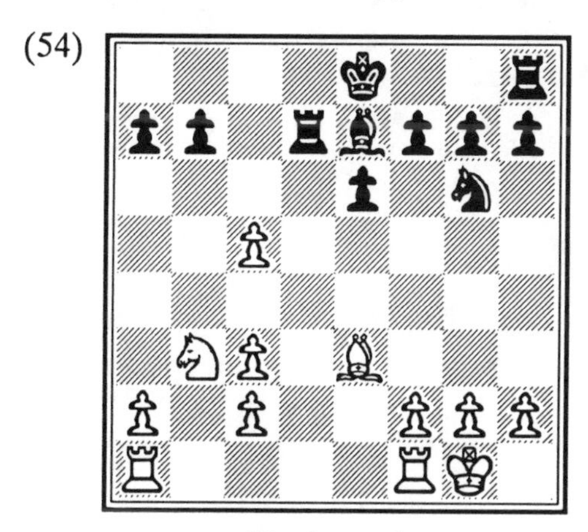

Black to play.

The position in the diagram was reached after 15 moves. Black, though a pawn down, undoubtedly thought that he stood well; after all, White's pawns hardly inspire confidence. However, Harold realized that these pawns gained space, tied up the enemy pieces, and allowed him to generate play against the opponent's remaining queenside pawns by moves like Rb1 and Na5.

16.Rad1

Harold challenges the d-file and tells the opponent that he can only castle if he is willing to give that file up.

16...Rc7 17.f4!

Following Steinitz's important rule: The way to beat Knights is to take away all their support points.

17...0-0 18.Rd3 Rd8 19.Rxd8+ Bxd8 20.Rd1 Bf6 21.Rd3

White is playing this game in a remarkably calm manner. Since Black has no real counterplay, White is able to slowly strengthen his position.

21...Nf8 22.Bd4 Be7 23.Be5 Rd7 24.Bd6

The White Bishop has taken up a powerful post. I love the way he methodically brought his Bishop to this nice square.

24...h6 25.g3 g6 26.Bxe7

Harold sees that this exchange will allow his Rook to penetrate into the hostile position.

26...Rxe7 27.Rd8 Rd7

—and now, instead of his hasty 28.Rxd7?? (which trades a very active Rook for its passive counterpart), White could have achieved a winning position with 28.Ra8! a6 29.c6 bxc6 30.Rxa6.

I suspected that most amateurs would take one look at those tripled pawns and proclaim their dislike of the White position. Is this view true or was I giving the chess playing masses less credit then they deserved? I set the same position up and gave another student the chance to prove me wrong.

1500 vs. J.S.

1500: Three isolated pawns on one file is bad, but on the other hand White is better developed, has an open b-file, and is a pawn up. Also Black has no pressure on White's game. White has the chance to sacrifice one of his isolated pawns with c6 and isolate Black's pawns; but first I would like to play my Knight to a5. I like this move but I want to concentrate on my development—I must use this before it goes away. I will play 1.Rfd1 and activate my Rooks.

(55)

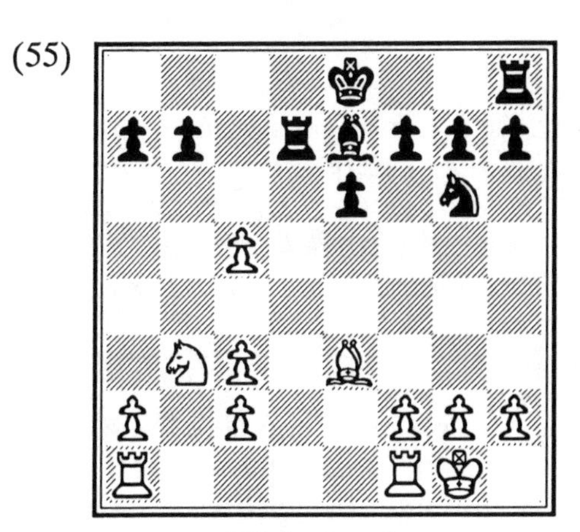

White to play.

JS: So I stand humbled—1500 also liked the White position! Is this because isolated pawns don't bother the average amateur, or are my students so well schooled that they are able to see beyond the typical chess bigotries that color most people's perception?

I was delighted when 1500 pointed out that he had to play fast if he were going to take advantage of his lead in development. Actually, just about all of 1500's comments were right on the money. Perhaps I am breeding a race of superplayers?

1.Rfd1 Rc7

1500: So I have taken control of the d-file. Now the Knight can go to a5.

JS: White's lead in development will soon be gone but he has managed to convert it into a long-lasting control of the important d-file.

2.Na5

JS: The b7-pawn is an excellent target but he is now rushing his position a bit. Harold's treatment, which held onto the c5-pawn and took squares away from the enemy pieces, was much better.

2...0-0

1500: I want to concentrate on the b-file and the b7-pawn.

3.Rab1 Bxc5 4.Bxc5?

JS: White thinks he is getting good value by trading off two of his tripled pawns for the healthy one on b7. This is quite wrong, though. Instead, White has freed the Black pieces from their prison and from the necessity of defending b7. The patience that I praised Harold for is quite lacking in this game.

4...Rxc5 5.Nxb7 Rxc3

1500: I would like to play Rd7 and take the seventh rank but I don't want to sacrifice my passed pawn. On the other hand, I don't want to play too defensively. I would like to trade one Rook, defend c2, and bring my Knight back so it can defend my pawns. The b4-square is good for this and can be reached via c6 or a6. White was better at the beginning and he still is. I should place a Rook behind my passed pawn.

6.Rdc1

1500: This Rook was chosen so I can follow up with Rb3.

6...Rb8

Here I stopped the game since White's advantage has completely disappeared.

Lessons From These Games:

1) A so-called weak pawn is only weak if it can be attacked! Don't fall for bigotries based on names (isolated, doubled, etc.). Each individual pawn has its own plusses and minuses and must be judged accordingly.

2) Patience is a real virtue in chess. If your opponent has little or no counterplay, then why should you feel compelled to force the issue? It is much better to take your time and add a host of little advantages to the plusses you already possess.

A backward pawn is a potential weakness because no other pawn can defend it, but its main problem is not so much the pawn itself but the square in front of it. The game that follows shows what happens if you ignore this simple fact.

(56) 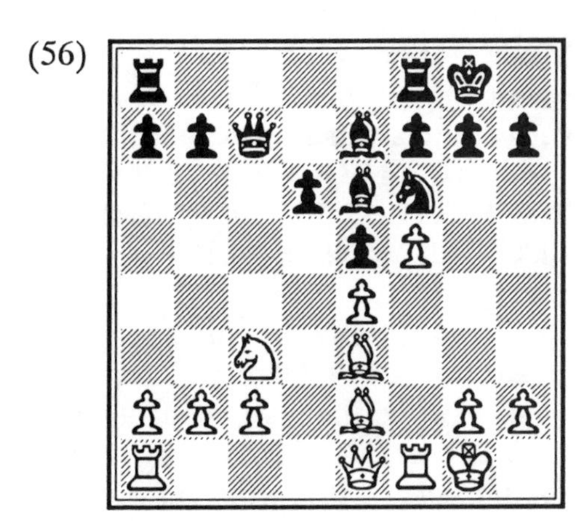

Smyslov–Rudakovsky, Moscow 1945
Black to play.

Black must move his threatened Bishop. Since 1...Bc8 seems wrong, that only leaves 1...Bd7 or 1...Bc4. Most players don't like having to retreat and prefer the more aggressive 1...Bc4. Indeed, that is what Black chose in the actual game.

1...Bc4??

Would you believe that this natural move leads to a positionally lost game? It does! As hard as it is to accept, 1...Bc4 is a positional blunder. To understand the position, we have to look at the backward pawn on d6. Is this pawn weak or in danger? No, it is well defended. However, the square in front of it, d5, only has two defenders—the light-squared Bishop and the Knight. Black's error with 1...Bc4 was that he traded one of the critical defenders of d5 for a piece that virtually had nothing to do with that square. Smyslov was quick to jump on this error.

2.Bxc4 Qxc4 3.Bg5!

Immediately chopping off the final defender of d5.

3...Rfe8 4.Bxf6 Bxf6 5.Nd5! Bd8

Black would lose the Exchange after 5...Qxc2 6.Rf2 Qc5 7.Rc1 followed by 8.Nc7.

6.c3

—and White's domination of d5 (and the superior minor piece that came with it) gave him a huge advantage that was confidently converted into a win after **6...b5 7.b3 Qc5+ 8.Kh1 Rc8 9.Rf3 Kh8 10.f6 gxf6 11.Qh4 Rg8 12.Nxf6 Rg7 13.Rg3 Bxf6 14.Qxf6 Rcg8 15.Rd1 d5 16.Rxg7**, 1-0, since 16...Rxg7 17.Rxd5 leaves Black with no answer to Rd8+.

All right, Smyslov played well, but could a student of mine do the same? I gave this task to 1330. First I gave him a lecture on strong and weak pawns. Then we spent a few weeks on other topics. Once I was sure that he had forgotten everything we had spoken about earlier, I threw this position at him.

J.S. vs. 1330

(57)

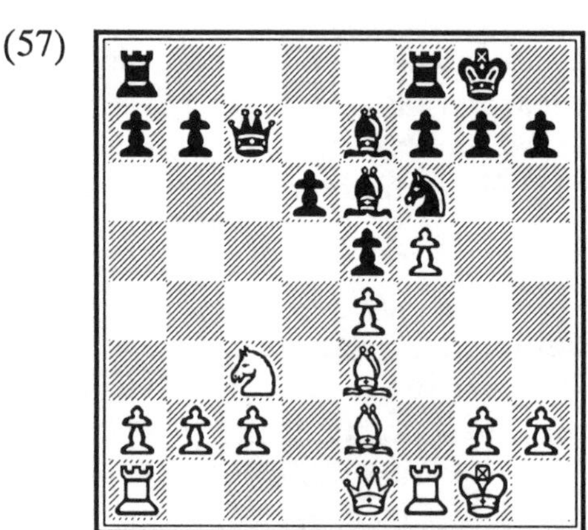

Black to play.

1330: Well, I have to move my Bishop to either c8, d7, or c4. At the moment White's Bishop is better than mine. I could force a trade on c4 but he would chase my Queen all over the board. d7 is possible but I hate to retreat and c8 is even worse. I like d7 since my Queen is safe and I keep pressure on f5.

JS: I began to search for the nurf bat. He didn't even mention the fact that Black was saddled with a backward d-pawn! As for his comment about his Queen being chased around, is this reality or laziness? Let's take a look. 1...Bc4? 2.Bxc4 Qxc4 3.b3? Qc6 and the c3 square has been weakened (which in turn weakens c2) by White's thoughtless one-move attack (b2-b3).

Was Black really going to leave his Queen on c4? Not if he is sober. That means that the Queen will be moved to a safe square. This would leave us with the question, "Did b2-b3 improve White's game in other ways?" Not at all. It just weakened squares and had no purpose other than the obvious attack on the Queen.

Don't make moves that have no purpose other than some obvious threat that can easily be parried.

1...Bd7!

JS: So 1330 played the right move for the wrong reason. 1...Bd7 is correct since it will go to c6 where it attacks White's e4-pawn and defends the delicate d5-square. Then Black can play ...a6, ...b5, ...Qb7, and ...b5-b4, undermining both d5 and e4.

2.g4

1330: He is starting a horrifying kingside attack. I'm concerned about g4-g5 when my Knight has no good squares. I could block that by ...h6 but that weakens my kingside. However, I like my Knight's position since it attacks e4 and defends d5.

JS: He mentioned the d5-square and the e4 pawn! Thank goodness for that. Unfortunately, he is beginning to panic and seems to be heading for the old "react to his threats and forget about my own play" state of mind.

2...h6

JS: This is a good move, but once again he made it for the wrong reason. I would have been happier if he had first played 2...Bc6 (bringing another piece to bear on d5), since I was sure that he was not aware of the proper follow-up to 2...h6.

3.h4

1330: He still has the same threat. Is this the time for 3...d5? I lose a pawn. I could go to h7 and defend g5.

3...Nh7

JS: 3...Bc6, attacking e4 and guarding d5, followed by 4...Nh7 was better.

4.Qg3?

JS: 4.Nd5 was strong (a move that could have been prevented by an earlier ...Bc6), but I wanted to give him the chance to find an all-star defensive move.

1330: The only way to free my Bishop on e7 is to play ...d5 and trade it with ...Bc5. My e7 Bishop is semi-bad and my light-squared Bishop is better. I need to counterattack since I have less space and he is attacking me. 4...Bc6 eyes his e-pawn and supports a 9...d5 advance. I can't do much now. However, his Knight has a terrific post on d5 so ...Bc6 at least takes that away from him.

4...Bc6??

JS: Too late. If White can successfully get g4-g5 in, he will have a winning attack. Black could have punished White for his last move by the retreating 4...Qd8!, a move that attacks h4 and covers g5. If White answered this by 5.h5 then Black would be free from the worry of g4-g5. If White played 5.Bf2, then the g5 square would still be in Black's hands and 5...Bc6 would be an intelligent move.

Just because a piece moves backwards does not mean that it is retreating.

5.g5 hxg5 6.hxg5

1330: What is the threat? My Bishop is practically worthless. I might be able to hole it up with 6...f6. If 7.g6 Ng5 8.Bxg5 fxg5.

JS: Driving a stake through his own heart. However, his game was already very bad. If you keep playing on the side where your opponent dominates then you will almost certainly lose.

6...f6?? 7.g6 Ng5 8.Bxg5 fxg5 9.Bc4+

Black resigned. Of course, 9.Qh3 was also promising.

Black lost this game because he reacted to the White attack and he never got his own play started.

Lessons From These Games:

1) The weak square in front of a backward pawn is often a greater problem than the pawn itself.
2) You can play to win a square by trading off its defenders.

Our final example takes us away from weak pawns and into the world of pawn structure as it relates to the plans for both sides. Deciding whether you want to keep the center open or allow it to be closed is an important decision in chess, and must only be made and can only be made with a firm knowledge of the other imbalances.

1650 vs. J.S.

The starting position arose after **1.d4 Nf6 2.Nf3 g6 3.Bg5 Bg7 4.Nbd2 0-0 5.e4 d6 6.c3 Bg4 7.Be2 Re8 8.h3 Bxf3 9.Bxf3 e5.**

(58)

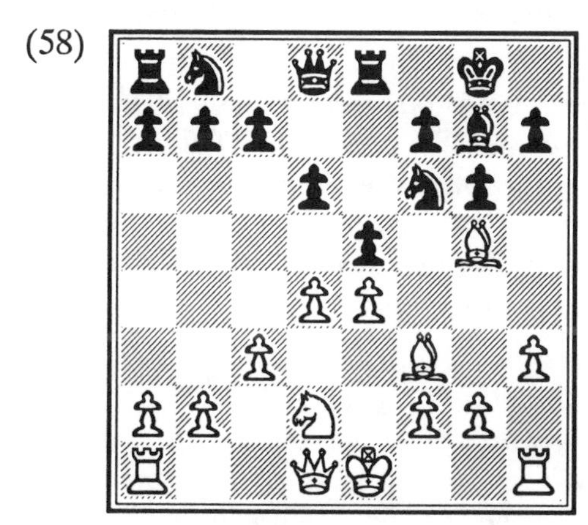

White to play.

1650: Though the Black pawns point towards the kingside, I should still castle on that side of the board. Black's Bishop is hitting granite and his b7 pawn might hang if he's not careful. After 10.0-0 if he plays 10...Nc6 then 11.d5 gains time and drives the Knight away. After 0-0 White will continue Re1 and Nc4 and then he can initiate the capture on e5. If Black takes the time to play ...h6 then White will take on f6. However, after 10.0-0 Nc6 11.d5 Ne7 he breaks the pin on the h4-d8 diagonal, so closing the center with d5 may not be very good. Back to my plan of 0-0, Re1, and Nc4. I'm not sure where my Queen goes, though, but after eventually placing a Rook on d1 his center will fall.

JS: When 1650 refers to the pawns pointing in a certain direction he is trying to make use of my rule of pointing pawns: In closed or semi-closed positions you will usually attack in the direction where your pawns point. In other words, the pawns on c7, d6, and e5 are aiming at the kingside—they act as a finger pointing the way. Why does this work? Because that is the direction where you have the most space, and you should usually play where you own more territory. Though it's a good sign to see him thinking about this rule, he is forgetting that the center is still in a state of flux and the pawn pointing rule only applies in a closed or semi-closed position. If you keep the center open and play in that sector then the pawn pointing rule has less validity. This is because the center is the most important place to play on the board and play in that sector usually takes precedence over play on the wings.

Another interesting but incorrect statement is that "10...Nc6 can be answered by 11.d5 with a gain of time." I often notice that amateurs love to attack enemy pieces with a pawn. The reasons for this are: 1) They are attacking something and this threatening gesture gives them a certain sense of security. 2) They think that they are gaining time.

Let's look at the flaws in this reasoning. Keep in mind that when you attack something it will move to safety (I am constantly surprised by the amount of players who harbor secret hopes that the piece will stay put and die). It is also important to understand that a pawn move only gains time if it chases a piece to an inferior square or places the pawn on a better post than where it started. In the present case, 10...Nc6 11.d5 Ne7 does not gain time for White because he is closing the position (something which favors the person with Knights), making his f3-Bishop a poor piece, and taking away the central play. White should not crow about any of these accomplishments.

Other things that were stated or ignored by Mike: 1) He is ignoring the important imbalance of the two Bishops. Since Bishops like open positions, an acknowledgment of this im-

balance would tell him that closing the center with d4-d5 might not be a good idea. 2) Black's Bishop is not hitting granite! It is a good piece and can easily become active after an eventual ...exd4. Admittedly, the center-closing d4-d5 makes Black's Bishop bad but this would also devalue White's two Bishops. 3) He says that after a certain series of moves Black's center will fall. Why should this be true? After a move like ...Nbd7 or ...Nc6 Black has a firm grip on his e5 pawn.

What is really going on? At some point Black can pressure Whites e4 and d4 pawns with ...exd4 (this also frees the g7 Bishop). White should try to kill off this counterplay and activate his two Bishops with 10.dxe5! dxe5 (10...Rxe5 11.Bf4) 11.0-0. White would then gain space on the queenside with a4 and b4 and get his light-squared Bishop into the game with Bf3-e2-c4. This plan would give the first player a small but safe edge because Black would have no points of attack and the Black Knights would have no advanced support points. On the other hand, White's Bishops would take up active posts on e3 and c4.

10.0-0 Nc6

1650: If I play 11.d5 Na5 is bad since b3 takes away all his squares. After 11.d5 the center is locked with his pawns pointing towards the kingside while mine aim at the queenside. I don't want to play d5 but I'm tempted because it drives the Knight and gains time. If I do that, where does my Knight go then? My white Bishop also seems poor. I'll tour my Knight to d5 via c4 and e3 instead of closing things.

JS: The comment about 11.d5 Na5 12.b3 (he is missing 12.b4, which picks up the poor beast) taking away all the Knight's squares is based on the lesson that the best way to deal with Knights is to take away all their advanced posts. However, why would Black want to place his Knight on the side where it is cut off from the rest of its army? Since he states that d5 leads to queenside chances for White and kingside play for Black, wouldn't it be more logical to bring the Knight to the side where Black intends to pursue his play? Thus 11.d5 Ne7 is much more sensible. Make your pieces work together—don't throw them all over the board without rhyme or reason! Do the same when you are trying to figure out your opponent's moves.

11.Nc4 h6

1650: If I go to h4 then 12...g5 13.Bg3 gives me pressure on e5.

JS: He tried to go to h4 but I warned him that something was wrong with the move. After a few moments he noticed that he would lose his e4-pawn to 11...exd4 12.cxd4 g5 so he panicked and blitzed out a few moves.

Let's devote a few lines to the subject of panic. Everyone has been unpleasantly surprised or has had the experience of noticing that their intended move is bad. If this happens you must not make any hasty decisions! Instead you must forget about the game and take a few moments to calm yourself down. Once this is done you can reassess the situation and avoid making a decision based solely on emotion.

12.Bxf6 Qxf6 13.d5

JS: Still riding high on emotion, White has ceased to think about his moves. The quiet 13.dxe5 keeps a very safe position.

13...Ne7

JS: Now that the center is closed, the pawn pointing rule comes into effect. Black will play for a kingside attack with ...f7-f5 while White should try to create a breakthrough on the opposite wing. Why? The center is closed so the wings are the only places where play can be initiated. Since most of Black's space is located on the kingside (his most advanced pawn is on e5), he should try to add to this with ...f7-f5 when his space advantage in that area is more apparent. In closed center situations you must play on the side where you have more freedom of movement and try to annex as much space as possible. Note that this is done with pawn advances since that allows files to be opened and the Rooks to enter the fray.

14.a4

1650: This stops him from chasing my Knight with ...b5.

JS: At the beginning of this game White did what he was taught and tried to break the position down into its component parts. Unfortunately, he failed to correctly assess matters because his thinking was vague and disjointed. After the shock of hanging material (see the note on the 11th move) he played a few hasty moves and from now to the end of the game he does nothing but play one-move attacks or defend against specific threats. In other words, he has been reduced to a purely reactionary role. To be fair, the move that Mike played (14.a4) is actually quite a good one. My criticism is that he only played it for a defensive purpose (to keep his Knight on c4). He should have been thinking in a more aggressive vein about gaining space on the queenside and trying to drum up an initiative there.

14...Qh4 15.Ne3

1650: I don't like his Queen being there so I'll harass her.

JS: Very interesting! A moment ago White was intent about keeping his Knight on c4. However, Black's move upset him—his King is being attacked and he feels the need to defend. Sadly enough, his statement about harassing Black's Queen is not based on accurate calculation. Instead he is bringing some pieces to the vicinity of the kingside and hoping that something positive happens for him. Never play moves with your fingers crossed! Never hope that he misses your threat or that things will somehow work out. All chess players should get rid of words like maybe and somehow. Clarify what's going on to the best of your ability. Perhaps you won't get it right but at least you will be creating some good habits. Mike has gotten lazy and is no longer putting his full energy into the game.

15...f5 16.exf5

1650: I like his pawn structure but I feel my King is safer than his.

JS: Another lazy and erroneous thought. Don't think that a King without a full pawn cover is in danger. A King is only in danger if the enemy pieces can get to it. I don't mind incorrect analysis or incorrect thinking—people can only perform at whatever level they have reached. Laziness, though, is a preventable disease that makes improvement impossible.

The capture on f5 is bad because it opens the g-file for Black's Rooks and makes Black's pawns on e5 and f5 mobile.

16...gxf5 17.a5

1650: A trap. I intend 18.Ra4.

JS: Why is this a trap? The one-move attack White gets on Black's Queen is hardly fatal. Notice how White is going more and more towards the reactionary role I discussed earlier.

17...Kh8 18.Ra4 Qf6 19.Bh5

JS: White's last two moves have been simple one-move attacks (please keep in mind that my criticisms usually refer to the thought behind the moves rather than the moves themselves). He is playing without any kind of plan.

19...Rg8

1650: We are both building up. I want to weaken the f5-pawn and put pressure on him.

JS: Finally some words of wisdom: White has identified a target. Now he should play 20.f4! when he holds back Black's pawns and threatens to initiate an attack on f5 with fxe5 at some point.

The comment about "building up" is less astute. You must first identify a target and only then build up your forces to attack it.

20.Qf3?

JS: Rather than stopping the advance of Black's central pawns, White places his Queen in a vulnerable position and makes the advance of the e-pawn all the more tempting.

20...Raf8

1650: He has a pretty good buildup. I'm not sure how to respond. I like Black's game now. It looks like the tables have turned.

JS: This new bout of depression comes with the realization that the f5 pawn is solidly defended. The rest of White's moves are all on the kingside. This is something that the attacker loves to see because that means White is reacting to what you are doing. Instead of this he should have been creating counter-threats on the opposite wing (the b7 and c7 pawns are undefended).

21.g3 e4

1650: I need to find a good location for my Queen. I would like to play it to g2 for defense but e2 is also tempting because it guards my Bishop on h5.

JS: All thoughts of a counterattack are gone. White is only thinking about ways to hold things together.

22. Qg2 Qg5

1650: I made the wrong choice. The e2-square was superior.

23.Be2 Be5

1650: I'm busted.

24.Kh1 f4 25.gxf4 Qxf4 26.Ng4 h5 27.Rxe4 Qd2, 0-1.

Lessons From This Game:

1) The Pawn Pointing Rule is useful to know in closed or semi-closed positions. If the center is locked you must attack on the wings with pawns. This increases your control of space and opens files for your Rooks. The pawn pointing rule enables you to tell which wing you are supposed to play on by pointing the way. See the note to Black's ninth move for a more detailed explanation.

2) Don't attack something for no reason! Attacking an enemy piece has no value in itself. You must always expect your opponent to play the best move, so he will most likely see the transparent attack and move away to safety. If you have gained something valuable, even if he sees your threat then the attack is useful. If there is nothing to be gained after his best reply then restrain yourself and leave his pieces alone! Remember: you are trying to follow a plan that benefits your whole army and takes advantage of the weaknesses in his camp. One-move attacks are only useful if they do something to benefit your plan.

3) Avoid vague thoughts. Concentrate on one or two important features of the position and go as far with them as you can. This will enable you to stay on track. If you find yourself saying

things like, "I'll somehow attack his King," you are being too vague. You must only attack the King (or anything else, for that matter) for a specific reason and you must be very clear with yourself on how you intend to go about doing it.

4) Don't allow surprise or depression to influence your moves. If something unexpected or bad happens you must sit on your hands until you regain your equilibrium. When this is done reassess the situation as if the game were starting over again and calmly figure out what the position needs.

5) Don't just react to the opponent's threats. At times defensive moves are called for. However, if you find that you have lost track of your own plans and are just reacting to your opponent's blows you must realize that you are on the road to defeat. Chess is a game where the opponent tries to impose his will on you. He wants you to do what he tells you to do. Fight like a madman and refuse to go along with his agenda!

PART FIVE

Material

Of all the imbalances in chess, a material plus carries more weight than just about anything else. An extra Bishop, or—in top flight events—even an extra pawn, is often more than enough to give you a victory. For this reason you must be very careful not to give away your units without just cause. Unfortunately, holding on to your pieces is not always so easy. I have noticed that the vast majority of games between amateurs are decided by some gross blunder of material. This means that if you can simply not give anything away—no deep strategy here!—you will see hundreds of points pad your rating.

How can we avoid this type of gross blunder? One useful method is to write your move down before you play it. Don't just scribble it, make the written move a work of art! The reason for this is that as we look deeply into a position, our mind goes off on tangents that often take us far afield of the reality of the moment. Writing the move down in this fashion brings us back to the here and now.

Once you have written the move down, you should ask, "When I play this move, does my opponent have any checks? Can he capture or threaten any of my pieces?" You will be surprised how often you will suddenly notice that your intended move, the move you placed so much hope in, is in reality a game-losing mistake. Instead of losing the game, though, you can now scratch out or erase your blunder and think of something new.

Even though so much importance is placed on material, we must remember that it is an imbalance, just like any other imbalance. Don't win a pawn if it gives the opponent an advantage in development, space, pawn structure, or several other things. Remember that a material plus is a static advantage; don't allow yourself to be beaten by the enemy's dynamics or by a combination of other static factors.

If you are lucky enough to find yourself with an advantage in material, you should follow these rules:

1) Material can beat the initiative if you can slowly neutralize the opponent's plusses and equalize the game. Then your extra material will bring him down.

2) Material gives you an extra unit of force. If you make this unit an active participant in the game you will have your opponent outnumbered.

3) Material edges like the Exchange (Bishop or Knight for a Rook—three points for five) are only useful if you can give the Rook an open file to fly on. An advanced, centralized Knight can easily beat an inactive, useless Rook. This means that you must be careful not to allow simple point count (the pieces' numerical value) to influence you more than the particular position.

(59)

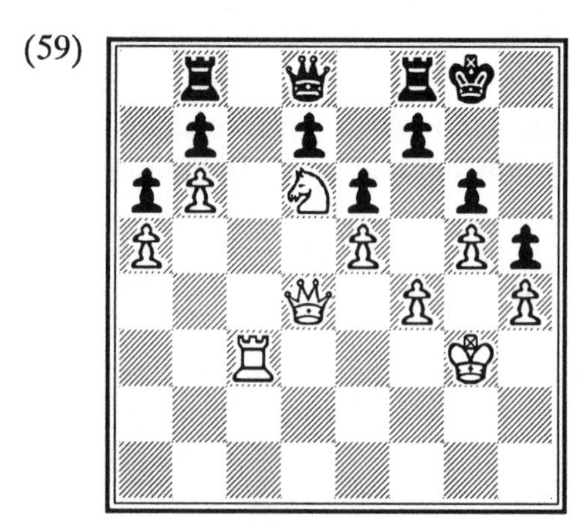

Black to play.

If we were to judge the position in diagram #59 on point count alone, we would have to say that Black seems to be an easy winner. He has a pawn and a Rook for a Knight (six points to three). However, his Rooks are completely helpless and his extra pawn on d7 is immobile. On the other hand, the White Knight on d6 dominates the board. Black cannot prevent White from playing Rc7 with a complete bind on the position.

4) When you win material you may find your pieces are off balance and without purpose. That is because they have fulfilled their mission and now need a new goal. If they are off balance, don't keep lashing out. Instead, bring your pieces back together, make everything tight and safe, and then prepare a new plan based on your material edge. Remember: extra material gives you a long-term advantage. You don't have to be in a rush to use it.

The Amateur's Mind

We will begin our look at material advantages with a seemingly simple position where White is an Exchange up for a pawn.

(60)

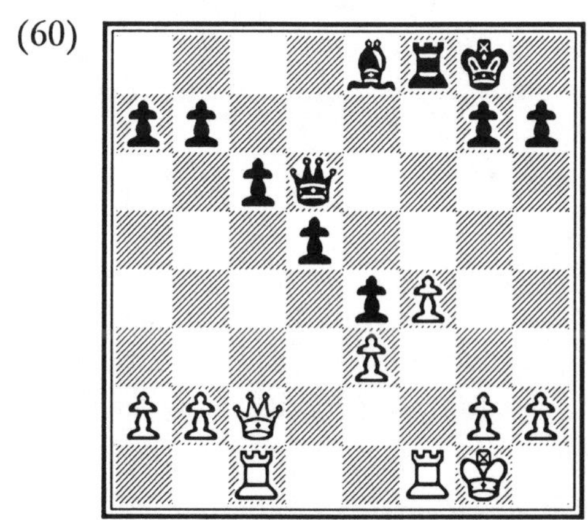

Kramer vs. Thomas, Utrecht 1949.
White to play.

In the position shown in diagram #60, Black enjoys more space due his strong pawn chain on b7-e4. The things that White can crow about are his kingside pawn majority and his material advantage.

I have stated over and over again: when you try to find a plan you must base it on the advantages (positive imbalances) in your position. Here you probably would not wish to rush your kingside pawns (one of your two advantages) forward (in an attempt to make use of your majority) since that would place your King in peril. This leaves you with that extra Exchange; how can White make use of it?

Rooks only reach their full potential on open files. Unfortunately for White, no completely open file exists. Still, if he wants to make use of that extra Rook he will have to find a way to create a file for it.

Before we go further we must ask what Black's advantages are. As stated before, he has that mass of pawns in the center. He also has to address the difference of Bishop for Rook. Rooks are better than Bishops but that doesn't mean that you must accept their inferiority and just wait to lose. Instead, you should play to make your Bishop as strong as possible. Black's plan is this: he will attempt to advance his pawns to b6 and c5 and then he will swing his Bishop around to the powerful d3 post via b5.

Armed with this knowledge, White's plan should be easier to find since you must always strive to prevent the opponent from succeeding in his plans at the same time as you fight to bring your own to fruition.

1.Qc3!

A simple but very fine move. White prepares to centralize his Queen on d4 and also covers b4 so that he can continue with b2-b4. This advance stops Black from advancing his own pawn to c5 and also prepares to force a file open with an eventual b5.

1...Bd7 2.b4 a6 3.Qd4 h6 4.Rfd1

Threatening to win a pawn with 5.Qxe4.

4...Qe7 5.a4 Kh7 6.b5!

White is happy to sacrifice a pawn if that allows his Rooks to break into the enemy position.

6...axb5 7.axb5 Ra8 8.bxc6 Bxc6 9.Ra1

White lays claim to the open a-file.

9...Ra3 10.Rxa3 Qxa3 11.Ra1 Qb3 12.h3

White has succeeded in most of his aims and now takes a moment off to see to the safety of his King.

12...Qd3 13.Qc5

White sees no reason to give Black a passed pawn on d3 with 13.Qxd3 exd3. Besides, the combined attack of White's Queen and Rook will soon lay waste to the Black King.

13...Kg6 14.Ra8 Kh5 15.Kh2!

This allows the White Queen to move without having to fear a check on e3.

15...Qe2 16.Rg8, 1-0.

It's clear that White is winning in our beginning position. Now let's see how amateurs handle this type of technically winning situation.

1000 vs. J.S.

(61)

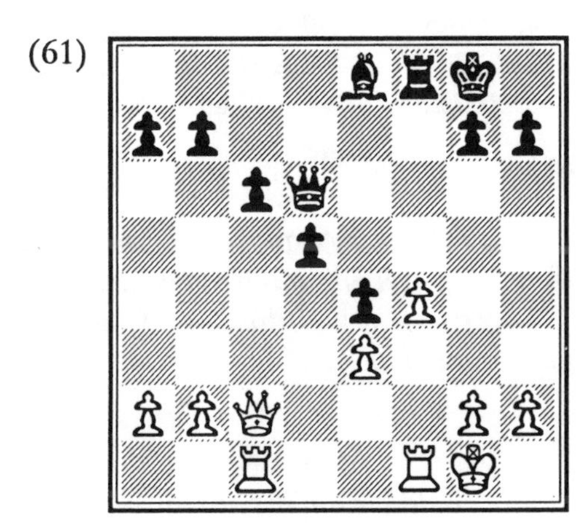

White to play.

1000: I'm a Rook for Bishop ahead but there are no open files for my Rooks. Black has one extra pawn and is more advanced then me. The pawns on a2 and b7 and a7 are undefended but I don't see any way either side can take advantage of this. His pawns are blocking his Bishop so that means his Bishop is bad. This is in my favor. Black can boast that he has more space. So how do I use these advantages? There is a possibility of pinning the d-pawn and attacking the one on e4. I must open a file for my Rooks and keep a close eye on my undefended pawns. One plan is Qb3, Rd1-d4 and Rxe4 winning a pawn due to the pin on the a2-g8 diagonal. Another similar idea is to place a Rook on d1 and play Qxe4 but that's no big deal since he should be able to defend against this type of thing. His e4-pawn stops my Rooks from going to f3 or d3. I'm inclined to advance my f-pawn and open a file. I'll do this by doubling Rooks on f2 and f1 and then advance the f-pawn by f5 and f6.

JS: He did an excellent job of picking the position apart; far beyond what one would expect from a 1000 player (we had just finished talking about good and bad Bishops so he was very much aware of that idea). Also impressive is the fact that he noticed some hidden tactical possibilities based on Rd1 and Qxe4. Unfortunately, his reasoning falls apart when it comes to the actual plan chosen. He notices that no open file exists and makes a plan that tries to create one. This is excellent. However, he completely fails to take into account his opponent's possibilities. Just because you have a superior or even winning position doesn't mean there is nothing for your opponent to do!

1.Rf2? b6

JS: Now White didn't ask why I played my move! You must always settle down and try to figure out what your opponent is up to. Instead White forges ahead with his own (erroneous) ideas and completely ignores his opponent.

2.Rcf1?

JS: Played instantly. 2.Rd2 with the threat of 3.Qxe4 would have been superior. White could then have put pressure on Black's central pawns and tried to discourage Black from advancing them. Of course, White could not expect Black to miss this threat (after 2.Rd2), but placing your pieces on centralized posts is rarely bad, and at the worst serves to make it hard for Black to make use of his center pawns.

2...c5

1000: I don't like the way your pawns are coming forward. I'll stop them with 3.b3.

JS: All of a sudden White starts to pay attention to Black's moves and now he forgets his own plans and begins to focus on his opponent's! You can't ignore your opponent's ideas but you also must avoid getting to a mental place where you do nothing but react to his moves and innuendoes.

3.b3?

JS: Now Black's Bishop gets outside the pawn chain (one of the most important things you can do with bad Bishops) and takes up an excellent post on d3. Black no longer has any problems whatsoever.

3...Bb5

1000: I'm not going to give you my Rook! I'll go to d1 and pin the d-pawn.

JS: Notice how everything White does is just a reaction to Black's moves.

4.Rd1 Bd3

1000: You have no threat other than the Queen so I'll go to c3 with activity.

JS: White has lost his grip on reality and thinks he stands better just because he is up an Exchange. This is not true: Rooks are no better than Bishops if you can't make use of them. Don't get trapped in the world of point-count and ignore what's happening on the board.

5.Qc3 d4

1000: I think I'm going to get my open file. After 6.exd4 Qxd4 I'd be happy to trade Queens.

6.exd4

JS: During the last few moves White should have begun damage control operations and given the Exchange back by Rxd3.

6...cxd4

1000: I'll retreat to c1 which keeps me dominant on the file.

7.Qc1? e3

1000: I like that. It's easy to defend my Rook, and his Bishop is hanging. His Queen is also stuck defending his d-pawn so I'm not unhappy about his move.

JS: Amazing! White is so possessed by the spectre of an open file that he ignores all the plusses that Black has created for himself (active Bishop, two powerful passed pawns, pressure against the White f-pawn).

8.Rb2

JS: Here 1000 tried 8.Rf3 but took it back when I pointed out the possibility of 8...Be2.

8...Ba6

1000: I'll play 9.a4 and try to kick his Bishop off the a6-f1 diagonal with b4-b5. Wait a minute! I just missed the excellent 9.Qxe3! Fortunately I noticed it before I did anything else.

JS: I give him credit for noticing this tactical shot (made possible by the undefended position of Black's Queen). It's just bad luck that it doesn't work out.

9.Qxe3 dxe3 10.Rxd6 e2

1000: I must retreat to b1. 11.Kf2 loses to 11...Rxf4+.

11.Rb1 Rxf4 12.Re1

JS: There was no defense.

12...Rf1+ 0-1

It's clear that White will become a much stronger player if he starts to pay attention to his opponent's possibilities as well as his own.

Our next try at this same position shows the amateur doing much better.

1550 vs. J.S.

(62)

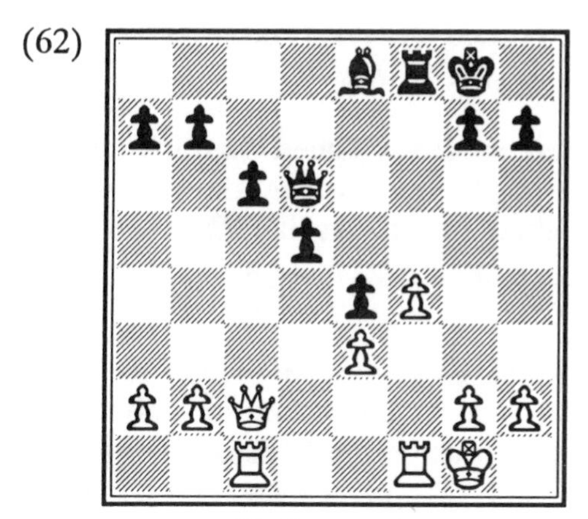

White to play.

1550: Black has a pawn majority on the queenside and in the center. White has pressure on the c-file. Black is down the Exchange. His pawns are on the same color as his Bishop so he will want to do something about that. Even though Black is down the Exchange, if he can keep the game closed and not allow the Rooks to be activated he will have a good game. If Black can get his Bishop to d3 he will stand very well and White may have to sacrifice a Rook to get rid of it. White on his end will use his kingside majority by trading Queens and prevent Black from activating his Bishop. If he can open up files for his Rooks he will win.

JS: Another excellent breakdown of the position. Notice how White considered some of Black's ideas also.

1.Qc5

1550: Centralizing my Queen and challenging his. Since Black's Queen is his most active piece, it's a good idea for me to trade it.

JS: I like his logic. In general, it is always good to trade off the opponent's superior pieces. However, in this case White could have used his Rooks in conjunction with his Queen. Another point that may make White want to retain the Queens is the fact that the Black King is now free to run to the center and help hold things together. With the Queens on, the Kings would both stay at home.

1...Qxc5 2.Rxc5 b6

1550: Must move my Rook since I want to double my Rooks on the c-file. I will play Rc3, which allows the doubling and defends e3 and allows for attacks like Ra3.

3.Rc3 c5

1550: White wants to challenge Black's pawns. Black has opened up the diagonal for his Bishop so White wants to move his Rook on f1; at the same time he also wants to protect his pawn on f4.

JS: So both amateurs (1000 and 1550) allowed Black to advance his pawn to c5. In this case White noticed the possibility but just allowed it to happen. You don't have to let your opponents do what they want—stop them!

4.g3?

JS: Absolutely horrible. White was worried about moving his f1-Rook since an eventual ...d4 would undermine his pawn on f4. By fixing his gaze on random will-o-the-wisps (I am reminded of a deer transfixed by the headlights of a car), he forgets about more important factors that are about to hit him on the head. A move like 4.Rd1 would have been much better.

4...Bb5

1550: That is what I was trying to avoid! Well . . . it's too late to do anything about it now. White's pressure is on the c-file so I'll play Rfc1, when both my Rooks are safe from the enemy.

JS: It is becoming clear that the most common error that the amateur makes (in any situation) is to ignore the opponent's possibilities.

5.Rfc1 Rd8?

JS: I played this poor move to see if he would panic at the prospect of the d-pawn rushing forward. However, White rises to the occasion and comes up with a wonderful reply. Black should have played the obvious 5...Bd3.

1550: Black is threatening a pawn push on the d-file so White will start a counter-attack on the c-file by sacrificing a pawn with b4.

6.b4!

(63)

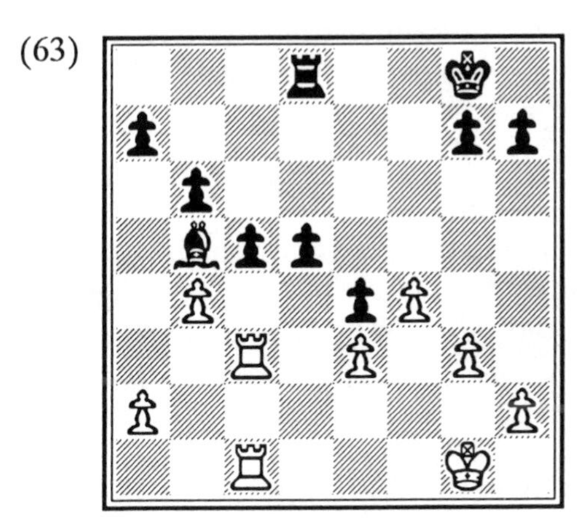

Black to play.

JS: Impressive. White is willing to give up a pawn to open a file for his Rooks. Now 6...c4 7.Rd1 leaves Black is a bad way. Black has gotten a passed pawn but all his potential activity has been permanently stopped. White would then play his King to d4 and advance his pawns on the kingside.

It's also important to point out that 6...cxb4 fails to 7.Rc8 Rxc8 8.Rxc8+ Kf7 9.Rc7+ Kf8 10.Rxa7 Bc4 11.g4 followed by f5 and Kf2-g3-f4-e5.

6...Bc4

1550: Black threatens the a-pawn. First I'll trade.

7.bxc5 bxc5

1500: Black has a bit of play but White's Rooks are also more mobile. White also wants his King in the game.

8.Kf2?

JS: It's interesting to watch White play a very thoughtful idea on one turn and then do some lazy "pass" the next. Instead of this useless time waster (Where is the King going? I'm sure that White has no idea), he had a couple of moves that deserved consideration. For example, 8.Ra3! a6 9.Ra5 ties Black down to the defense of his pawns, and 8.Rb1!? Bxa2 9.Ra1 Bc4 10.Rxa7 with a Rook on the seventh and the threat of Rc7 is also possible.

It's strange that White worked so hard to create an open file for his Rooks and when he succeeds in his plan he refuses to make use of them.

8...Rb8

1550: Ouch! I missed this move. Now he is getting activity and creating some threats so I'll sacrifice the Exchange back and put pressure on his other pawns. This should put me in charge.

JS: Here he goes again. After the bad 8th move (8.Kf2?) he comes storming back with a nice idea.

9.Rxc4!? dxc4 10.Rxc4 Rb2+ 11.Kg1 Rxa2 12.Rxc5 a5?

JS: A bad move. Black could (and should!) get an easy draw with 12...Ra3 13.Kf2 Ra2+ but I didn't want the game to end yet. Instead I play to see what he remembers of our endgame lessons.

13.Re5

1550: Might as well eat the e-pawn and get a passed pawn of my own.

13...a4 14.Rxe4 Kf7

1550: I will advance my g-pawn to g4 to limit Black's King activity and at the same time expand my majority. If I can get his queenside pawn for one of my kingsiders I will be a clean pawn up.

JS: I wasn't happy to hear this last comment. I had told him in the past that a Rook ending with three vs. two pawns (or two vs. one) that are all on the same side of the board is drawn. If Black can trade his a-pawn for White's pawn on e3 then a draw would result in spite of White's extra pawn. At this point White is winning and he should do everything he can to avoid any kind of drawish situations. The fact that his opponent is much higher rated is no excuse.

15.g4

JS: Fortunately for White, he can't find any way to trade the a-pawn for the e-pawn so he instead continues to play good moves and soon builds up an overwhelming position.

15...h6

1550: I will keep advancing and claim more space.

16.h4 Kf6

1550: I will move my Rook along the fourth rank, which allows the e-pawn to advance.

17.Rb4 h5

1550: I want to prevent Black's King from entering the battle so I will first drive him away with a check.

18.Rb6+ Kf7 19.g5

1550: Now I have three vs. one. If I took it would just be two vs. one since the doubled h-pawns would be useless.

19...a3

1550: White would like to get his King into action since it's doing nothing at the moment. First I'll activate my f-pawn by pushing it to f5. Then if ...g6 I will advance to f6 and White should win.

JS: This is the very moment that I was waiting for when I went into this ending in the first place. I wanted to see if he remembered the extremely important rule: Rooks belong behind passed pawns. If he had played 20.Ra6! I would have been delighted, though 20.g6+! first and only then 21.Ra6 is probably even more accurate.

20.f5??

JS: If White's Rook were on a6 then this pawn move would be completely winning. Unfortunately for White, Black is actually able to win the game now.

20...Rb2

1550: This is not good. I think I made a big error. White can't trade Rooks.

21.Ra6 a2

1550: I can't believe it. I'm actually losing now.

22.g6+ Kf8 23.e4 Rb1+ 24.Kf2 a1=Q 25.Rxa1 Rxa1

—and the game was stopped.

Lessons From These Games:

1) Once you learn how to break down the imbalances in a position, you have to practice coming up with a plan *based on these factors*.

2) Use this same understanding of the imbalances to figure out what the opponent should be doing and then make some effort to stop his plans.

3) Don't ignore your opponent's threats or ideas. Just because you have a superior or even winning position doesn't mean there is nothing for your opponent to do!

4) You must also avoid getting into a place where all you do is worry about your opponent's intentions. Then you will spend the game reacting to his moves and will almost surely lose.

5) Avoid the quick, lazy move. This is the one move that will almost always turn out to be the losing blunder.

6) A material advantage doesn't just win by itself. You have to make use of the extra wood and demonstrate its usefulness. A Bishop or a Knight can easily beat a Rook if the Rook doesn't find a useful file. Point-count chess is a useful guide but it doesn't mean anything if you don't *prove* why your numerical superiority gives you an advantage.

7) Basic endgame knowledge is very important. Rules like Rooks belong behind passed pawns is knowledge that everyone of every class must have!

In our next example we see that owning a material advantage does not mean that you can ignore the positional factors that are normally so important in any given game. Often a small material edge (like an extra pawn) can be used as endgame insurance but has no enormous meaning right away. In this case you must play to earn new advantages, i.e. space, superior minor piece, etc.

(64)

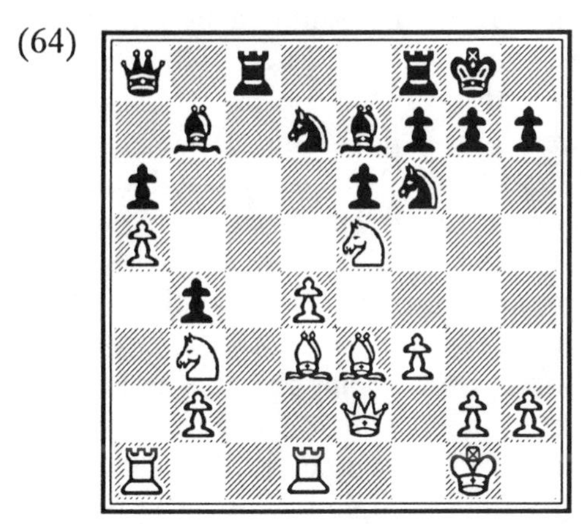

Silman-Blankenau, National Open 1989.
Black to play.

White has an isolated d-pawn but the Black pawns on a6 and b4 will also need attention. White enjoys some advantage in territory while Black can use the hole on d5 for his pieces. At the moment White has placed his Knight on e5 and Black must figure out what he wants to do about it. Should he leave it on this strong post or should he chop it off? Black makes a very bad decision.

1...Nxe5?

Giving White's dark-squared Bishop more scope and turning the potentially weak pawn on d4 into a strong attacking e5-pawn.

2.dxe5 Nd7?

Leaving the Knight undefended on d7. The amateur must be very careful when he sees that his pieces might be undefended; many bad things can befall them when this happens.

3.Bxh7+

A simple combination that nets a pawn.

3...Kxh7 4.Rxd7 Rfe8

White has won a pawn and could easily fall asleep with the thought that his game will win itself. How many promising positions are lost in this way?

Since the extra pawn is not going to make itself felt for a long time, White must work hard to insure that other positional factors will be in his favor. The most glaring thing about the position is the fact that Black has two Bishops. What are the rules for this type of situation? Going back to the chapter on minor pieces, we see that the side with the Bishop and Knight should trade off one of the enemy Bishops and create a Bishop vs. Knight position. Then you must concentrate on making your Knight superior to the enemy Bishop. With this in mind, White comes up with a detailed plan designed to make his Knight as good or better than any Bishop.

5.Qf2!

Covering the important c5 square with gain of time since Black must do something about the threatened 6.Rxe7 Rxe7 7.Qh4+, picking up a piece.

5...Kg8 6.Bc5!

Trading off a set of Bishops and preparing to give the Knight a nice home on c5.

6...Bxc5 7.Nxc5 Bd5 8.Na4!

The c5-square was nice but it was not permanent since no pawn defended it. Due to this the greedy Knight heads for greener pastures on b6.

8...Qc6 9.Nb6 Rcd8 10.Rxd8 Rxd8 11.Qd4

—and White was in complete control. The final moves saw White give the material back in order to weaken the Black King: **11...Qb5 12.h4 Rb8 13.h5 Rb7 14.h6 gxh6 15.Rc1 Qxa5 16.Rc8+ Kh7 17.Qg4 Qxb6+ 18.Kh2 h5 19.Qxh5+ Kg7**

20.Qh8+, 1-0.

This game is certainly nothing special, but I was quite interested to see how a strong amateur player would handle the technical questions that arose after White won the pawn.

1700 vs. J.S.

(65)

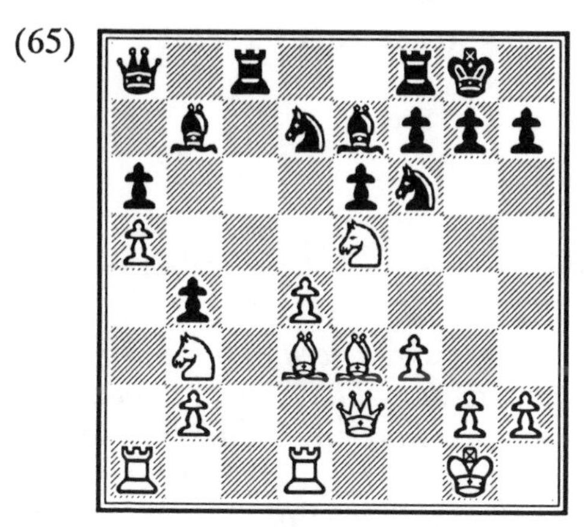

Black to play.

1700: Black's pawns on a6 and b4 are weak while White's weaknesses can easily be protected. White has more queenside space than Black. b6 is a weak square that White might be able to use (also c5). Black has an ideal square on d5, though White could exchange pieces there.

JS: I reminded him that this was the wrong strategy. In a past lesson I had taught him that the way to beat isolated d-pawns is to trade off all the minor pieces and then double on the d-pawn with a Queen and Rook. The lack of minor pieces would take away all the isolated d-pawn's dynamic strength and turn it into just a weakness.

Due to this rule, it is Black who would be happy to make trades on d5, not White.

1700: I forgot about that stuff. Anyway, White would attack on the queenside and Black on the kingside. Does White want to allow ...Nxe5, exchanging a good Knight for a limited Knight? I would not allow this Knight on e5 to be exchanged. I would have played it to c4 and b6. Black should take on e5.

Overall, I think White is a bit better due to his space, control of key squares, and Black's weak queenside pawns. On second thought, if ...Nxe5 then dxe5 makes the dark-squared piece very dangerous!

JS: What is this talk about a kingside attack for Black? As usual, the amateur player is always thinking of attacking the enemy King, even if such a thing is unlikely in the given position.

1...Nxe5 2.dxe5 Nd7 3.Bxh7+ Kxh7 4.Rxd7

1700: That was easy to see.

4...Rfe8

1700: I would like to get a Knight to b6. Also the Bishop could go there.

JS: Bishops don't necessarily need to be advanced to be effective, but Knights do! He should have given a lot of thought over his Knight's future. Note how any thoughts of superior minor piece never entered his head. I would have been so happy if he had thought of trading one pair of Bishops, but though my students are well aware of this rule, they have trouble recognizing and implementing it during actual play.

5.Bb6 Bd5

1700: Do I want to exchange my bad Knight for his good Bishop? Should I give it to him and win it back by Qd3+? Can his c-Rook penetrate along that file? No, it can't. This means that I can take the time to double.

JS: I was very happy to see him not panic over ...Bxb3, which is really not a threat at all due to the reply Qd3+. However, why does he want to double on a file that is not open due to the Bishop's presence on d5?

6.Rd1? Kg8

1700: I might be able to trap his Queen with Ra7 at some point. Can I let him take on b3 and get a check on d8? No, I will just centralize my Knight. I also threaten Nf5!

7.Nd4 Bc5

1700: Trying to exchange a pair of Bishops. I thought *I* was the one who was supposed to do this? However, he *is* weakening my a5 pawn and pinning my Knight. If 27.Bxc5 Rxc5 my pawns on a5 and e5 are both weak. I think my game has gotten worse than it was at first. Critical is 27.Ra7 going after a6.

JS: He remembered the rule about trading one set of Bishops in order to de-fang the Bishop pair. This knowledge would have been more useful to him if he had done something about it earlier.

27.Ra7 Qxa7! 28.Bxa7 Bxa7 29.Kh1 Bxd4 30.Rxd4 Rc1+ 31.Rd1 Rfc8

—and we stopped the game since Black, for a small material price, had gotten a firm grip on the initiative.

PART SIX

The Gratification that Development and Initiative Bring

Things like development and initiative are almost invisible. They don't show territory, nor do they revolve around pawn structure or any particular weakness. Instead, these terms belong in the mysterious realm of *dynamics*, compared to the *statics* that most of our other imbalances correspond to.

A static advantage is something that is sitting around on the chessboard, plain for all to see, and will be there for a long time to come. Material is a static advantage, as are weak pawns and squares, and, of course, extra territory.

A dynamic advantage is composed of something less tangible and permanent. Here things like timing, tactical vision, and playing with verve become important. The goal of a dynamic advantage is to make quick and energetic use of it in the hopes of trading in the temporary activity for a permanent static edge.

The two dynamic advantages we will discuss here are development and initiative.

Development

A lead in development is easy to spot. Simply put, you have more pieces out than your opponent. Of course, normally you would expect one side to get the rest of his pieces out and eventually catch up in development. That is why a development lead is a temporary advantage—you only have a few moves until it disappears! Because of that, you must make immediate use of it or you will end up empty-handed. How is this done? What is the goal? The following rules should clarify these points:

1) A lead in development usually means that you must start some sort of aggressive act. Quiet play puts no pressure on the opponent and will allow him to get the rest of his forces out.

(66)

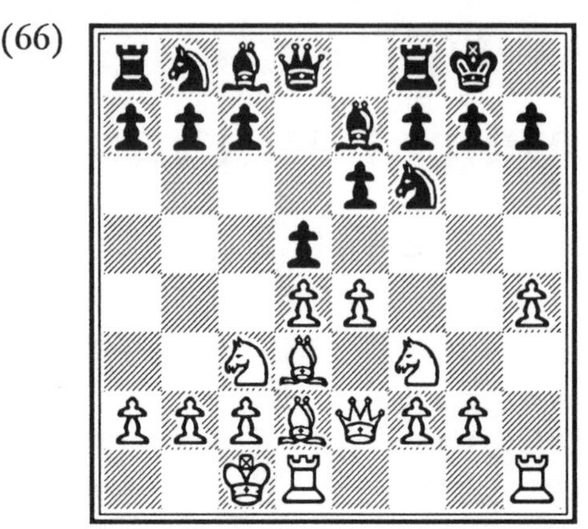

White to play.

White enjoys a clear lead in development in diagram #66. He could play in the center with 1.exd5 exd5 2.Rhe1 followed by 3.Ne5, but instead White decides to advance his pawn and chase Black's main kingside defender away. **1.e5 Nd7** Now quiet play might allow Black to get some counterplay in the center and on the queenside by ...c5 and ...Nc6. White has the use of a greater force at the moment so he decides to strike while the iron is hot. **2.Bxh7+!** Notice how White's last two moves have not allowed Black the time to get the rest of his forces out. When you are ahead in development, <u>take the battle to the opponent!</u> **2...Kxh7 3.Ng5+ Kg8 4.Qh5** and Black will be mated (4...Bxg5 5.hxg5). Poor Black was overwhelmed by the superior force of the White army.

2) A lead in development means the most in open positions because the open central files should enable your army to penetrate into the hostile position with relative ease. If you have more pieces out and the position is wide open (or even semi-open), **ATTACK!**

After **1.e4 c5 2.Nf3 d6 3.Bb5+ Bd7 4.Bxd7+ Qxd7 5.c4** Black can win a pawn with the greedy **5...Qg4?!** However, this move, which does give Black a static material edge, allows White to build up an enormous advantage in development. **6.0-0 Qxe4 7.d4** White opens up as many lines as possible. These open files should be looked upon as highways into the hostile position. **7...cxd4 8.Re1 Qc6 9.Nxd4 Qxc4?**

(67)

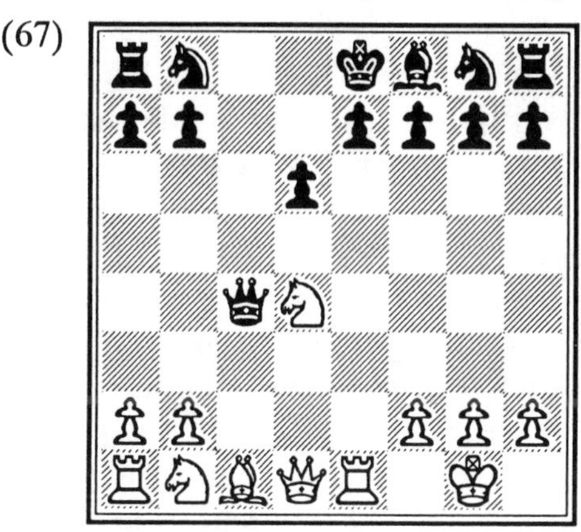

Browne–Quinteros, Wijk aan Zee 1974.
White to play.

Black wants two free pawns instead of one. However, few things in life are really free, and this suicidal capture gives White more development and more open lines. If you are the defender in such positions, remember that it is rarely a good idea to open lines if your King is still in the center. **10.Na3** From this point on, White will play with threats and never allow his opponent to bring his lazy troops out. **10...Qc8 11.Nab5** Threatening 12.Nxd6+. **11...Qd7** White answers the obvious 11...e6 with 12.Nf5! **12.Bf4** Renewing the threat against d6. **12...e5 13.Bxe5!** It's time to crack open the Black King. Normal material considerations no longer exist. White is now trying for a quick knockout. **13...dxe5 14.Rxe5+ Be7 15.Rd5!** Black is not given a moment's rest. **15...Qc8** Taking on d5 was not possible due to 16.Nc7+. **16.Nf5** Another fork is threatened on d6. **16...Kf8 17.Nxe7 Kxe7** Mate follows 17...Nxe7 18.Rd8+. **18.Re5+**, 1-0. Black has taken enough punishment. 18...Kf8 19.Qd6+ does not paint a pretty picture.

3) If the enemy King is still in the center and you enjoy more

development, consider these factors an invitation to rip the opponent's head off! Start an immediate attack. At the very least, you will keep his King stuck in the middle and make him suffer for a long time to come.

4) A closed position often nullifies a lead in development because the blocked files stop you from effecting any real penetration. If you have a big lead in development and think you can blast the pawns out of the way, then by all means give it a try. However, more often than not, the side with the deficit in development will find that he has ample time to cure this problem if the central situation is locked up.

A common opening that leads to a closed center is **1.d4 Nf6 2.c4 c5 3.d5 e5 4.Nc3 d6 5.e4 Be7 6.Bd3 0-0 7.Nge2 Ne8!** Black allows himself to fall behind in development because he knows that White's pieces cannot get to him due to the traffic jam in the middle. After **8.0-0** Black shows that he is willing to lose even more time by **8...Bg5!**, trading off his bad Bishop for White's good one. Black shows disdain for development and instead accomplishes a good strategic goal, secure in the knowledge that he can catch up in development later.

5) The goal is not mate (though anyone would be quite happy with such an outcome)! If you start an attack and win material (or get the two Bishops in an open position, or leave him with weak pawns, etc.) by the time he gets his forces out, then you would be in possession of a fine static advantage. Don't go crazy and attempt to force an immediate decision where none exists.

(68)

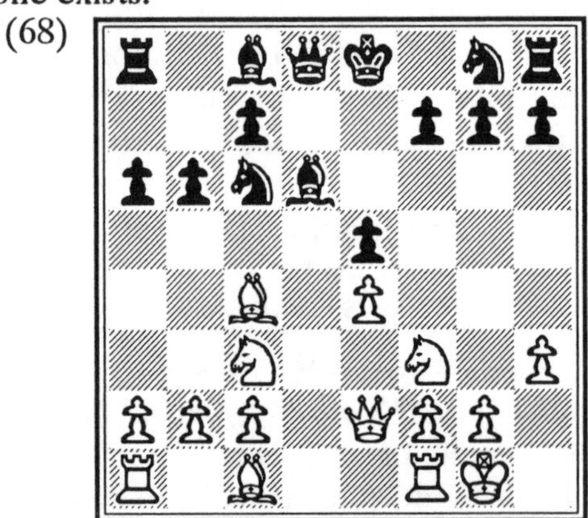

White to play.

In diagram #68, White could attempt to make use of his development lead and try to attack in some way, but why not grab material with **1.Bxf7+ Kxf7 2.Qc4+** followed by Qxc6 with a solid extra pawn? This would give White something to use for the rest of the game.

Initiative

When you have control of the game you are said to possess the initiative. The initiative can be based on static or dynamic factors. For example, if you are attacking a weak pawn (a static plus) and your opponent is reduced to a passive defense, you have the initiative. You would still own the initiative if you have a poor pawn structure but your lead in development gives you an attack (this time you have an initiative based on dynamics).

In general, top players look upon the initiative with great favor—it is always advantageous to have the initiative. The question is, will you be able to retain it and will it prove more important than a static advantage that the opponent might possess?

For example, you may have sacrificed a pawn to take control of the game (the initiative). Will he eventually be able to equalize the game when his extra pawn will become a force, or will your initiative lead to gains that are greater than the sacrificed material?

(69)

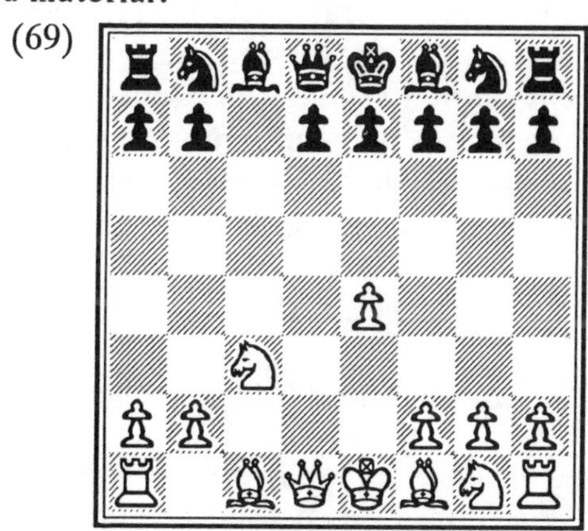

Black to play.

The position in diagram #69 comes about after the moves **1.e4 c5 2.d4 cxd4 3.c3 dxc3 4.Nxc3**. Why did White sacrifice a pawn? He *does* gain a lead in development, but in this case Black expects to eventually catch up. The real reason White made the offer was, aside from the development, to create two open files and a space advantage. Of course, this particular gambit is considered somewhat unsound at the top levels, but the concept is a good one: One must always fight to take control of the game. If you can do this and retain static advantages, then who could ask for more? However, if you are about to get pushed around, then why not give up material or grant the opponent some other type of static plus in order to try to become master of your own fate? The example in the diagram is somewhat extreme. White immediately goes after the initiative and feels that a pawn is a good price to pay. However, why should White give anything away? Why not fight for the initiative by positional means and attempt to get it all at no cost whatsoever?

The answer to these questions is, perhaps, a matter of taste. One thing is perfectly clear, though: An understanding of that invisible thing known as the initiative is critically important for anyone who wants to make progress in the game of chess.

The Amateur's Mind

An eight-year-old student—rated about 1100 and visiting me for the first time—recently showed me a game which he lost to an opponent (another youngster) with a rating of just 800. He wasn't sure where he went wrong, but a glance was sufficient to show me that he lost due to passive play. His opponent grabbed the initiative and literally blew him off the board.

800 vs. 1100

1.e4 c5 2.Nf3 e6 3.Nc3 Nc6 4.Bb5 Nd4 5.0-0 Nxb5 6.Nxb5

So far both sides have played really well. White enjoys a lead in development while Black has a solid position and owns a pair of Bishops.

6...d6

Quite playable, but this move caused some concern in me. I would have been happier to see 6...a6, chasing the Knight back to obscurity. If Black had taken lessons from me earlier, he would have known that you battle Knights by taking away all their advanced support points.

7.d4

This guy is just 800 strength? White is trying to open up the position so he can make use of his lead in development.

7...b6?

The first poor move of the game. Correct was 7...a6 8.Nc3 cxd4, when White's Knights are being contained and Black can hope to catch up in development and eventually make his two Bishops work for him. Remember that you are supposed to create imbalances in the opening and then develop your pieces around those differences.

8.Bf4?

White's heart is in the right place but he falters anyway. He should have made immediate use of his advanced Knight by playing 8.dxc5 bxc5 9.Bf4. Now Black is given another opportunity to chase the annoying horse away.

8...Ba6?

(See diagram #70)

This pins the Knight but allows it to stay on its fine post. 8...a6 was still correct.

9.c4

I would prefer 9.a4, when 9...Bxb5 10.axb5 opens a file for White's Rook.

9...Qd7

So what is Black doing wrong? Several things! He is not

(70)
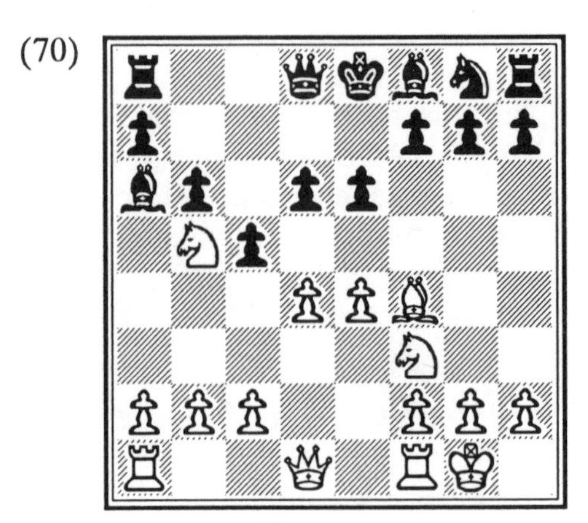

White to play.

aware of the possible battle between the minor pieces—we know this because he is not doing anything to make his Bishops active—and he is allowing the enemy Knights to remain on active posts.

Black is also not aware of the danger of leaving one's King in the center for too long. Once you castle and get your King to safety, you can play for a long time. However, if your King is sitting in the middle then you might get nuked at any moment. Finally, Black is not aware of the dangers inherent in a lack of development. At the beginning of this game he bought the two Bishops for the price of development. Now it's time to replenish his store of cash (development) but he refuses to do so. Moves like ...b6 do nothing for development at all, and ...Ba6 and ...Qd7 leave all the kingside pieces at home.

10.a4 0-0-0

White threatened dxc5 with a multi-attack on d6. Castling long defends this square but places the King in another vulnerable area.

11.e5!

White is doing everything he can to open up the position and get to the Black King. This is exactly what you want to do when you enjoy a huge lead in development.

11...d5 12.cxd5 exd5 13.e6!!

The 800 rating kept swirling around in my head. I wish my students with class A ratings would play like this! In one move White, who is playing with a lot of energy, brings two pieces into the attack.

13...fxe6 14.Ne5 Qe7?

Note that 14...Qb7 is still met by 15.Nc6! when the Rook and the a7 pawn both hang and 15...Qxc6 fails to 16.Nxa7+.

15.Nc6

—and White went on to win.

This game raised some questions. Do most amateurs see a lack of development as a major problem? Do most amateurs attack with the verve that White demonstrated in this game? To answer these questions I had two of my students take the White side from the diagrammed position and try to blow me off the board.

1400 vs. J.S.

(71)

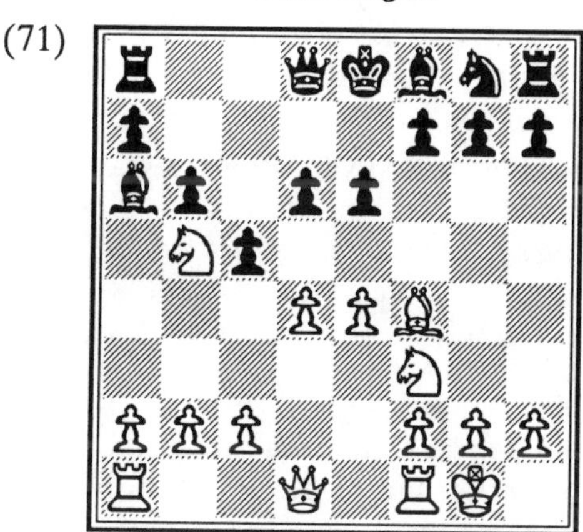

White to play.

1400: Black has an advantage in space on the queenside and owns the two Bishops. However, Black is a long way from being castled so I am not sure if he can make use of these things. White has a space advantage on the kingside and in the center, plus he is way ahead in development. I also see a possible weak square on c6. White should break open the center by any means possible. Even a pawn sacrifice would be justified if it meant getting to that King.

Now for something concrete. I have to protect my pinned Knight. 9.c4 defends, aims at the center, and breaks the pin.

JS: I really like what White said about breaking through the center by any means possible*—that is just the type of attitude that I am trying to cultivate. However, when it came down to particulars he had surprisingly little to say. That's because he started to concentrate on his attacked Knight. Notice how he never gets too far away from this defensive thought.*

9.c4 Qd7

1400: I will bring my Queen up to d3 where it will defend c4. This move also connects my Rooks.

JS: I prefer White's 10.a4 followed by 11.e5, as in the original game. White has become so concerned about defending b5 that he never gets his dreams for an attack started.

A large part of chess success is based on attitude. If you decide that your advantage consists of something that demands quick and vigorous play and you insist on moves from yourself that conform to those particular needs, then you will be a fearsome opponent. However, if you pay too much attention to the enemy's threats, then your mind will click into this defensive mode and you will become sensitive to every threat or non-threat that arises. You will start playing a game of reaction and your own ideas will never have a chance for expression.

10.Qd3 cxd4

1400: Now the recapture dumps a piece to ...e6-e5. I'll play e5. This opens the center but blocks my Bishop.

JS: He has already lost the game mentally. If someone's King is in the middle then feel free to sacrifice a pawn or even a piece in order to get your army to it. In this case White should play 11.Qxd4! e5 (the move he feared. 11...Bxb5 12.cxb5 e5 13.Qd5 is great for White) 12.Nxe5! (blasting his way through) 12...dxe5 13.Qxe5+ Be7 14.Nc7+ and White regains his sacrificed piece. White didn't see this because he stopped looking when he saw the fork by ...e6-e5. This is how blind spots are created—we see a move or two ahead, notice a problem, and completely stop looking. Instead we should look one or two moves ahead, stop, and treat this future situation as our starting position. When you analyze from this new starting position you will often be amazed at what you find!

11.e5 d5

JS: Notice how White has been reacting to Black's threats for the last several moves. In chess there are two wars being waged; one is on the physical chessboard. The other is the subtler battle of mind vs. mind. In the present contest White is doing whatever Black tells him to do. This means that Black has already won the mental part of the fight.

12.b3?

JS: No words or thought; he just played it right away. He is still reacting to everything Black does.

12...dxc4 13.bxc4 Bc5

JS: Now White has a permanent weakness on c4 and he has also given Black use of the c5 square.

1400: I want to take on d4.

JS: He tried 14.Nfxd4 Bxb5 15.Be3?? (15.Qe4) and didn't notice that he was a piece down. I pointed this out to him and had him do something else.

1400: That's not good! I'll just keep up the pressure by moving my Rook to d1.

JS: White is making things easy on Black. He has to get control of the game before Black develops his Knight and castles—he <u>*has*</u> *to make something happen before the long-term disadvantages of the White game make themselves felt. White should play 14.Nd6+ Bxd6 15.exd6, when the pawn on d6 is quite strong and the pawn on d4 will quickly fall. Remember: Chess is a game where you come up with an idea that supposedly improves the plusses in the position; and then you do everything you can to implement that idea. In the present case White is just doing what his opponent wants him to do.*

14.Rad1 Ne7

1400: I want to trade one of my Knights for his Bishop to get rid of his Bishop pair. I'll do this by Nd2-b3xc5.

JS: He's lost all sense of reality and reverts to rules used only in static situations. Taking the Bishop on c5 only helps Black retain his extra pawn on d4. White should have taken his pawn back by 15.Nfxd4.

15.Nd2? 0-0 16.Nb3? Bxb5 17.Nxc5? bxc5 18.cxb5 Qd5

JS: Threatens both ...Qxa2 and ...Ng6 followed by ...Nxe5.

—Stopped the game.

So White noticed what was going on in this game but he never made a real effort to realize his ideals. It was becoming clear to me that mental toughness (this is something that can be learned) is a major part of chess strength. You have to insist on accomplishing your goals and you can't allow anything distract you from this path.

The next game is still from the same position, but this student's collapse comes even faster.

1300 vs. J.S.

(72)

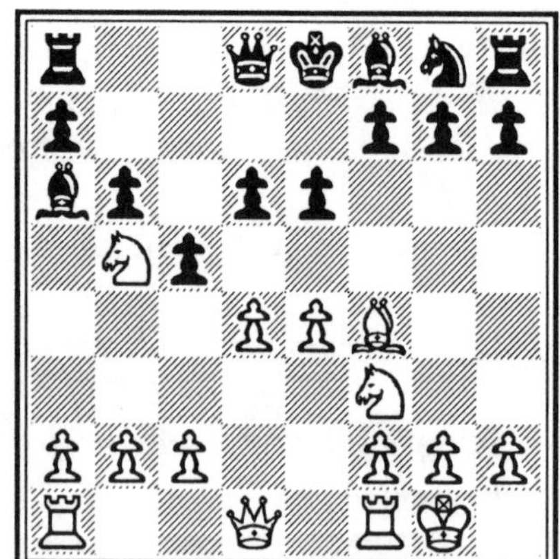

White to play.

1300: My Bishop is undefended on f4 and my Knight is attacked and pinned. White has a space advantage in the center but this is evened out by Black's space edge on the queenside. I have a lead in development . . . actually I'm almost completely developed while Black has only one piece out. I'm probably just slightly better due to my development, though I'm bothered by my pinned Knight on b5. I would like to move it to safety but then he would take my Rook. I'll go to d3 with my Queen. Then if he takes my Knight I can recapture with check.

JS: All this talk about Black's space advantage on the queenside is rather strange since he will never get a chance to use it. Evidently, White doesn't realize that a huge lead in development on an open board takes precedence over most static principles.

9.Qd3

JS: An interesting move. Now the Bishop on a6 can hang to tactics based on Nc7+ or Nxd6+.

9...cxd4

1300: 10.Nxd6+ is possible—he gets my Knight and I get his Bishop on a6. Wait! After 10.Nxd6 Bxd6 11.Qxa6 I lose a piece to 11...Bxf4. I'll just take back on d4.

JS: Very interesting. White faces his first tough decision and promptly falls apart. When you are trying to make use of a dynamic edge you should take your time and look long and hard for a knockout. This doesn't mean that you are playing only for mate. Far from it! A superior ending, the win of a pawn, a huge positional plus; all of these things are good value for your dynamic dollar. In the present situation White should have played 10.Bxd6! Bxd6 11.Nxd6+ Qxd6 12.Qxa6 when threats like 13.Qa4+ or 13.Rad1 guarantee that White will pick up the d-pawn and be a solid pawn to the good.

10.Nfxd4 e5

1300: I didn't see that at all. I better attack.

JS: White more or less just gives up. I would have been happy if he hunkered down and tried hard to find a way out (It didn't matter if he actually found a saving idea, I just wanted to see some effort. If you don't make an effort, you won't get results). Instead he took a few seconds and makes a one-move threat.

11.Nc6 Qd7

1300: My c6 Knight and my f4 Bishop are hanging. Things have gotten out of hand.

12.Nc7+

JS: Mental and physical surrender.

12...Qxc7 13.Qxa6 Qxc6 0-1

In this game White had an idea but noticed that it didn't work at the last moment. Instead of calmly reassessing the situation, he panicked and went berserk!

It is interesting to note that the amateurs took note of the development leads and realized that it was a favorable factor, but they were not able to make use of this advantage.

Lessons From These Games:

1) Figure out if the position is a dynamic one or a static one. If it's dynamic then you must play with tremendous energy.

2) Once you decide on a goal (for example: you want to break through in the center) you must take as long as necessary to accomplish it (on the clock and on the board). A static goal might take twenty moves. A dynamic goal calls for some sort of instant result—this means that speed is extremely important. If it takes you forty minutes to figure out how to do what you want done, then take forty minutes!

3) Never let the opponent dominate you mentally! If you notice that you are meekly reacting to everything he does, you must snap yourself out of your trance and fight to establish some sort of psychic control.

4) Castle quickly! When your King is safe you can do what you want and play without fear of a mating surprise. If you see a King in the center, do everything you can to blast things open and execute it. No subtleties here, just pure brutality!

Our next example shows what happens when one of the greatest attackers of all time gets his hands on the initiative: He never lets up until the opponent is dead.

Even more interesting is how he creates the initiative in the first place. It's almost like he treats his opponent like a sheep—he herds him in a certain direction and the opponent obeys the commands given to him.

(73)

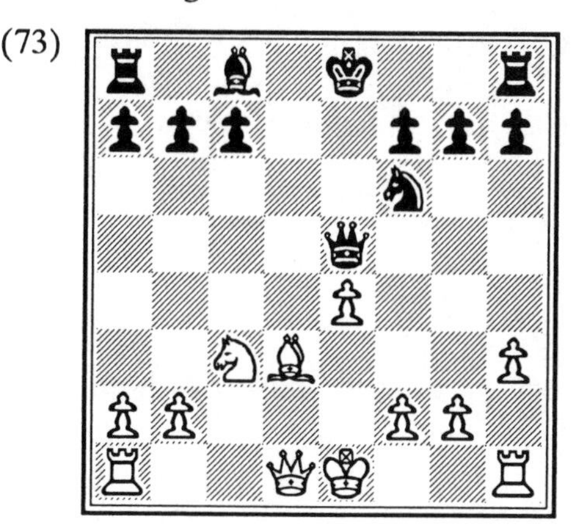

Alekhine–Marshall, Baden-Baden 1925.
White to play.

The main imbalance in this position is created by the mutual pawn majorities. White has a central majority and Black has a majority of pawns on the queenside.

Seeing that the key to his success will be whether or not he can make use of the power of his majority, Alekhine takes immediate steps to get his pawns underway.

1.Qd2

A flexible move. White prepares to make use of his kingside majority with f2-f4. He can also castle queenside.

1...Bd7

Since White's pawn majority influences the center and kingside, Black hopes to place his King on the other side of the board. Naturally, White takes immediate steps to prevent this.

2.Qe3!

A very fine idea. Black is prevented from castling queenside and the Black Queen is also kept out of the d4 square. We can see how Black made use of this square in the games that follow.

2...Bc6?!

Black decides to castle kingside but it is rarely wise to castle into the strength of the enemy. In this case the kingside is White's strength due to his majority of pawns.

Better was 2...Qa5, when Black could safely castle on the queenside.

3.0-0-0

With his king safely tucked away on this side of the board, White can advance his kingside pawns without being worried about weakening his King.

3...0-0

Kings that are castled on opposite sides usually denote a wild struggle where both sides play for an attack on the enemy monarch. However, in this case Black will hardly be able to strike a blow. Why? Because the Black majority is unable to take part in the attack. White gets the first blow in and he keeps on punching till the opponent falls to the canvas. This type of active control is known as the initiative.

4.f4

The first threat. White takes over the initiative because the advance of his pawns gain time by attacking the Black pieces.

4...Qe6 5.e5

Another threat. Once again Black is forced to react to White and not bother with his own ideas.

5...Rfe8 6.Rhe1 Rad8 7.f5

White's assault is in full swing while Black's counterattack has not even started.

7...Qe7 8.Qg5 Nd5 9.f6 Qf8 10.Bc4!

White never gives his opponent a moment's respite.

10...Nxc3 11.Rxd8 Rxd8 12.fxg7!

Taking advantage of the fact that Black's Queen is the only defender of the Rook on d8.

12...Nxa2+

Also hopeless is 12...Qe8 13.Bxf7+ Kxf7 14.Rf1+ Ke6 15.Rf6+, etc.

13.Kb1!

The automatic 13.Bxa2 would give Black a saving check on c5.

13...Qe8 14.e6! Be4+ 15.Ka1

A self-mate can be had by 15.Kxa2?? Qa4 mate.

15...f5

White wins more mundanely after 15...fxe6 16.Bxe6+ Qxe6 17.Qxd8+ Kxg7 18.Qd4+ followed by the capture of Black's Bishop.

16.e7+ Rd5 17.Qf6 Qf7 18.e8=Q+

—and mates in two moves.

This powerful performance by the legendary Alekhine was accomplished due to his insight into the possibilities of the opponent. He didn't just note that his kingside majority was strong. He also took into consideration the opponent's possible counterplay and made a point of first preventing it, and next playing in such a manner that the enemy never had a chance to do anything but defend.

Now let's see how mortals play the position that Alekhine handled so magnificently.

1500 vs. J.S.

1500: White has a space advantage. Black has the more active Queen but it could also turn out to be a target. White can activate his majority with tempo by playing for f2-f4. How do I do this? I'll castle and play for a quick f4.

(74)

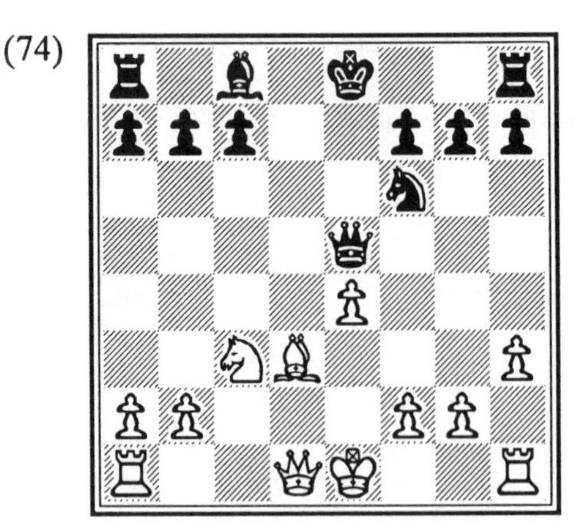

White to play.

JS: White, to his credit, notices the advantages that an active central majority can bring. Unfortunately he neglects to take Black's plans into account.

1.0-0 Be6 2.f4 Qd4+

JS: It is worth noting that Alekhine was very careful not to give his opponent access to this square.

3.Kh2 0-0-0

1500: I should have prevented this. I'll play 16.Rf3. What else can I do? No! It's too passive.

4.Bc2 Qe3

1500: Can't play 5.Qe2 because of 5...Qxe2 and 6...Rd2. I need to trade Queens.

5.Qf3 Qxf3 6.Rxf3 Rd2

1500: Ugh. Have to defend my Bishop.

JS: Ever since Black placed his Queen on d4 and castled queenside, White has forgotten his own plans and done nothing but worry about the threats of his opponent. This all stemmed from White's refusal to look for Black's plan on the first move.

—Game ended due to lesson time running out.

1700 vs. J.S.

(75)

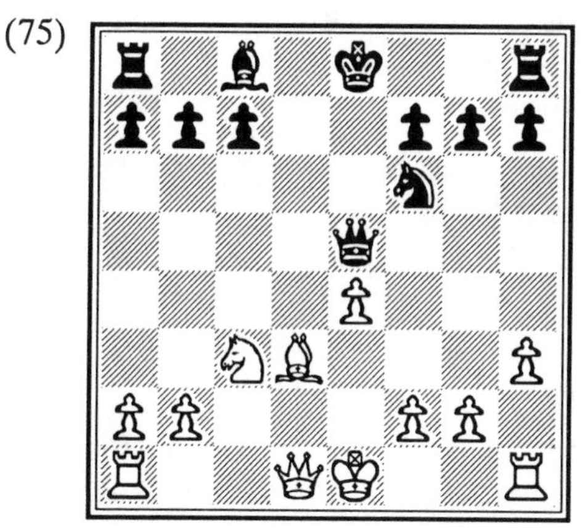

White to play.

1700: White has a pawn majority on the kingside. Black's pieces are farther advanced and Black has a bit less development. White's pawn majority gives him a space advantage on the kingside so Black would be well advised to castle long.

White will castle short and prepare f4.

JS: 1700 realized that Black should not step into the brunt of White's onrushing pawns. This is excellent. However, like the student before him, White fails to notice the potential weakness of the dark squares in the center. This seems to be a typical weakness of the amateur player: he can see tactical threats to win material or go after the King, but he has real trouble seeing that a square can also be a target.

1.0-0 Be6

1700: If I play f4 he can check me with ...Qd4 but then he has to move his queen because he can easily lose it to a Bishop discovery on b5. He could also check me on c5 when his queen might be safer. I could just move out of the way, though, and continue my attack.

JS: This student tends towards excessive optimism. While confidence is an important thing to have, you also need a touch of realism. Like 1500 before him, 1700 is not really giving the possibilities of the opponent a thorough examination.

The initiative in open positions will often go to the player who is first to control an open central file. In the Alekhine game, White went ahead with his pawn expansion only after stopping any counterplay on the d-file.

2.f4 Qd4+

1700: Looks risky for him.

JS: At this point White is transfixed by his threat to win Black's Queen by Bb5+.

3.Kh1 0-0-0

1700: Now he's attacking my Bishop and stopped my threat of Bb5+. I can move my Bishop to c2 or play Rf3.

4.Bc2

JS: Incredibly enough, we have reached the same position as in the previous game, with the insignificant exception of the King's placement on h1 instead of h2.

Perhaps we have stumbled onto something important. Perhaps the amateur typically has some sort of idea about what he wishes to achieve but rarely takes an honest look at the opponent's plans.

4...Bc4

1700: I have to defend my Rook.

JS: Now White was in pure defensive mode. He seemed shocked that things had turned around so quickly and this depressed state of mind soon led to a blunder.

5.Re1 Qf2 6.Qc1

JS: He moved quickly and without thought.

6...Rd2 0-1

Well, that was a disaster for White! Note how routine play keeps giving Black the initiative in these games. Now compare them to Alekhine's play and you will get a greater appreciation of two things: how he stopped Black's counterplay before it began and how he claimed the initiative for himself.

1800 vs. J.S.

(76)

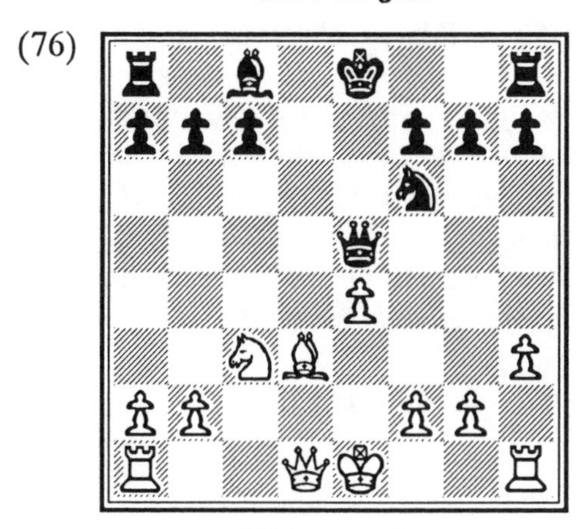

White to play.

1800: I like White. He has his minor pieces out and he has a pawn controlling the center. He has both the d-file and the half-open c-file to work with. He has a pawn majority on the kingside while Black has a majority on the queenside. We have to kill his majority and get ours going. How do we do this? 1.Qb3 slows down his development, but he just goes 1...b6 and fianchettoes. At some point I could play b4 stopping his pawns. I can't do this at the moment so I'll just castle and prepare to get my pawns going by f2-f4.

JS: As a higher rated player, 1800 looked at more than his predecessors. Nevertheless, his error is basically the same. By seeing the game as some mad race between rival majorities, he fails to take into account other possibilities for Black and falls victim to the pressure on the d-file that the others ran afoul of.

1.0-0 Be6

1800: He has a pin coming up but there is nothing he can do with it yet. I'll get my majority rolling.

JS: Like 1700, White sees Black's first move but discounts its usefulness.

2.f4 Qd4+ 3.Kh1 0-0-0

1800: I'm pinned and I don't see any counterplay for me.

JS: Here we go again! All of these players saw the punch coming but refused to give it credence until their teeth were knocked out!

How do players of C-A strength avoid this type of reversal? You have to work much harder at the board than these guys did! They gave the position just a cursory examination. It's good to come up with an aggressive plan for yourself (based on the positive aspects of your position, of course), but you must also figure out what the opponent is going to do and strive to cross his plans. This is made possible if your plan is faster, or by simply stopping him from doing what he wants to do.

4.Bc2

1800: I need to consolidate and this does it.

4...Qe3

1800: He's in my position! I don't know what to do.

JS: The once confident commander of the White pieces succumbs to panic.

5.Qf3 Qxf3 6.Rxf3 Rd2

1800: Black stands better. I need to sacrifice a pawn and get out of the bind.

JS: White is a little too eager to give up material. Your position may be unpleasant but you must hold on tight and refuse to give up anything!

7.Bb3?

JS: So panic leads to the loss of material. The calm 7.Rc1 was much better.

7...Rxb2

—Stopped the game.

Ready to do this one more time? Let's go to the strong expert class and see if someone of this strength can handle the position any better.

2100 vs. J.S.

(77)

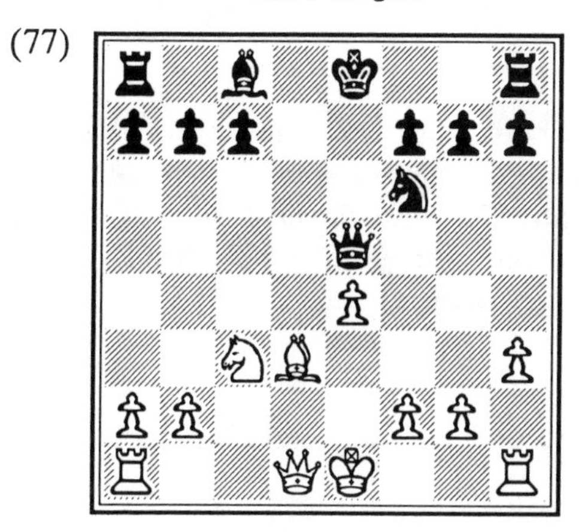

White to play.

2100: The major imbalance is a kingside majority vs. a queenside majority. If White can break the blockade on e5 and push his pawn to that square, his Bishop will be more active and his pawns will push the Black pieces backwards.

Of course, this sounds good but not so easy to accomplish. On 1.0-0 Black can play 1...Nh5 and create a blockade on f4. My dark squares would then be conquered. I have three moves to consider: 1.0-0 with the idea f4. I already found a good reply to this: 1.Ne2 giving up the b-pawn. I don't think I can open up the center fast enough to justify this sacrifice; 1.Qc2 with the idea of Ne2. This covers the f4 and d4 squares. 1.Qd2 is also possible but Qc2 gives extra protection to the e-pawn.

From Black's point of view: Black wants to retain his blockade and prevent f4. He doesn't want to castle queenside 'cause there are several open files. Black could try to work on the e4 pawn but that might be slow. He should probably try to use his queenside majority and get his King to safety with ...0-0.

For White, I like 1.Qc2 because there are potential attacks on the c-pawn.

JS: This was nicely done! He was off on his assessment concerning the correct location for Black's King, but his efforts to take the dark squares away from Black are highly praiseworthy. Notice how he also looked for ways that Black could fight against his plans (1.0-0 being met by ...Nh5). This was some-

thing that the C-A players didn't do.

1.Qc2 Bd7

2100: Now I'll take away those squares on f4 and d4.

JS: Notice how the other players never even mentioned the existence of "squares." Any class player will make great strides if he realizes that the control of individual squares is as important as any other strategy in the game.

2.Ne2 Bc6

2100: Now 3.f3 or 3.Nc3 will make me look stupid so f4 is forced.

3.f4 Qa5+

2100: I knew he was going there. If 4.Qd2 he can simply trade. 4.Nc3 is my best option; the Knight's already done its job in allowing me to play f4. After 4.Nc3 I can also castle queenside and get my kingside majority into play.

4.Nc3 0-0-0

2100: Now I have to decide between queenside castling and e5. Risky to play in the center when your King is still sitting there. I'd better castle since he threatens 5...Nxe4! 6.Bxe4 Bxe4 7.Qxe4 Rhe8.

5.0-0-0

JS: Though White's play was not the very best, he came up with a logical plan and this sufficed to give him a good position with a safe King and an active central majority.

The game was stopped here.

Lessons From These Games:

1) Don't become entranced with your own plans. You must also take note of the opponent's possibilities and gauge just how dangerous they really are.

2) Part of your plan can be the prevention of his goals. For

example, you can be playing to win a weak pawn but take time out to prevent his Knight from reaching a strong central outpost.

3) In an open position, the first person to dominate an open central file will usually gain the initiative.

4) The initiative will usually go to the first person who turns his plan into a reality.

During my years of teaching experience I have noticed that nothing freaks out the amateur player more than the threat of an attack against his King. Though the amateur's play on the queenside or in the center may be highly promising, when the opponent goes boo to his King all thoughts about his own plans are quickly forgotten and his pieces rush to the kingside in an effort to defend their leader. Funnily enough, *it is then not the opponent's kingside attack that wins the game but rather the amateur's lack of threats due to his having given up on his own plans.*

This leads us to the following simple but effective rule: When players are attacking on opposite wings it is important to follow your plans with unerring devotion. Certain defensive moves *are* acceptable, but the first person to crack and go into purely defensive mode will most likely end up as the loser. Why? Because the attacking side can then take his time and build up his forces to his heart's content, secure in the knowledge that his opponent has ceased to make threats of his own.

How is it that the side with the initiative must play quickly and actively in one game, and in another he can play in a slower vein? The answer is simple: If the opponent is also pursuing an active plan then you must play a fast, active game. However, if he stops his own plans and just reacts to you, then you have all the time in the world—he is no longer doing anything that can hurt you!

The following two games both show cases where White (the amateur) is given a position with very promising queenside play. Will they panic in the face of Black's kingside counterattack? If they do panic, does this mean that such a reaction is typical of most amateurs, or is it simply a matter of style and individual temperament? Perhaps the games will provide an answer to these questions.

1400 vs. J.S.

The starting moves were: **1.d4 d5 2.c4 e6 3.Nc3 Nf6 4.cxd5 exd5 5.Bg5 Be7 6.e3 c6 7.Bd3 0-0 8.Nf3 Nbd7 9.0-0 Re8**

(78)

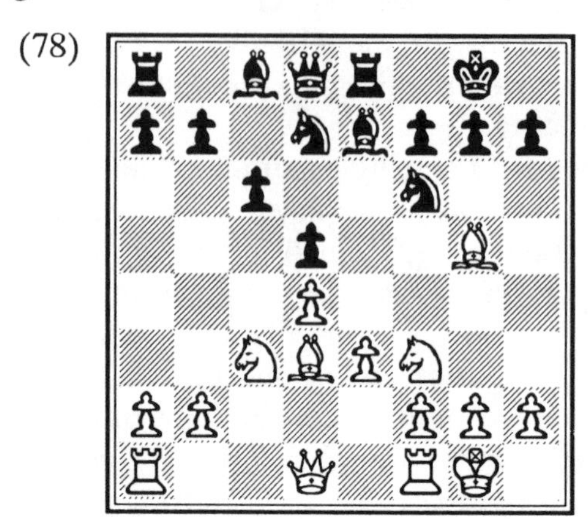

White to play.

JS: This, the Exchange Variation in the Queen's Gambit Declined, features one of the most useful positional ideas in chess: the Minority Attack. *The beauty of this plan is that White is able to implement a strategy that goes beyond the middle game and right into the endgame. The idea is to play Rb1 followed b2-b4-b5 and bxc6 (White is attacking a majority of pawns with a minority of pawns), when Black will be left with a weak pawn on c6 which will bother him forever. Does this mean that Black is doomed to defend passively and hope for a draw? No, note that Black's pawns are pointing towards the kingside. The pawn pointing theory (discussed in other chapters) states that Black should play in the direction his pawns point, so this means that Black must try to generate a kingside attack. Thus the battle lines are drawn: White will play on the queenside (this gives him a long-range advantage since endgames are favorable to White), Black on the kingside (Black hopes for a middlegame decision).*

My students in these two games were given a complete lecture on the minority attack so it should prove interesting to see how much they retained of this plan.

1400: The position looks even. White's light-squared Bishop appears to be pretty good. Looks like Ne5 followed by f4 with a kingside attack might do well here. Black has a queenside pawn majority and White has a majority on the kingside. White therefore has the possibility of a minority attack on the queenside. The other plan with Ne5 is interesting but Black has a lot of pieces aimed at the kingside and his pawns point there also. White's pawns aim at the queenside so a minority attack must be correct. I'm considering Rb1 followed by b2-b4 starting a minority attack. I'm not sure if that is correct or if a3 followed by b4 is better.

10.a3?!

JS: The best move is 10.Qc2, which gives added support to the e4 square and connects the Rooks. When the time comes for the b4 advance, though, correct is Rb1 instead of a3 since after an eventual b2-b4-b5 and bxc6 the Rook will be nicely placed on the open b-file. Another problem with 10.a3 is that after b4 Black can play ...a6 when White must move the a-pawn a second time by a3-a4 if he wishes to get in the desired b4-b5 advance. Note that Rb1 followed by b4 allows White to advance his a-pawn (if needed) in just one move.

10...Ne4

1400: Looks like I have to trade Bishops by Bxe7. By doing that I'm allowing Black to further back up his Knight. Due to this 10.Bf4 is possible. Trading the Bishops probably helps me on the queenside with my minority attack so I will go ahead and snap it off.

JS: So far White is thinking only of his minority attack, which is a good sign—he has a plan and he wants to implement it!

11.Bxe7 Qxe7

1400: I'm now concerned about his Knight on e4 and an ...f7-f5 advance on the kingside; how do I get rid of his Knight? However, my pieces are posted towards an advance on the queenside and I don't see how he can kill me right away so let's advance!

JS: Here we see the start of 1400's fatal weakness as a chessplayer: he becomes so worried about the threats (real and imagined) of the opponent that he starts to forget about his own ideas and even misses elementary tactical tricks. At this point 1400 played 12.b4?? which hangs his face to 12...Nxc3. I had him take the move over.

1400: I can play 12.Qc2 to guard c3 and put pressure on e4.

12.Qc2 Nf8

1400: Black is definitely setting his sights on a fierce attack against my King. In order to counteract that I can play Nce2-g3.

JS: White's fear of being mated has left all his previous dreams of a minority attack in the dust. From this point on he plays a fearful defensive game and hands the initiative to Black. Funnily enough, the time White takes to defend himself allows Black all the tempi he needs to set a real attack in motion.

13.Ne2 Ng6

1400: Now I'll bring my Knight around and get more protection for my King.

JS: White is now so preoccupied with thoughts of defense that he no longer entertains any hopes at all of continuing his queen-side play.

14.Ng3 Bg4

1400: Now I have an opportunity to get rid of his Knight by Nd2. However, my f3 Knight is protecting against a Knight advance to h4 but I don't want him to capture on f3 and double my pawns.

JS: The game was stopped here since time was running out. However, it's obvious that White's mental state is rapidly deteriorating. He has reduced himself to just reacting to the opponent's ideas and is getting so confused about stopping all of the enemy's possibilities that he has become afraid to move anything at all!

In the next game I played pretty much the same position but this time I brought in my ever-confident 1700 student. Would he bravely follow his own plans or would he, like 1400 before him, succumb to the whims of fear and panic?

1700 vs. J.S.

The starting moves were: **1.d4 d5 2.c4 e6 3.Nc3 Nf6 4.cxd5 exd5 5.Bg5 Be7 6.e3 c6 7.Bd3 0-0 8.Nf3 Nbd7 9.0-0 Re8 10.Qc2 Nf8**

(79) 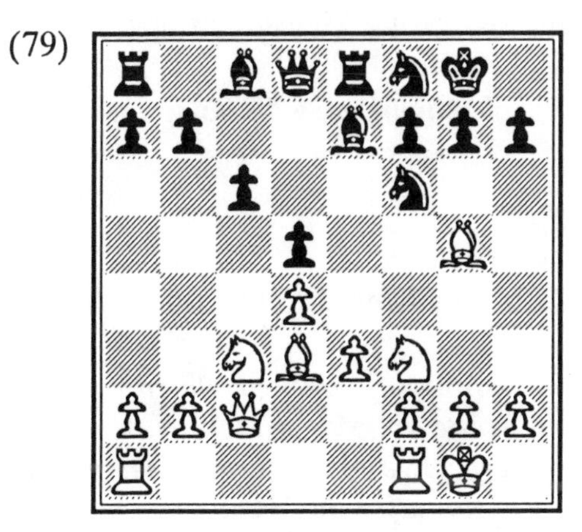

White to play.

1700: I want to take the f6 Knight, which prevents ...Ne4 and allows me to play b4 immediately and begin my minority attack.

JS: This is more like it! White is going after his plan with as much speed as possible. However, how long will he retain this positive mental attitude?

11.Bxf6 Bxf6 12.b4 Be7

JS: Seeing that his Bishop is doing nothing on f6, Black wants to redirect it to d6 where it will menace the White King.

1700: He's attacking my pawn. I can now push my pawn up or guard it with the Rook. If I play b5 then he can try ...c5. So maybe it's better to guard it first.

JS: He didn't try to figure out why I played ...Be7 (other than to attack his b4-pawn) and what my plan was. We also get to see a bit of laziness present itself: he notices the possibility of answering b5 with ...c5 but doesn't take time out to see if that idea works for Black. After 13.b5 c5? 14.dxc5 Bxc5 15.Rad1 Black would experience real problems with his weak d-pawn (after all, Black's original plan was the creation of a pawn weakness and the lame creature on d5 certainly qualifies) and the undefended Bishop on c5. Don't look at a move for your opponent and just decide that it works for him. Prove it!!

13.Rab1 Bd6

1700: He's going right for a kingside attack. I should ignore that and continue with my idea.

JS: Bravo! As the old saying goes, "The best defense is a good offense."

14.b5 Re6

1700: Still going for my King. I will capture on c6 and create a target there.

JS: Black wishes to mix offense with defense. His Rook will defend c6 and join in the kingside attack. Note how both sides are following their respective plans (both sides are fighting for the initiative) and are not allowing side issues to distract them.

15.bxc6 bxc6

1700: I can bring my Knight back to e2 where it guards the kingside and uncovers my Queen on c6.

JS: Now that a weakness has been created on c6 White can spend a little time shoring up his kingside. However, great care must be taken to insure that his own threats on the queenside never let up. He must also make sure that he does not fall into a defensive frame of mind.

16.Ne2

JS: Instead of this somewhat passive reassignment of the Knight, better would have been 16.Bf5! (Since endgames favor White, trades can only make the first player happy. In this case the c8 Bishop was aiming at White's King so this equals one less attacking piece for Black) 16...Rh6 17.Bxc8 (17.h3!? followed by 18.Rfc1 may be better. With the light-squared Bishops gone, White suddenly has access to the f5 and b7 squares) 17...Rxc8 (and not 17...Bxh2+?? 18.Nxh2 Qh4 19.Bh3) 18.h3 (Stopping the threatened 18...Bxh2+ 19.Nxh2 Qh4) 18...Ng6 (Bringing up reinforcements. Neither side is losing sight of his goal) 19.Rfc1 (Threatening 20.Nxd5) 19...Nh4! (This allows the remaining

Black forces to get closer to the enemy King) 20.Nxh4 Qxh4 and now 21.Rb7 or even 21.Qf5 Rd8 22.Rc2 Rf6 23.Qg4 keeps Black's kingside play under control, still leaving him to deal with the weaknesses on c6 and a7.

Admittedly long-winded, but the point should be clear enough. Even in the face of a kingside attack you must keep a clear head and not lose sight of simple goals like trading pieces if endgames favor you (after all, White owns the static advantage, while Black's play is based on dynamics).

16...Rh6

1700: I can't take on c6 due to ...Bxh2+ winning my Queen. I should block his Bishop on d6 by 17.Ng3 or 17.Nf4.

17.Nf4??

JS: Black first played Ng3 and just before letting go placed it on f4 saying, Here is better. Naturally, this type of last second change of plan can only lead to trouble. If you touch a piece and suddenly have a change of heart, put the piece down, take a deep breath, and rethink the position. You do have to move the piece you touch but at least you can make sure that you place it on a good square.

17...g5

1700: Attacking my Knight. I have to move it when he can continue to advance via ...g5-g4. Then I will play Ne5.

JS: White's mistake on the 17th move has given Black several free moves and a firm grip on the initiative. White must now ride the storm and allow Black to dictate the play.

18.Ne2 g4 19.Ne5 Bxe5 20.dxe5 Qh4

1700: I have to play h3. I don't like it but I no longer have any choice.

21.h3

JS: White's last few moves have all been forced. Though things look hopeless, Black's lingering weaknesses on c6 and a7 give White some hope of surviving if a mate or further loss of material can be avoided.

21...gxh3 22.g3 Qg4

1700: He threatens to go to f3 with mate on g2.

The game was stopped here due to lack of time. For those that have always wondered what the initiative is, this game provides an excellent example. White was forced to deal with all the Black threats and was not able even to think of continuing his own play on the queenside.

Lessons From These Games:

1) Don't panic in the face of a kingside attack. Size up his real threats, make defensive moves when needed, and continue with your own plans.

2) Follow your plans with gusto. Be devoted to your plan and it will serve you well.

3) Don't play with fear in your heart. If you play with courage the worst thing that can happen to you is a loss. Since we will all lose many games in our lifetime, we might as well go down with honor and make every game as instructive as possible. Playing passively and getting routed is no fun at all and teaches you nothing.

4) Worry, confusion, and hasty moves leads to gross blunders. If you find your mind fogging up, sit back, relax, and take a fresh look at the position.

5) Chess is a game of will power. Don't let the opponent's will dominate yours. Stick to your plans and don't allow him to distract you from them.

6) Take nothing for granted. Don't feel or hope that some line is good or bad. Make sure that it is!

7) The best defense is a good offense. When you have to defend, try to make a move that also furthers your own plans.

PART SEVEN

Many Imbalances, One Board

The vast majority of chess games contain battles between several different types of imbalances. One person may have high hopes for his advantage in space and superior pawn structure, while the opponent will insist that his two Bishops and greater activity is what really counts. Often it is not clear which particular imbalance will triumph, but no one doubts that the first player who stops trying to make use of these positive attributes will allow the opponent to dominate.

There are no general rules concerning many kinds of imbalances. What you must do is be aware of the rules pertaining to the individual imbalances (given in the earlier chapters) and see if one negates or strengthens the other. When listing your imbalances, be sure that they complement each other. For example: you may have two Bishops (vs. a Bishop and Knight), a passed pawn, and the chance to gain extra space by advancing and locking the pawns. The desire to gain space may be great, but will this decision aid or hurt your Bishops (remember that they don't like closed positions)? Will the passed pawn be useful or will it make the enemy Knight (which might sit in front of the passer and act as a blockader) stronger?

The Amateur's Mind

Our first example of several imbalances interacting with

each other is obviously in White's favor. He clearly enjoys the superior pawn structure and he also has a fine Knight vs. a poor Bishop. Is this enough to win? Yes, White should win, but the process is far from easy.

(80)

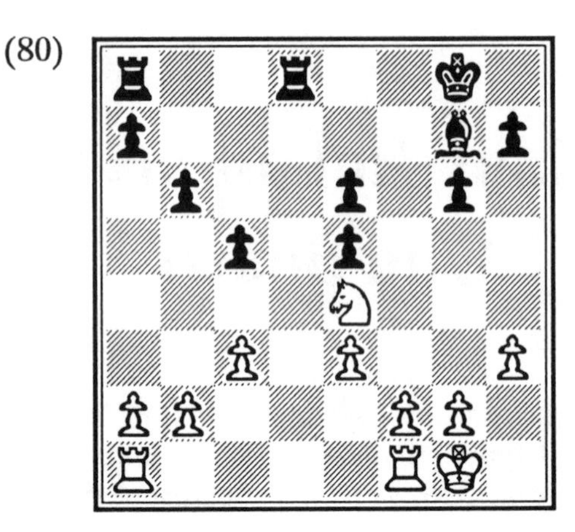

Alekhine–Euwe, London 1922.
White to play.

1.Rfd1

Staking a claim to the d-file. To win this game White will play to keep the Black Bishop bottled up while attempting to create new weaknesses (points of attack or penetration) on the queenside.

1...Kf8 2.Kf1

More obvious stuff. Once an endgame is reached, both sides should rush their Kings towards the center.

2...Ke7 3.c4!

This does two things: It keeps a Black Rook out of d5 and it fixes the Black c-pawn on c5 where it blocks its own Bishop.

3...h6 4.Ke2 Rxd1 5.Rxd1 Rb8

To quote Alekhine:

"Black cannot exchange Rooks, since after 5...Rd8 6.Rxd8 Kxd8 White wins as follows:

"1st phase: 7.h4 followed by g2-g4 and g4-g5, against which Black has nothing better than ...h5, since the exchange of pawns will give the White Knight the square h4.

"2nd phase: b2-b3 followed by Kd3, Nc3 and Ke4.

"3rd phase: the transfer of the Knight to d3, which ties the Black King to d6, in order to hold the twice-attacked e5 pawn.

"4th phase: finally f2-f4, forcing the win of the g or e pawn, after which White wins easily.

"By avoiding the exchange of Rooks Black makes his opponent's task more difficult."

6.Rd3 Bh8 7.a4!

White intends to play a4-a5 and create new weaknesses in the Black position. Since 7...a5 8.Rb3 wins material for White (the threat of Nxc5 is hard to stop), Black is unable to prevent this advance by White.

7...Rc8 8.Rb3 Kd7 9.a5! Kc6 10.axb6 axb6 11.Ra3

White will use the a-file to penetrate into the Black position. Black cannot do the same along the d-file since the White King and Knight cover all the entry points.

11...Bg7

And not 11...Kb7?? 12.Nd6+. White's Rook becomes more active than its Black counterpart mainly due to the fact that his Knight is taking part in the effort. Compare it to the pathetic Bishop on h8 and you will see the vast difference in strength between the two pieces.

12.Ra7 Rc7

Now White could trade Rooks and carry out the winning plan that Alekhine mentioned earlier; however, he decides that his Rook is better than the enemy's and should offer him a way to a quicker decision.

13.Ra8! Re7 14.Rc8+ Kd7 15.Rg8! Kc6 16.h4

Now White has the superior minor piece, a structural advantage, and a more active Rook. Since Black is unable to do anything active, White takes his time and plays to tie Black up. If you have an opponent backed up against a wall, take away any and all potential counterplay before going for the final kill.

16...Kc7 17.g4 Kc6 18.Kd3 Rd7+ 19.Kc3 Rf7 20.b3

Still taking his time and doing little things that make his position more compact and safer.

20...Kc7 21.Kd3 Rd7+ 22.Ke2 Rf7 23.Nc3! Re7 24.g5 hxg5 25.hxg5 Kc6 26.Kd3 Rd7+ 27.Ke4

White has just added a superior King to his list of advantages.

27...Rc7 28.Nb5 Re7 29.f3! Kd7 30.Rb8 Kc6 31.Rc8+ Kd7 32.Rc7+ Kd8 33.Rc6 Rb7 34.Rxe6 1-0

We have seen that in top flight chess the diagrammed position is considered to be a matter of technique, but at the amateur level virtually anything can happen! Let's see what kind of mistakes the amateur makes while trying to realize his advantage.

1467 vs. J.S.

1467: My Knight is better than his bad Bishop and the open d-file is not a problem since White can easily challenge it. The

(81)

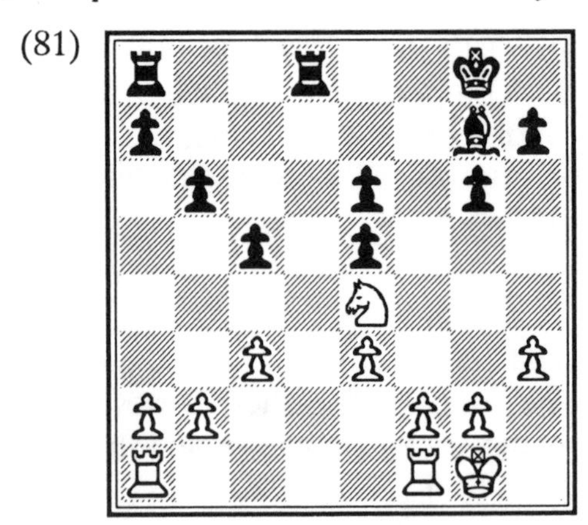

White to play.

queenside seems even. The only thing I can see is to play Rfd1.

JS: He saw the basics (though I was surprised that he never mentioned Black's doubled pawns) but was not sure how to make use of his advantages. In this type of static position a player should look for ideas rather than concrete moves.

I certainly don't expect 1467 to come up with the plans that Alekhine laid out, but there are three things that a player of any rating can do: 1) make each of his pieces better than or at least equal to their enemy counterparts; 2) If the opponent cannot do anything active, then don't rush the position; instead you should let him sit there, suffer, and beg you for a draw; 3) Try to make your plusses expand while making sure that his negatives don't cure themselves.

1.Rfd1

1467: Now if 1...Rxd1+ 2.Rxd1 White threatens Rd6 and Rd7.

1...Kf7

1467: I can check on g5 and win a pawn!

JS: He decides that I just hung a pawn and rushes to take it. This type of decision should be made slowly; after all, White is moving his Knight from a dominant central location and placing it on the far rim of the board.

Instead of this impulsive act, White would have done well if he had simply brought his King to the center.

2.Ng5+ Ke7

1467: I don't know if this is good even though it wins a pawn.

JS: He should have figured this out before he made the check.

3.Nxh7 Bh6

JS: White's ill thought-out idea, which forced the Black King to the center, has left him with a poorly placed Knight.

4.h4

JS: The only way to free the poor Knight. White has now taken on the role of the defender—someone who must react to his opponent's will. How did this transformation take place? White failed to make his pieces better than or equal to the Black ones and he failed to make use of his fine Knight (instead he stuck it in a ditch).

4...Rh8 5.Ng5 Bxg5 6.hxg5

1467: I probably should have exchanged Rooks first.

JS: He is no longer thinking of positive things to do. Instead he is living in the past. This means that his concentration has also left him.

6...Rh5 7.f4 Rf8

1467: Attacking me.

8.g3 Rfh8

1467: I have a bit of a problem here.

9.Rf1 e4!

1467: I should have exchanged a pair of Rooks while I could.

JS: The sickly doubled pawn now controls f3 and contributes to an attack on the White King.

10.c4 Rh1+

1467: Damn! Now he wins the b2 pawn. I should have played b3.

11.Kf2 R8h2+ 12.Ke1 Rxf1+ 13.Kxf1 Rh1+ 0-1

He lost this game because he did a series of negative things: allowed his proud Knight to be exchanged for the horrible Bishop; centralized the enemy King; tried to cash in his advantage too quickly. Remember: If you have a long-lasting advantage take your time and improve your game slowly while taking away the opponent's counterplay.

1467 was so upset about losing this nice endgame that he insisted that we try it again.

1.Rfd1 Kf7 2.Kf1

1467: This time I will leave my Knight on its dominant

(82)

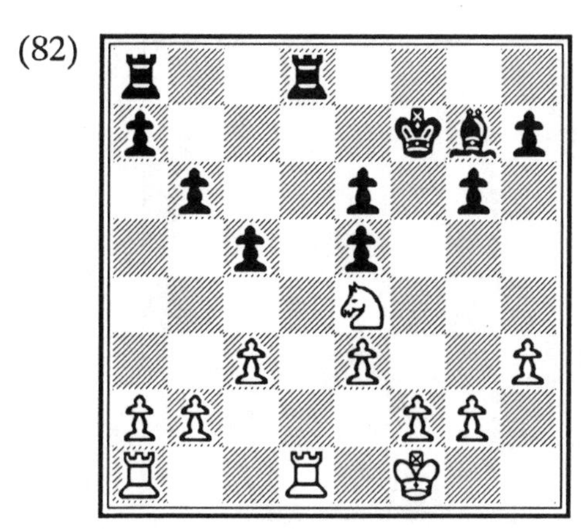

Black to play.

square and bring my King up to the middle. No more adventures for me.

2...Ke7 3.Ke2 c4

1467: I should have played c3-c4. This would have kept his pawns on the same color of his Bishop.

JS: He is living in the past again. If he had asked himself how he could have made sure that the bad Bishop stays bad, he would have found c3-c4. Always ask yourself: "How do I make his bad points even worse?"

4.Rd2 Rxd2+ 5.Kxd2 Rd8+ 6.Ke2 Rd5 7.Rd1 b5

1467: My game has deteriorated.

JS: White is still better but Black has made some progress: His Rook is happy on d5 and the Bishop can eventually find some life on the f8-a3 diagonal.

We stopped the game here since he wanted to try it one last time from the beginning.

1467 vs. J.S.

1.Rfd1 Kf7 2.c4

1467: All right! I don't know what I have to do to get this

(83)

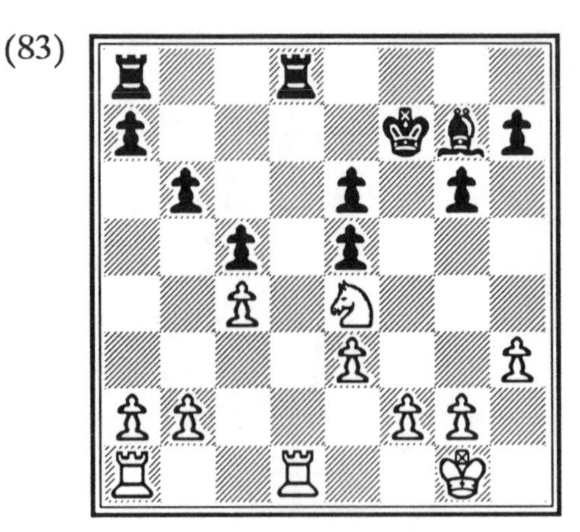

Black to play.

right, but I actually have the feeling that I kind of know what I am doing.

2...Ke7

1467: Now I can bring my King up.

3.Kf1 h6

1467: I'm not penetrating but right now I don't see how to do it. I need to activate my King and Rooks. A good plan is 4.a4-a5 when ...bxa5 Rxa5 leaves him with a weakness on a7 and c5.

JS: Quite a difference from the other two games! Here he is killing my counterplay, centralizing his pieces, and probing for weaknesses.

4.a4 a5

1467: His Bishop is even weaker and now I have b5 for my Knight. I could bring my King up and change all the Rooks, but does that win? I need to get his g6 pawn to go to g5, when his Bishop is a horrible piece. To get him to play ...g5 I must threaten his pawn, but how? I guess I should play b3 first to improve my game. I have time.

JS: He must have taken vitamins or something! Keep in mind that 1467 has not yet seen the Alekhine game but now, after a couple of trial runs, he is actually coming very close to the World

Champion's ideas.

Why the drastic change? I think he suddenly realized that his advantages are not going away and that a slow handling of the position leaves Black without any play at all.

5.b3 Rab8 6.Ke2 Bf8

1467: I'm thinking of playing Nc3 and e3-e4 to close the position. I don't like that, though. I should expand on the kingside via h4. Then I can consider Rh1-h3-g3.

JS: His original idea of playing e3-e4 was horrible since it killed a square that was a potential home for his Knight and his King. However, his 7.h4 followed by Rh1-h3-g3 deserves quite a bit of praise since it gains space and begins to pick on some of Black's weak pawns.

7.h4 Kf7 8.Rxd8 Rxd8 9.Rd1

1467: I know I can at least draw this position.

JS: I wish he had given his original idea of Rh1-h3-g3 a try. Though 9.Rd1 is far from terrible, it was mainly played to avoid defeat (which it certainly succeeds in doing). Do not play moves that are influenced by the rating of the opponent!

9...Rxd1 10.Kxd1 Be7 11.g3 Ke8 12.Ke2 Kd7 13.Kd3 Bd8 14.Nc3 Ke7 15.Ke4 Bc7

1467: Now 16.Nb5 Bb8, so I need to get my Knight on d3 or f3 when I attack e5 with many pieces.

JS: I like the way he first picks a weakness to attack and then brings all his pieces to bear on that target.

16.g4 g5 17.hxg5 hxg5

1467: Now I'll get my Knight to f3 to attack both g5 and e5.

18.Nb1 Kf6 19.Nd2 Bb8

1467: I can't chase him from g5 and e5. I needed to get my Knight on g4 to win. Now it is a draw.

We stopped the game.

Lessons From This Game:

1) If you own a long-term advantage, don't be in a hurry to make use of it.
2) If the opponent has a passive position, never allow him to get counterplay.
3) Even if you already have several advantages, always be on the lookout for ways to create new targets.

When it comes to positions with several differences, humans, computers, and other chess playing creatures may find themselves with differing views about who has the advantage. I recall once having a little argument with a well known chess writer in the pages of a certain American chess magazine. In one of his books he declared that Black stood better in the following position.

(84)

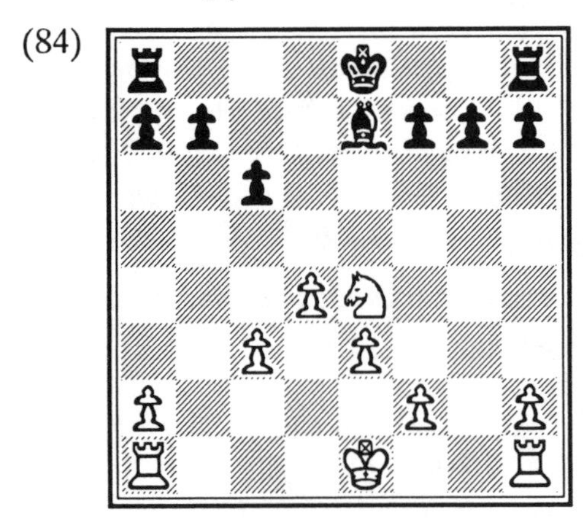

White to play.

I disagreed, saying that the ending was far from clear (I actually preferred White but decided to be kind). He disagreed with my disagreement and pointed out that his chess computer validated his opinion. I . . . well, we never did come to terms on this position.

Why the difference of opinion? Why would a computer be in error? This example showed me why some players and many computers run into trouble: When the heart of a position takes accepted principles and turns them inside out, many players find themselves at a loss to understand what's really going on. This means that though basic laws such as *Always capture towards the center*, *Don't move the same piece twice in the opening*, *Doubled pawns are bad*, and *Bishops are better than Knights in open positions* are often correct, they also lead to a close-minded bigotry that can stunt the growth of just about any student of the game.

Computers, of course, are even more vulnerable to this type of thing than humans are. They are told specific things and they stick faithfully to them—often to the exclusion of everything else. Us biological organisms, however, can go beyond this one dimensional view.

In diagram #84 we have a situation where the basic laws of chess add up to give Black the better position: He has a Bishop vs. a Knight in an open position and White has three pawn islands vs. Black's two. However, placing any credence in these two laws serves only to blind a player to the truth—which is that White's mass of center pawns are far more threatening than their Black counterparts.

This unwavering faith in beginning principles has harmed many players who have come to me for help. How many times have I recommended a position with doubled pawns and how many times have they cringed in horror. How often have I caught myself in this situation: During lesson #1 I say, "Why did you move the same piece twice in the opening? You should know better than that." Then, during the next lesson I find myself pointing out how they could have gotten a strong game by breaking that rule and moving the same piece twice or even three times!

This confusing state of affairs is enough to drive anyone crazy. Indeed, I have even run into cases where masters get trapped in the world of basic rules. A good example of this is the position in diagram #85.

Here the players agreed to a draw since White was exhausted from a long trip and Black was disgusted that she had blown a winning position from the opening. At the time the players and the tournament's other participants thought that

Beatriz Marinello–Sharon Burtman
1993 US Woman's Invitational Championship

(85)

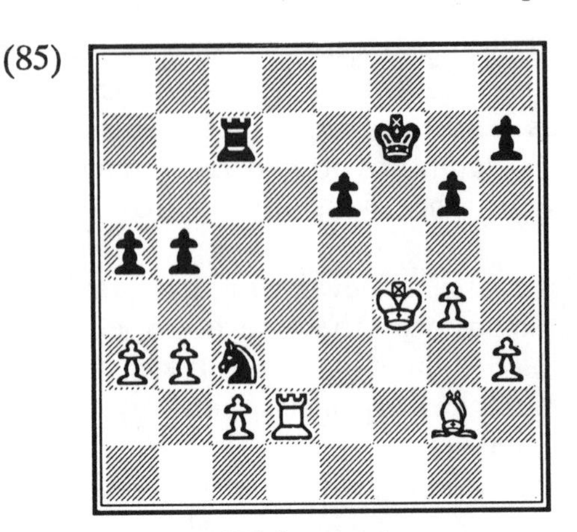

White to play.

White had the advantage and should have continued the battle. A glance shows that this is a reasonable assessment: White's Rook is on a completely open file, White's Bishop is very active, White has a queenside majority of pawns, Black has an isolated pawn on e6, and White enjoys a clearly superior King position.

An impressive list, but I shocked Sharon when I declared that Black's position looked quite nice to me. What was I seeing that the others didn't? Nothing at all! I just preferred to look at all the so-called negatives in a positive light.

Here is what I mean: 1) White's Bishop is indeed slicing down that h1-a8 diagonal, but what is it doing there? On the other hand the Black Knight is quite bothersome and threatens to pick up the a3-pawn by ...Nb1. 2) White's Rook is on a completely open file but it is not attacking anything there. The Black Rook, though, is eyeing the morsel on c2. 3) White does have a queenside majority but the purpose of such a majority is to create a passed pawn. Black's so-called weakness on e6 is in reality a tower of strength since it is already passed. Thus I will not look at it as isolated—instead I look at it as passed! 4) The White King is better placed than the Black one. You got me on that point!

Naturally, I immediately gave this position to a class C student and had him play me one of my patented "talk out loud games."

1470 vs. J.S.

(86)

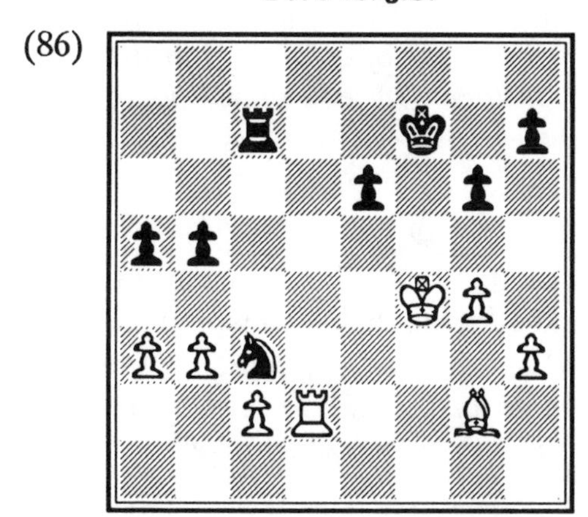

White to play.

1470: Black has an isolated pawn and a passive King. My Bishop is also dominating his Knight, though the pawn on g4 makes my Bishop bad. I think that I should be able to do something really good here—Black must be busted. I will use my superior King to march into h6 and win the h7 pawn.

1.Kg5?

JS: By looking at the e6 pawn as a weakness, White was unable to see its dynamic potential. Something is only weak if you can attack it. Names such as "doubled" or "isolated" don't make things weak!

White's best try is probably something like 1.Rd6. This activates the Rook and prepares to attack the Black queenside pawns from behind by Ra6.

1...e5!

1470: Oh-oh. This pawn is threatening to go to e4, e3, and e2! Have I done something really stupid or can I stop the silly thing? I can't believe that this pawn can really go too far! I will continue with my plan and make him defend. That way he will never have time to push the pawn.

2.Kh6

JS: Winning the h-pawn will not worry Black. He is after a new Queen and certainly won't blink an eye at such a tiny threat. White is making the mistake of assuming that Black will go into a panic at this first threat. Instead he will ignore White's King walk and continue with his own ideas.

2...e4

1470: Giving me material. There is no turning back now, I have to take it and dare him to do his worst!

JS: Black could have dispelled White's illusions with 2...Ke6 but felt it was more instructive to give up the h-pawn and demonstrate the strength of the runner on e4.

3.Kxh7 e3

1470: I expected this but I think I have a good defense. I will check him on f3 and . . . wait! If I play 4.Rf3+ he can play 4...Ke8 and check me laterally with his Rook! Can't allow that.

4.Re3 Re7

We ended the game. That weakness on e6 took White right out of the game!

The next time I gave the position to a student, I made a couple of small changes to make things look even more attractive. Incredibly, my student insisted that Black stood better, so I found myself with the White side!

J.S. vs. 1650

1650: So we have an endgame with Rook and Knight vs. Rook and Bishop. The question is, what is better, the Knight or Bishop? White has a queenside pawn majority. White's Bishop controls a nice long diagonal. White has a hidden weakness on c2, so his Rook is forced to stay on the second rank to defend it. Black's Knight is kind of trapped on c3 so that covers the weakness at the moment. However, the threat to move it to b1 and win the a3 pawn is very annoying for

(87)

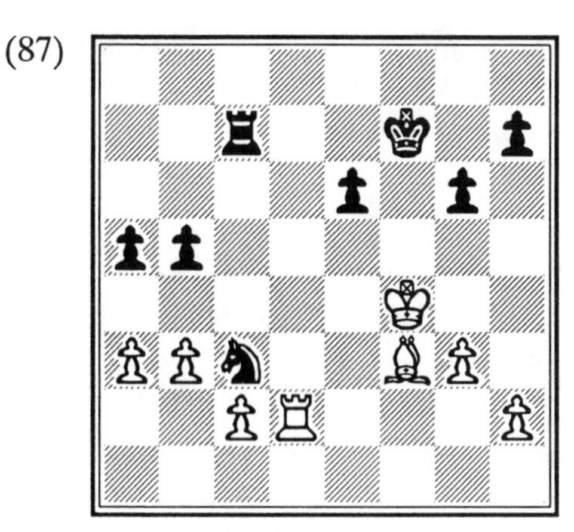

White to play.

White. So overall, I will give the edge to Black.

I think that way because, aside from the threat of ...Na3, Black also has three pawns to two on the kingside.

JS: Not bad at all! Black is not trapped with memorized preconceptions and instead tries to figure out the present position in a fresh way. I decided to try to freak him out with a central King rush.

1.Ke5

1650: White is aiming for d6 with an invasion on the queenside. I want to prevent this!

1...Ke7 2.Bg4

1650: He is going after my pawn but this is an easy threat to stop.

2...Rc5+ 3.Kd4 Rc7?

1650: Time to bring my Rook back to safety.

JS: Missing two strong possibilities. The first (but weaker) of the two is 3...Kd6! when 4.Ke3+ Ke5 leaves Black with the superior King or 4.Bxe6?? Kxe6 5.Kxc5 Ne4+ picks up a piece.

The second possibility is 3...Rd5+!, a move that he looked at but rejected due to 4.Kxc3 (Note that 4.Ke3 Rxd2 5.Kxd2 Nb1+ wins a pawn for Black). Now Black can take advantage of the loosely guarded White Rook by 4...b4+! 5.axb4 axb4+ 6.Kxb4 Rxd2 with an extra Exchange and a sure win. If a piece is not well defended you should always look for ways to win it.

4.Ke5

1650: He wants a draw but I hate draws and I won't allow him to get one! I will just go after his pawn.

JS: I like his attitude but he makes the mistake of placing the Knight on the side. Of course, it ends up being out of play there.

4...Nb1? 5.Rf2 Nxa3

1650: I hope my Knight can get back in the game!

JS: Whether he can get it back into play or not is beside the point—he should have asked this question before putting it on the side.

6.Bxe6 Rc5+? 7.Bd5

1650: This doesn't scare me. He wants to check me on f7 and win the h-pawn. He has no mating possibilities so it all comes down to a race.

JS: He was not aware (though we had discussed this point several months before) that a Knight is much worse than a Bishop in a mutual pawn race situation. The speed of a Bishop puts a Knight to shame in those cases.

7...Nxc2 8.Rf7+ Ke8 9.Rxh7 Ne3

1650: I think I have him!

10.Ke6

1650: He had a way out. He wants to mate me but that is easily stopped. I'm still doing well.

JS: He also missed 10.Kd4 (attacking Black's two undefended pieces at once), which would have led to a draw.

10...Kd8 11.Be4

1650: A trap! He is hoping for 11...Rc7 12.Rh8 mate! I will play 11...Nf5 which defends my g-pawn and threatens ...Nd4+. Then I will follow up with ...a5-a4 and try to queen my pawn.

JS: Note how the Bishop is dominating the Black Knight. This Bishop is so much better than the Knight that White is now winning.

11...Nf5?

JS: Leading to a quick finish.

12.g4

1650: I expected that, but I don't mind giving up my g-pawn for his b-pawn.

12...Nd4+ 13.Kd6

1650: Oh no! He threatens both Kxd6 and Rh8 mate.

—And we stopped the game. It should be apparent that leaving one's pieces in vulnerable, undefended positions is asking for trouble.

Lessons From This Game:

1) The basic rules we learned when we started out are good guidelines but must be broken often. Don't fall in love with these concepts and become blind to the reality of any given situation.

2) Every imbalance is capable of doing something positive. Don't look at a thing as negative just because it is supposed to be weak or bad. You have to ask: is it bad in this particular situation?

3) Undefended pieces can easily lead to trouble.

4) When pawns are racing to queen on both sides of the board, a Bishop will usually beat out a Knight due to its ability to jump from one side of the board to another in one move.

The next game shows a battle based on very different imbalances. Both sides nurse what they have and try to make it grow but, of course, only one side's vision will be proven correct.

2120 vs. J.S.

1.c4 Nf6 2.Nf3 e6 3.Nc3 Bb4 4.Qc2 0-0 5.g3 b6 6.Bg2 Bb7 7.a3 Bxc3 8.Qxc3 d6

2120: Lots of moves: 0-0, b4, d3. What's my plan, though? Black's plan is to play ...c5 and ...d5 and break open the center. How am I going to activate the dark-squared Bishop? I could play Bg5 with a pin or place it on the long diagonal. 9.d3 controls e4 and keeps options open.

JS: While it is all right to play an obviously useful move (like 9.d3), there is also a bit of laziness in the equation. White should really have at least a partial plan mapped out for himself. For example: White has the two Bishops and would like to make them better than the Knights. Since the dark-squared Bishop is the one piece that Black does not have, White should try his best to make it as active as possible. Thus d3 (limiting the enemy Knights), followed by b2-b4 and Bb2, placing the Bishop on the fine long diagonal, would be a simple but effective plan.

9.d3 Nbd7

2120: Where is his Knight heading to? If I develop my Bishop on the long diagonal he could play ...e5 and block it. 10.Bg5 is also silly due to ...h6.

JS: He is still not quite sure what to do so he holds off on any clear decisions and simply castles. This is fine here, but in many situations such trepidation might lead to problems.

10.0-0 c5

2120: Takes away this square from the Knight. Now he can't play ...e5 since d5 would be weak. I could play b3 or b4. On 11.b4 cxb4 opens up the a-file for me. I could also play d4 and open up the d-file so as to get play on d6. He wants to play for d5. My Knight on f3 is not doing anything so where do my pieces go? I'll get play by b2-b4.

JS: In closed or semi-closed positions you should lead with your pawns. For this reason Black had no intention of playing ...Nc5 since it would just get chased back by b2-b4. Instead Black gains space with ...c7-c5 and keeps his pieces flexibly posted behind his pawns. A d3-d4 advance would give Black use of the e4 square and activate his Knights. It should also be mentioned that Black will have no problems playing an ...e6-e5 advance. True, it leaves a hole on d5. But can White actually use that hole? No, he can't. So, since this weakness is more illusion than reality, Black will be happy with ...e6-e5 since it blocks the a1-h8 diagonal and gains central territory.

11.b4 Qe7

2120: Playing for d5. My Queen is nothing special and I would like to mix things up. A good slow plan is b5 and a4-a5.

JS: Black has no intention of playing ...d6-d5 (unless it achieves a very particular goal) since that would open up the position for the enemy Bishops. Instead he will place his Rooks on squares that will inhibit White from playing in the middle. Once that is done, Black will seek counterchances on the kingside.

12.Bb2 Rac8

2120: Threatens to take and get in ...d5 so I will own the queenside with b5.

13.b5 Rfe8

(88)

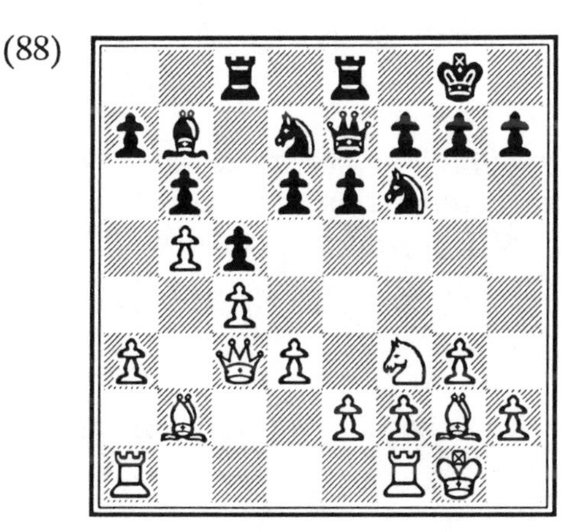

White to play.

2120: A wealth of riches. What do I want to play? I'm ignoring the center, which is bad. 14.d4 gives him the e4 square.

What does he do here? ...d5? My g2 Bishop is doing relatively nothing. How do I get my pieces into play? I'd like to play for a4-a5 but that has nothing to do with my b2-Bishop.

JS: It is strange to see a guy with such a wealth of riches be so confused about how he is going to get play! His 13.b5 took the tension out of the middle so he might as well continue on the queenside with a3-a4-a5.

Funnily enough, it is Black who has most of the options here. He can play ...e6-e5 or he can play ...d6-d5 with the idea of ...d5-d4.

Where are White's riches?

14.Nd2

2120: To transfer it to b3 in anticipation of a4-a5.

14...Bxg2 15.Kxg2 e5

2120: He has no threat. I could play e4 when my Bishop could get into play via c1 since d5 still scares me. e4 leaves me with play on the queenside.

JS: So White has stopped ...d6-d5 once and for all. However, his dark-squared Bishop is now all but useless (the locked position will be friendlier to the Knights) and the whole game will now come down to a race between White's queenside play (he will open lines with a3-a4-a5) and Black's kingside play (he will play for ...f7-f5).

This game has seen a few imbalances parade by: first we had a Bishop vs. Knight battle (which still exists) and now the emphasis is on mutual wing attacks (made possible by the closed center).

16.e4 Nf8

2120: Transferring to e6 and d4. I will go ahead with my plan.

17.a4

2120: I'm only worried about a kingside attack, so I would like a Queen trade.

JS: I like this comment very much. He is quite aware that his chances lie on the queenside and he knows that the presence of the Queens only helps Black, who will do his utmost to break through on the kingside.

17...Ne6

2120: I see no threat.

18.a5 Nd4 19.axb6 axb6 20.Ra6 Nd7

2120: Does he want to transfer his Queen to that side? Since my Bishop is doing nothing I will try to trade it off.

21.Qa3 Ne6 22.Ra1 Rf8

2120: Trying to get activity.

JS: Black wasted time with his Knight maneuver to d4; once it got there it moved away since it did not want the pathetic Bishop to snap it off.

23.Nf1 f5

2120: I could take and gain a tempo with Ne3 or I could play Ne3 and sink at f5 or d5. Does he have anything? He has no threat right now.

24.Ne3 f4

2120: Now I have two squares. Nd5 wins b6. I'd like to get my Queen into the defense. 24.Nf5 attacks d6 and closes the file. I am winning a pawn.

JS: Yes, White will win a pawn, but his King is far from safe.

25.Nf5 f3+

2120: Is he really going to mate me? I refuse to believe it!

JS: A good attitude, but the reality of the situation is quite different. White's King is in grave danger.

26.Kh1 Qg5 27.Qb3

2120: My Queen will come back and defend the g2 mating square.

27...Rxf5 28.exf5 Qxf5

JS: By giving up a very tiny bit of material, Black has made his pawns safe and is free to pursue his kingside desires.

29.Qd1 Rf8

2120: I will trade Rooks.

30.Ra8 Nf6 31.Rxf8+ Nxf8 32.Bc1 Ng4 33.Kg1 Ne6

2120: More pieces into the attack.

JS: The Black Knights are suddenly looking quite good. In the meantime, the White Rook and Bishop are unable to help out on the kingside.

34.Ra8+

2120: Can't be bad.

34...Kf7 35.Ra7+ Kg6 36.h3 Nf6

2120: Now 37.g4 Nxg4 38.hxg4 Qg4+ is complicated and gives him several pawns and an attack for the Rook. Since he has no threat I will be safe.

37.Kh2 Nd4

2120: If g4 he will retreat since 38.g4 Nxg4+ 39.hxg4 Qxg4 40.Qg1 Qxg1+ 41.Kxg1 Ne2+ picks up the Bishop but leads to a favorable endgame for White.

38.g4 Qe6

2120: What do I do about ...Ne2 when ...Nxg4+ is really strong? It's time I went for his King!

JS: A panic reaction. I would have been happier to see 39.Ra2 intending 40.Be3 and 41.Bxd4. Then 39...Ne2 would be met by 40.Rxe2, sacrificing the Exchange back.

39.Bg5?? Kxg5 40.h4+ Kxh4 41.Rxg7 Nxg4+ 42.Kg1 Qh6 43.Rg8 Qf4 0-1

White lost this battle because he did not work hard enough to make his Bishop active and then, once he closed the center (and as a result lost the minor piece duel), he did not take proper precautions on the kingside.

PART EIGHT

How To Play The Opening

When we first learn how to play, we are forced to learn the basics of opening strategy: develop our forces, castle so that our King can be safe, and then attempt to control the center with our pieces and pawns. Soon after, we learn that the same piece shouldn't be moved twice in the opening; this makes us feel that we understand everything there is to know (discounting memorization of variations) about this phase of the game.

This is excellent advice when we are starting out; however, as we progress up the rating ladder we lose more and more games in the opening phase and we begin to suspect that there is something missing in our knowledge. Sadly, we invariably discover that we can't find this mysterious bit of knowledge in any books. We memorize more and more lines in an attempt to shore up our opening I.Q., still lose countless games, and, in a fit of despair, run off to Tibet to seek the mystical light that will eventually lead us to the discovery of the inner game of chess.

What is the *real* purpose of the opening? Is it really correct to mindlessly develop our pieces, only to discover that we often stand badly when everything is out? The answer is repeated again and again in the earlier parts of this book: we are trying to create favorable imbalances (or imbalances that have the potential to eventually become favorable) and develop our pieces and pawns around the differences that we have created at the beginning stages of the game.

For example, after **1.d4 Nf6 2.c4 e6 3.Nc3 Bb4 4.a3 Bxc3+ 5.bxc3**, White accepts doubled pawns for the two Bishops and a space advantage in the center. White will play to increase this edge in territory via f3 and e4, while Black will strive to show that White's weakness on c4 is of greater consequence (via ...b6, ...Ba6, and ...Nb8-c6-a5). It is this battle of ideas that determines where we develop our pieces, where we place each and every pawn, and delineates the fight that will be waged throughout the middlegame.

Another common opening battle that is created in the first few moves comes about from the popular French Defense: **1.e4 e6 2.d4 d5 3.Nd2** So that White can meet the ...Bb4 pin with c2-c3. **3...Nf6 4.e5 Nfd7** White has an obvious space advantage in the center while Black will attempt to place pressure on the d4 and e5 pawns. **5.f4** Greedily claiming even more space. This makes a lot of sense. White gained a certain advantage and he wants to place his pawns on squares that enable him to increase it. **5...c5** Black claims some space of his own on the queenside and simultaneously attacks the White pawn on d4. Mindless developing moves like 5...Nc6 would leave Black without territory or threats after 6.c3. **6.c3** White follows the rule that you must try to make your center as strong as possible so that the opponent will eventually be engulfed in its space-gaining coils. **6...Nc6** And Black devotes a lot of energy into attacking d4. This forces White to make concessions and defend his pawn. **7.Ndf3!** Why would White move an already developed piece a second time? Wouldn't 7.Ngf3, bringing a new piece out, be more logical? No, after 7.Ngf3?! Qb6 (keeping up the pressure on d4) White would have trouble guarding d4; he would be forced to place his Knight (it would have to move again after all!) on the unpleasant b3 square. The correct 7.Ndf3 allows White to support his center with all his pieces. **7...Qb6 8.Ne2** and d4 is well defended.

These two examples have shown us that both sides use the opening to create some difference and then try hard to demonstrate that their difference is more important than the enemy's. This means that the opening is not really about development at all, it is about ideas and their implementation.

The Amateur's Mind

Our first game shows both sides sparring to gain anything that might be of use later in the game. Targets, space, good and bad minor pieces; all these things come into consideration when we start out a serious game of chess.

2100 vs. J.S.
Reti/Orangutang Opening

1.Nf3 d5 2.b4 Nf6 3.Bb2 e6 4.a3 Be7

JS: I made him play these first few moves. White has gained some queenside space and has a powerful Bishop on b2 that eyes the central dark squares. Black has a solid position and some central space but, at the moment, does not have any clear plan or targets to aim at.

2100: I can fianchetto my other Bishop if I want to. I have space on the queenside. I could play for e2-e4 via d3. I must make use of my dark-squared Bishop. Since I like the e2-e4 push, I should fianchetto, castle, and play to advance with that move.

JS: The kingside fianchetto does not make much sense to me since the h1-a8 diagonal will be firmly blocked by the pawn on d5. I would prefer 5.e3 (gaining more control of d4) followed by Be2, 0-0, and c2-c4. This increases White's advantage on the queenside by adding to the territory that he already possesses.

5.g3 0-0 6.Bg2

2100: I don't understand the point of b4 since he can play ....a5 or ...c5. If 6...a5 then both 7.b5 and bxa5 are possible.

JS: Moves like ...a7-a5 and ...c7-c5 could be answered by b4-b5 (gaining more space) if the White Bishop stood on e2 (where it would defend b5). The light-squared Bishop does not participate in queenside operations on g2.

Remember: White gained space there on move two, so he should continue to add to the gains that he has already made. All his pieces should work together in this (or any other) effort.

6...c5

2100: There's no life to this game. If 7.b5 the pawn might be weak since nothing is defending it. I could take. Any pawn sacrifice fails and 7.c3 is extremely ugly. My plan is to utilize the dark-squared Bishop and play on the kingside. Since he is playing on the queenside, I could try to hold with b5 but I don't like it due to ...a6 when the a-file might open and a3 could become weak.

7.bxc5 Bxc5

2100: I could either castle or play d3. Oh, oh! I just noticed that 8.d3 loses to 8...Qb6 with a double attack on f2 and b2. I have to castle.

JS: I mentioned earlier that Black wanted a clear plan and targets. His last two moves have left him with play against White's isolated pawn on a3 and possibilities of creating pressure down the half-open c-file (the c2-pawn might become weak).

8.0-0 Nc6

2100: I have to come up with a plan. My b2 Bishop is undefended and bothers me in many lines. Change of plan! He has too much control of open center squares for me to do a kingside attack. I'll just play for e4 as originally intended.

JS: With 8...Nc6 Black developed and tried to regain some control of his central dark squares on e5 and d4. White's whole plan of e2-e4 is incorrect since that would leave him with a weak c-pawn on a half-open file. Better is a plan involving c2-c4. This would help to crack open the h1-a8 diagonal for the light-squared Bishop and it would get rid of the c-pawn.

9.d3 Qe7

2100: I will continue to develop my pieces and play for e2-e4.

10.Nbd2 Rd8

2100: Does he really want to play d5-d4 himself? I'm probably choosing incorrect plans. I can't tell if I want an open or closed position. I want to play e4 but that doesn't work at the moment due to 11...dxe4 with a nasty pin on the d-file. So I'll play e3 and if 11...d4 then 12.e4.

JS: Usually a player with two fianchettoes wants the position to be as open as possible since that would benefit his heat-seeking Bishops. A closed position would block them and make them both useless.

As stated earlier, White should play 11.c4 when 11...d4 12.Nb3 opens the h1-a8 diagonal and gives White play on the queenside because of the extra space there and the open b-file. If Black answered 11.c4 with 11...dxc4?, then 12.Nxc4 would lead to a beautiful position for White. Both his Bishops enjoy wide open diagonals, his Knights both aim at e5, all his pawns are safe, and he could generate play down the open b- and c-files.

11.e3?

JS: Now a c2-c4 advance would leave the pawn on d3 weak.

11...b6

2100: Playing to fianchetto on b7.

12.Qe2

2100: Still preparing for my central advance.

12...Ba6

2100: He's hampering my intended e2-e4 so I will switch to a

(89)

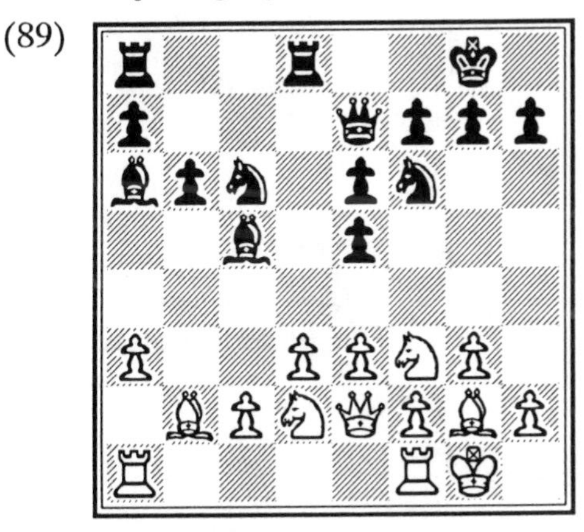

different plan. His c6-Knight gives him good control of the dark squares so I will trade it off.

JS: Notice how Black has slowly placed his pieces on squares that fight for central squares and restrain any central pawn advances by White. At the same time Black has opened a key file (the c-file) and left White with weaknesses on c2 and a3.

White, on the other hand, hasn't done much of anything. He has allowed weaknesses to appear in his position and, aside from randomly developing his pieces, he has not made any effort to create points of attack in the enemy camp or to gain space for himself.

13.Ne5 Nxe5 14.Bxe5 Rac8

2100: He is trying to hit c2. I'm not active enough. My kingside stuff is not happening since f2-f4 is slow. I also have to worry about the a3 pawn. It may be time to push it out of harm's way.

15.a4 Bb4

2100: What's the point?

JS: Black understands that pawns are not the only things that can become weak. The new target is c3, and Black rushes to claim it.

16.Nb3 Bc3

2100: He is getting rid of my strong Bishop.

17.Bxc3 Rxc3 18.a5

2100: I need to try to get rid of everything.

JS: Exchanging off a weak pawn is a good idea, but unfortunately he forgets that his Knight on b3 is not as safe as it appears to be.

18...Bxd3! 19.cxd3 Rxb3

I stopped the game because White is a pawn down for nothing.

Lessons From This Game:

1) If you gain space early you should continue to add to the gains that you have already made. All your pieces should work together in this (or any other) effort. The same can be said for an early minor piece advantage (make all your pieces and pawns help to improve your piece and restrict his), a structural edge (show that his pawns are weaker than yours), or virtually any other imbalance.

2) Don't just develop pieces. You must make gains with every move.

3) Bishops on long diagonals want those diagonals to stay open. Only allow them to close up if you feel that you are getting something good in other areas.

Admittedly, this was a rather one-sided contest. Our next game shows a more balanced battle.

2100 vs. J.S.
English Opening.

The moves that I forced him to play were: **1.c4 c5 2.Nc3 Nc6 3.g3 g6 4.Bg2 Bg7 5.e4 d6 6.Nge2 Nf6 7.0-0 0-0 8.d3 Ne8**

(90)

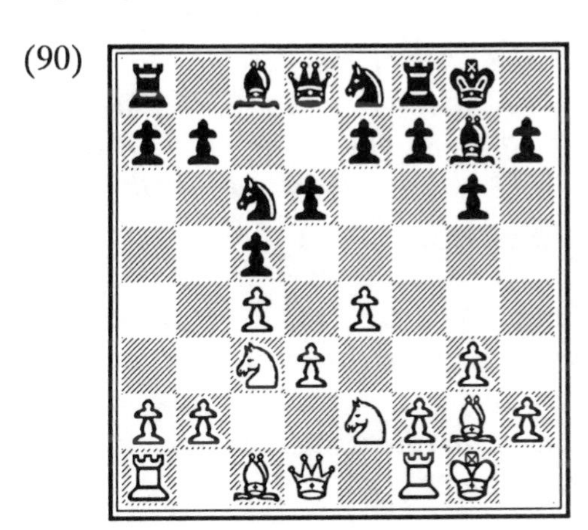

White to play.

2100: He's going to c7 to guard d5, prepare ...b5 and his Knight retreat also allows for a defensive ...f7-f5. Black's

fianchettoed Bishop is annoying. I want to play f4 but the position does not call for the move. The hell with it!

JS: Why doesn't the position call for f2-f4? The move gains more kingside space and prepares for f4-f5 with a dangerous kingside attack.

The Black Knight on e8 is heading for c7, but it may continue on to e6 and d4 if given the chance. White's opening with pawns on c4 and e4 gives the first player plenty of space but it also leaves a hole on d4 which Black would like to make use of.

9.f4 f5

2100: I wanted to provoke that. I knew he would not let me play f5. Now I have many possibilities. If I go Nd5 he will kick it out with ...Nc7. I will just develop and defend the d4 square and perhaps push to d4.

JS: 10.Be3 is a good all-purpose move that eyes his weakened d4 square and connects the Rooks.

10.Be3 Nd4

2100: He doesn't want me to play d4. I have an idea to sacrifice a pawn to get some sort of activity with 11.Nb5 when the b2 pawn goes but I get lots of open lines. I want to get a quick d4 in to take advantage of his lack of development.

JS: I don't like the idea of him bringing his c-pawn to the vulnerable b5 square but I do like the fact that he is trying to open the position and take advantage of his lead in development. He is forcing the play and making Black dance to his tune.

11.Nb5 Nxb5 12.cxb5 Nc7

2100: Didn't fall for 12...Bxb2 13.Qb3+. The b5 pawn is not threatened at the moment so I can do anything I please. My original plan was to play d4.

JS: He had an idea and he is sticking to it. White can easily take over the game if Black is not careful.

13.d4 cxd4 14.Bxd4

2100: Weakening his King.

14...Ne6

2100: Now there's lots of pins coming up. If 15.exf5 Nxd4 and ...Qb6 kills me. I have two moves. Either 15.Bxg7 or 15.Qb3. Since I'll probably take on g7 anyway I should try to win a tempo.

JS: White, due to his edge in space and his extra development, has taken the initiative. However, Black has a majority of pawns in the center and play against the loose pawn on b5.

15.Qb3 Kh8

2100: No choice.

16.Bxg7+ Nxg7

2100: I want to play Kh1 but it's so slow. I'll let him do it for me.

17.Rad1 Qb6+ 18.Kh1 Be6

2100: I have no idea what's going on here. Should I sacrifice the b-pawn? No . . . I'll make him work for it!

JS: The opening stage is over. Black has caught up in development and is now trying to take over the initiative also. This won't be so simple, though. True, Black does have the long-range advantage of a superior pawn structure, but White has potential pressure down the e-file (against the e7-pawn) and his pieces are more active than the Black guys. Note that both sides came out of the opening with certain plusses and are now trying to milk these advantages for all they are worth.

19.Qd3 Rac8

2100: Hitting c4. I could play Rc1 but I will go for b3 which controls some squares but gives him the c-file.

20.b3 Rc5

2100: I'm starting to regret b3. I'm giving you time to double up. I have to continue with my plan.

21.Nd4 Bd7

2100: It may be time for my a4 advance. It gives him a free move but may be the only way to defend b5.

22.a4 Rfc8

2100: I still can't assess this. I have to get some counterplay to challenge his domination of the c-file. I have to get something going on the e-file.

JS: He finally notices his potential down the e-file.

23.Rfe1 e6

2100: Saying no to my counterplay. But now I have a new target.

24.exf5 gxf5

2100: Whose King is weaker? What are my ideas here? His Knight looks silly but it guards lots of squares. I could sacrifice an Exchange or a Rook but maybe I don't need to go for any wild stuff. I'll force him to create holes.

25.Qf3 d5

2100: Cool! It feels great to push him around for a change. Now I can run to e5.

26.Qe3 Qd6

2100: I hate that! He wants an endgame. I want to play Nf3-e5 but that weakens b3!

27.Nf3

2100: I'm going to get mated . . . my King is so weak.

JS: I don't know why he felt that his King was weak; it looks perfectly safe to me. The advantages acquired from the opening are still influencing the moves for both sides. White still has to defend his queenside pawns while Black, due to the doubled White pawns, is virtually a pawn up in the center. White's biggest plus is his control of the juicy dark squares on d4 and e5.

27...b6

2100: Still have no idea. I'll play Ne5 cause it looks nice. Is that a bad reason?

JS: Making a move because it "looks nice" is not a good

reason at all. I prefer keeping the Knight on d4 where it guards b3, blocks the d-pawn, keeps the enemy Rooks out of c2, and eyes e6.

28.Ne5 Kg8

2100: Now I can challenge the file.

29.Rc1 Be8

2100: I will re-maneuver the Knight.

30.Nd3 d4 31.Qd2 Rc3

We stopped the game due to lack of time. The battle is still raging around the imbalances created in the opening.

Lesson From This Game:

1) The advantages you create in the opening often still have influence deep into the middlegame or endgame.

This type of cut and thrust battle becomes more and more common as your rating and the rating of your opponents grow. However, a beginner never looks at these things. Instead, he simply wants to get his stuff out and have some basic idea of what to do once his development is completed.

The game that follows shows some of the typical mistakes that players in the 1100 range and below often make.

900 vs. J.S.
Ruy Lopez, Exchange Variation

1.e4

900: Attacks the middle and the f5 and d5 squares. Also helps develop the Queen and Bishop.

1...e5 2.Nf3

900: Attacks e5, develops, and prepares to move the Bishop and castle.

2...Nc6

900: Protects and develops.

3.Bb5

900: Attacks the Knight and will someday threaten to win the pawn on e5. I remember you telling me that an immediate 4.Bxc6 dxc6 5.Nxe5 fails to 5...Qd4 with a double attack on my Knight and pawn.

3...a6

900: Attacks the Bishop.

JS: You must always ask why your opponent played his move. That way you won't experience any horrible surprises.

4.Bxc6

900: Chops off a piece with no loss of time.

4...dxc6

(91)

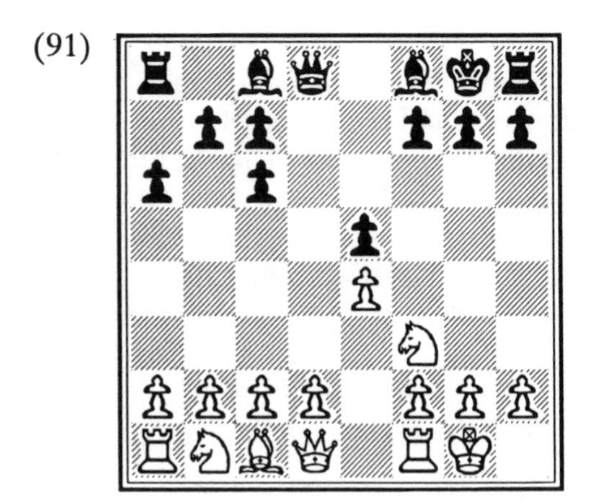

White to play.

900: I want to castle but I am a bit worried about him getting a Bishop to h3 and a Queen to f3. Then I may be mated on g2. I will just develop and see what happens.

JS: While I was happy that he thought about mating patterns of that type, I was quick to point out that you can't live in fear of every shadow that comes your way. Getting the Black Queen to f3 and the Bishop to h3 would only be possible if White lost or advanced his g-pawn and White made other blunders as well. The usefulness of seeing such patterns in advance is that once you are aware of them, you can make a point of not allowing them to happen.

A more advanced player would know that Black has gotten the two Bishops in exchange for a slightly compromised pawn structure. White should play for d2-d4 and exchange the d-pawn for Black's e-pawn. Then White would own a healthy 4 vs. 3 majority of pawns on the kingside.

I didn't go into this stuff too heavily with 900 since I just wanted to concentrate on some easier concepts first. For example, one of the biggest problems a beginner has is making use of his Rooks. He just doesn't know how to get these pieces into play. If he had tried d2-d4 with the idea of opening the d-file for his Rooks, I would have been delighted. Instead I constantly see players of this class play d2-d3 and then wonder how they are ever going to find an active place for the Rooks.

5.Nc3 Bc5

JS: Putting the Bishop on an active square and playing to stop White from opening a file with d2-d4.

6.0-0

900: Since you told me that I don't have to worry about his Queen and Rook coming down on me, I suppose that castling will be okay.

JS: He never even noticed Nxe5, which, however, can be answered by 6...Qg5 or 6...Bxf2+ 7.Kxf2 Qd4+ when Black has taken advantage of the undefended piece on e5.

6...f6 7.d3 Ne7

900: I remember that you once told me that 8.Be3 Bxe3 9.fxe3 would be a good idea. However, I really am attracted to 8.Na4 with an attack on his Bishop.

JS: White finds another typical error. One-move attacks are useless if they don't do something else that's good also. Here White is sticking his Knight on the rim and after Black moves his

Bishop to safety the first player will have to deal with the stupid placement of the poor horse on a4.

Much better was his first thought of 8.Be3 Bxe3 9.fxe3 which brings a pawn to the center (where it controls the useful d4 and f4 squares) and opens the f-file for his Rooks. Compare this with 8.Na4 Be7 which does nothing at all to improve White's position.

8.Na4? Ba7

900: I would like to play d2-d4 but I can't. I will play 9.Qe2 which connects my Rooks and prepares Be3.

JS: A really good idea. White would love to trade off Bishops with Be3 since that develops, gives White more control of d4, and gets rid of Black's Bishop pair.

9.Qe2

We stopped the game since the lesson time had run out.

Lessons From This Game:

1) Don't play mindless one-move attacks which, after he moves his attacked unit to safety (and you must believe that he will see your threat), leaves your attacking piece on a useless square.

2) If you advance your pawns in the center you will be able to open central files for your Rooks. Be attentive to the needs of your Rooks and they will serve you well.

PART NINE

Using The Rooks

Most chess players are aware that Rooks need open files to be effective. However, these files don't just appear out of thin air (well . . . sometimes they are just there waiting for you, but don't grow to count on this type of lucky manifestation), you must go out of your way to create them.

The amateur player often has trouble using his Rooks; they just seem to sit there, trapped behind their own pawns, and often don't play a part in the game at all. The following thoughts should prove worthwhile to those who have trouble with Rooks:

1) Use your pawns to blast open files. This holds true in open and closed positions.

(92)

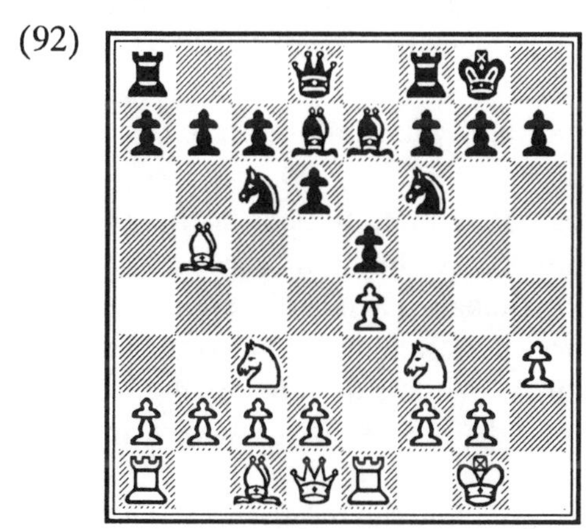

White to play.

In this diagram (#92) many amateurs might play 1.d3, which gives another defender to the e-pawn and frees the dark-squared Bishop. However, what does this do to help your Rooks? Nothing at all! Much better would be **1.d4** followed by Be3, Qd2 and Rad1. Now the White Rooks are showing a hint of activity on the d-file.

(93)

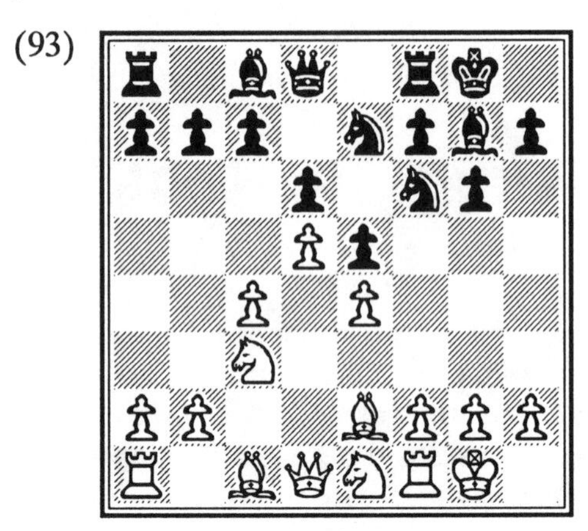

Black to play.

The position in diagram #93 also seems to offer a bleak prospect for the Rooks. Because of this, both sides play to open files and get these towers of uselessness into the game. **1...Nd7! 2.Nd3!** and Black will play **...f7-f5** with a gain in kingside space and possibilities of opening files on the kingside. White will play for **c4-c5** (with b2-b4), which will blast open the c-file.

2) Don't open a file if you think that the opponent will take it away from you.

3) If the creation of an open file has nothing to do with your other positive imbalances, then don't waste your time creating it. In diagram #93, Black's pawns pointed to the kingside so he not only played to open files, but he also played to gain extra territory in that area. White's dreams of c4-c5 also attempt to open files on the side of the board where he enjoys more space.

4) At times you can allow the opponent to dominate an open file, as long as you make sure that no penetration points exist along it.

Black appears to have pressure along the open b-file in

(94)

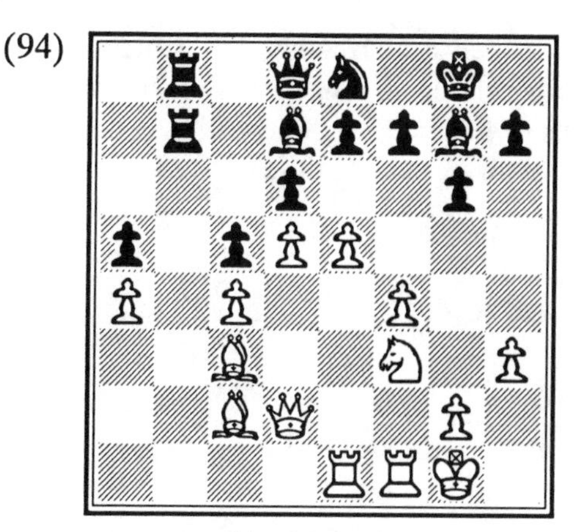

Black to play.

diagram #94, but this is really an illusion because these Rooks can't penetrate into the enemy position. The squares b5, b4, b3, b2, and b1 are all covered and are taboo to the Black Rooks.

The Amateur's Mind

Our first example shows that a file without penetration points is more or less useless.

(95)

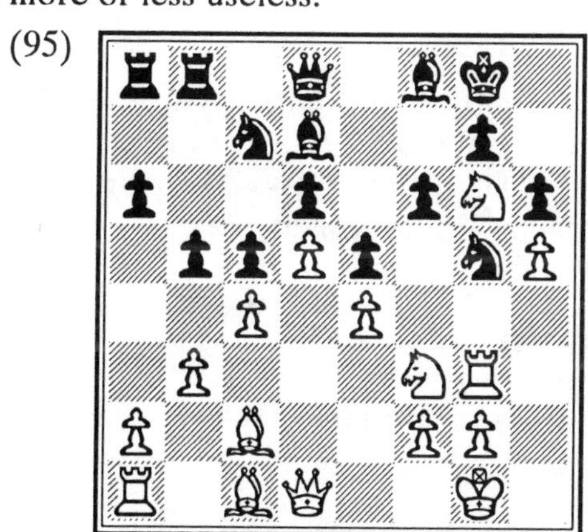

Black to play.
Karpov–Andersson, Stockholm 1969.

The center is closed and Black's superiority on the queenside is just as obvious as White's on the kingside. Hoping to add to the flames of his queenside assault, Andersson played to open as many files there as possible.

1...a5

Intending to blast everything open with ...a4.

2.a4!

An excellent move that stops the a-pawn dead in its tracks. True, Black does gain the open b-file. True, White has weakened the b4 square. However, White feels that he can successfully deal with one open file. He certainly did not want to allow Black two of them!

2...bxc4 3.bxc4 Na6 4.Qe2

Karpov knows that his chances on the kingside are not going away, so he plays to take away all the entry points along the b-file. Once this is done and the enemy Rooks are neutralized, White will be free to play for his own attack in relative safety.

4...Ra7 5.Bd2 Rab7 6.Bc3 Nb4 7.Bd1 Na6 8.Nd2

White's pieces keep Black out of b5, b4, b3, b2, and b1.

8...Nb4 9.Re3 Be8 10.Nf1 Qc8 11.Ng3 Bd7 12.Qd2 Nh7 13.Be2

White goes about another positional plan before he starts an attack. He wants to trade off his light-squared Bishop for its counterpart on d7. Then the f5 and g6 squares will be permanent homes for the White Knights.

13...Kf7 14.Qd1 Be7 15.Nf1 Bd8 16.Nh2 Kg8 17.Bg4 Ng5 18.Bxd7 Qxd7 19.Nf1

Now that the Bishops are gone, White heads for the nice home on f5.

19...f5

Getting rid of the hole before White can use it. This does

not work out very well, but to allow White Ng3-f5 followed by g3 and f2-f4 would also be hopeless.

20.exf5 Qxf5 21.Ng3 Qf7

Black sees that 21...Qc2 22.f4! would give up material, since 22...exf4 23.Re8+ leads to mate.

22.Qe2

With all his basic positional goals taken care of (the nullification of the b-file and the trade of his bad Bishop), Karpov plays to open files of his own. He knows that if his Rooks get in the game the Black position will fall apart.

22...Bf6 23.Rf1

White will play f2-f4, when both his Rooks charge into play.

23...Qd7 24.f4 exf4 25.Rxf4 Bxc3 26.Rxc3 Re8 27.Re3 R7b8 28.Qf2

Threatening 29.Re7! Rxe7 30.Rf8+.

28...Nh7 29.Nf5 Rxe3 30.Qxe3 Nf6 31.Nge7+ Kh8 32.Nxh6 Re8 33.Nf7+ Kh7 34.Re4! Rxe7

Giving up, since he saw that 34...Nxe4 35.Qxe4+ leads to a quick mate.

35.Rxe7 1-0

A beautiful game in which Karpov nullifies the enemy files and uses his own to create threats of a decisive penetration into the hostile position.

I thought that this idea of taking away penetration points along a file is unfamiliar to most amateurs. To test out this view, I tried the same position out on several of my students. Sure enough, none of them knew how to keep Rooks from penetrating along an open file. Here is the most instructive of these contests.

1400 vs. J.S.

(96)

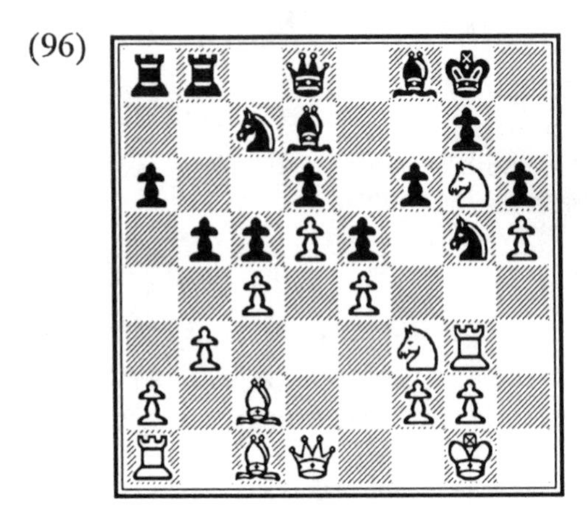

Black to play.

1400: Black's dark-squared Bishop stinks. White has more space in the center and a great Knight on g6. Black has more territory on the queenside and would like to open the b-file. Though it's Black to move, I still like White. Black would like to trade pieces, particularly the g6 Knight.

1...a5

1400: Continues with his queenside space edge. I like 2.a4 because it will kill his pawns, though it does open up the b-file and weaken b4.

2.a4! bxc4 3.bxc4 Na6

1400: Heading for b4. Since the center is closed I will start to get things going on the kingside.

4.Nxg5

JS: Before this White had played just like Karpov! However, now he shows that he feels it is a race on opposite wings (which means that you must proceed with speed). While this shows a good understanding of wing situations, this is simply not true here. White could and should keep the enemy pieces out (via Bd2-c3, which, by the way, also eyes the Black a-pawn) and then take all the time he wants on the opposite side.

4...fxg5

1400: Trying to figure out the best way of getting in. Since the center is locked I would like to use my kingside pawns. An immediate f2-f4 fails but I do want to push f2-f4. The only way to do it is a Rook move followed by g3 and f4. Seems like it's too slow, though. Well, I have to get my Rook out of the way but I don't know where to put it.

JS: Notice how he played 4.Nxg5 without detailed thought. This move was an act of aggression on the kingside that made him feel better but did nothing to open lines on that side of the board. On the contrary, it made it harder for White to play the file-opening f2-f4.

5.Rc3 Be7

1400: He wants to play ...g5-g4 followed by ...Bg5, trading off his bad Bishop. I will stop this with g2-g4, when his dark-squared Bishop remains very bad.

6.g4?

JS: He thought he saw a threat and became so distracted by it that he forgot all about opening lines on the kingside. Instead he stopped the "threat" of ...g5-g4 (which in actuality places the pawn in grave danger after Bd3-e2) and closed up the kingside.

Don't become so entranced by the enemy's ideas that you forget all about your own.

6...Bf6

1400: That makes it hard to push f2-f4. I still want to play for f4 and if he takes exf4 then e5 is possible. So 7.Qe2 is an idea.

JS: Black is making sure that any tactically based e4-e5 advance fails. Once he does that he will have a free hand on the queenside. In a way, this is the reverse of what happened in the Karpov-Andersson game.

7.Qe2 Be8

1400: That was inevitable. I want my Queen to go to h2 so f3 clears the 2nd rank.

8.f3 Bxg6 9.hxg6 Qe8

JS: I wanted to see how he would react to the loss of material. I was hoping he would see lines like 10...Qxg6 11.f4! gxf4 (11...exf4?? 12.e5. Black does best to simply ignore the f-pawn) 12.Bxf4.

10.Qh2?

1400: Eyeing h6 and if he takes on g6 I go to h5 and trade.

JS: What is this stuff about trading? Why would he want to go into an endgame after he has lost a pawn? The threat to the g6-pawn seems to have blown one of his fuses!

10...Qxg6 11.Qh5 Qxh5 12.gxh5 g6 13.hxg6 Kg7

1400: Black has an extra passed pawn but I don't know if that pawn makes such a big difference. My two Bishops help and his Knight is useless since b4 is a nowhere square. I will trade Rooks since all his pawns are on dark squares which makes his Bishop bad. Ideally I would like to trade my bad Bishop for his Knight.

JS: I was very pleased how he continually thought about getting rid of bad Bishops. However, his desire to trade when down material concerned me. Usually it is the person who is up material that wants to trade!

14.Rb1 Rxb1 15.Bxb1 Rb8 16.Bc2 Kxg6 17.Rb3 Rb4

1400: He is threatening 2 pawns. I will trade and if he retakes with either one I can block on b3 with my Bishop.

JS: Still trading away to his doom.

18.Rxb4 cxb4

JS: Now Black has a new passed pawn and a nice square for his Knight on c5.

19.Be3 Bd8

1400: He has 2 passed pawns. I have to improve the position of my King.

20.Kg2 Nb8!

1400: I think the push works now.

JS: Black intended to trade his bad Bishop (or get it outside the pawn chain) by ...Nd7 followed by ...Bb6.

21.c5 dxc5 22.Bxc5 Nd7 23.Be3 Bb6

1400: Trading his bad Bishop for my good one. I don't want his Bishop to go to d4 but what can I do about it?

24.Bd2 Bd4 25.Kg3 Nc5

I stopped the game at this point.

Lessons From This Game:

1) Trading bad Bishops is fine, but don't think about that to the exclusion of everything else.

2) Open files are only valuable if you can effect some sort of penetration on them.

3) If you can stop the opponent's play, you don't have to be in a hurry with your own.

In the diagram that follows we see a position that is far from enticing for Black. Aside from having the inferior pawn structure, he is also about to lose a pawn. Masters know that in Rook endgames it is of the utmost importance to keep one's

(97)

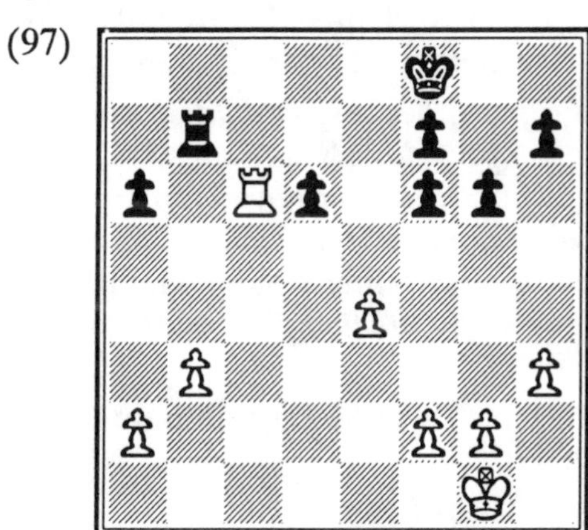

J.S. vs. 1480
Black to play.

Rook active. This rule should be followed even if you have to sacrifice a pawn. However, I suspected that in the amateur ranks this well-known principle was unknown.

How would an amateur defend such a position? I tried it against several students to see if their reactions were uniform or varied from individual to individual.

1480: The position is miserable for Black. I need to give up a pawn and penetrate with my Rook so it gets active. However, 1...Ke7 2.Rxa6 leaves him with two connected passers on the queenside. My Rook could penetrate then and his Rook would be in front of his pawns but that probably doesn't make any difference. The other problem is that if I let him chop on d6 then the f6 pawn would also hang. I would consider the game lost here and I would not have a positive attitude. I would play 1...Ke7 2.Rxa6 Rc7 and penetrate with the Rook. Maybe I could get some play.

1...Ke7?

JS: Poor 1480 didn't enjoy this position at all! Apparently, he was not aware of the old saying, "All Rook endings are drawn." This is actually an old joke saying but there is more truth to it than one would imagine. Why? Because all Rook endings take patience and skill to win. Such qualities are not always present, and a dogged resistance can easily bring rewards.

He gave up the a-pawn because he had already given up the game. When you adopt a loser's attitude you will play loser moves. You must believe that you have a chance. If you don't then your moves will echo this sentiment. His 1...Ke7 gave White two connected passed pawns after 2.Rxa6, and these two pawns will easily win the game for the first player.

We stopped the game since 1480 was too disgusted with the position to continue!

J.S. vs. 1500

1500: I can't save both pawns so I have two choices. One is

to save the d6 pawn and advance the f-pawn and create a passed d-pawn. Second is to try to keep the a-pawn by advancing it and give up the d6 pawn. I can get my Rook behind his pawns and try to prevent him from Queening. The first plan gives him two passers on the queenside so the second is the way to go.

I have 1...a5 or 1...Ra7. 1...a5 allows 2.Ra6. I'm not crazy about 1...Ra7 because it dooms my Rook to passivity, so 1...a5 is better.

JS: I was pretty happy about what he had to say. He wanted to avoid a passive Rook and did not want to give White two connected passed pawns.

1...a5

1500: If 2.Ra6 Rb5.

2.Rxd6 Ke7

1500: Protects the f-pawn, centralizes my King and attacks the Rook.

JS: So far, he has done quite well. This natural move, though, just forces the White Rook to a better square. For the superior 2...a4! see the next game.

3.Ra6 Rb5

Here we stopped the game since Black is a pawn down with a passive position.

(98)

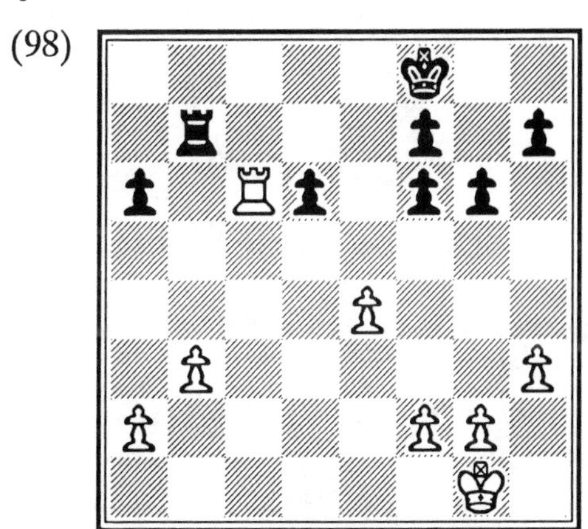

J.S. vs. 2100
Black to play.

2100: Losing the a6 pawn is fatal because connected passed pawns on the queenside is hopeless for me. However, my Rook is not active and ...Ra7 does nothing to help. I have to activate my Rook *and* stop his queenside pawns. I must hold the a-pawn and ...a5 followed by ..Ra7 is the only way to do it. I don't care about my d-pawn but my a-pawn is everything. Unfortunately, my King can't be activated either. So 1...a5 is forced since ...Ra7 is death. After 1...a5 2.Ra6 Rb5 or 2.Rxd6 a4! and if he takes on f6 I liquidate and the 4 vs. 3. should draw.

JS: Excellent! He intends to play this as actively as possible in order to avoid a passive pawn down Rook endgame. I was especially pleased that he noted the drawn four vs. three endgame—whenever you have pawns on only one side of the board you create excellent drawing chances.

1..a5 2.Rxd6 a4!

2100: 2...Ke7 does not really activate my King so I have to liquidate. White has to get his King into play. If 3.bxa4 Rb4 gives counterplay.

JS: He is doing a really excellent job. White's best chance for victory is 3.bxa4 Rb4 4.f3 Rxa4 5.Rd2 when White is the one with the passive Rook. Nevertheless, White could still torture Black by bringing his King over to the queenside and relieving his Rook from guard duty. Whatever the result, Black has done his utmost to make the win hard for White to achieve.

3.Rxf6 axb3 4.axb3 Rxb3 5.h4 h5 6.Kh2 Kg7 7.e5 Rb5 8.f4 Rb4 9.Kh3 Rb3 10.g3 Rb2

Draw agreed. 1/2-1/2.

Lessons From These Games:

1) A game is always easier to draw if there are pawns on only one side of the board.

2) A bad, defeatest attitude will get you only defeat.

3) Two connected passed pawns almost always win in a Rook endgame.

4) In Rook endgames, do everything possible to make sure that your Rook stays active.

PART TEN

The Curse of the Mindless King Hunter

Everyone likes to attack an opponent's King. If it works you get a quick win with a lot of flash. However, it drives me to distraction when a player tries to do this without any regard for the particular position. The amateur must learn that you have to do what the position *calls for*, not what you *want* to do! This means that you may be the finest attacker of all time; however, if the position calls for a queenside attack against a weak pawn, then that is what you should be doing.

Attacks against the enemy King only make sense in the following situations:

1) If the center is locked you should play in the direction that your pawns point. You play where your pawns point because that is where your territory is.

(99)

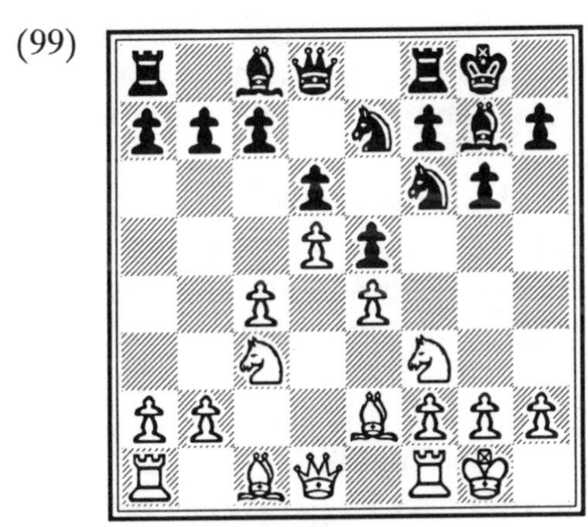

White to play.

Black's pawns point towards the kingside in diagram #99, so he should be playing for a kingside pawn storm by ...Nd7 and ...f7-f5. White's pawns flow towards the queenside so he would like to eventually play b2-b4 and c4-c5, gaining queenside space and opening up the c-file for his Rooks.

2) If the center is locked you should try to attack with pawns. This gives you extra space and allows your Rooks to come into play.

3) It is very important to understand that you play on the wings when the center is closed, but if the center is open the middle is the most important area to concentrate on.

(100)

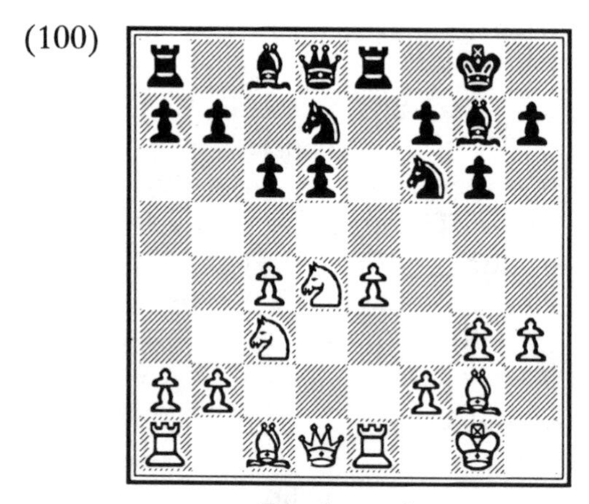

Black to play.

In diagram #100, Black would not even think of a kingside attack since there is too much play in the center. Instead he would concentrate on strengthening his position in the middle by ...a5, ...Nc5, ...a4, and ...Qa5 with piece pressure on the White position.

4) You only play where you have a favorable imbalance or the possibility of creating a favorable imbalance. In other words, if you have nothing positive on the kingside you cannot expect to be successful on that side of the board.

In diagram #101, White is justified to look at the kingside since his main imbalance (the Bishop vs. the Knight) is aiming in that direction. By **1.Qd4 Kg7** (the only move. Any Knight move would have allowed mate on h8) **2.g4!** (threatening g4-

(101) 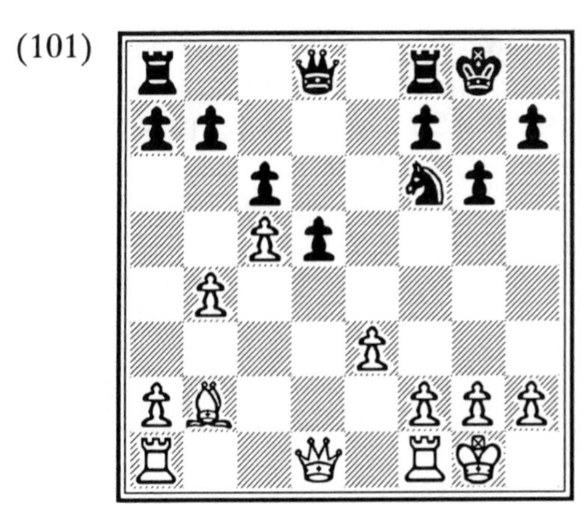

White to play.

g5) 2...h6 (or 2...g5 3.f4 when the Rook on f1 joins in the attack) **3.f4!** Black is overwhelmed.

5) You may also start a King hunt if you have a large lead in development and think you can land a knockout blow before he can recover his balance.

After the moves **1.e4 e5 2.Nf3 f6?** we get the position in the diagram.

(102) 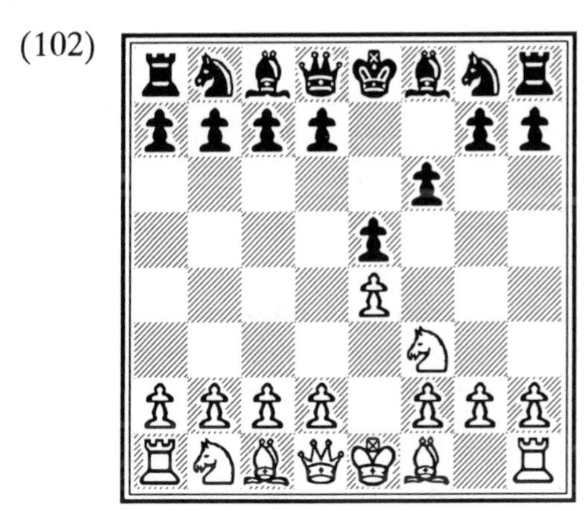

White to play.

White has a lead in development and Black has weakened his King position by playing the horrible ...f7-f6. It is this weakening of the a2-g8 and h5-e8 diagonals that makes White feel that he is justified in trying **3.Nxe5! fxe5 4.Qh5+ Ke7**

(4...g6 5.Qxe5+ picks up the Rook on h8) **5.Qxe5+ Kf7 6.Bc4+** (White's army comes out with gain of time) **6...Kg6 7.Qf5+ Kh6 8.d4+ g5 9.h4** and Black cannot stave off White's threats.

The Amateur's Mind

In the game between amateurs that follows, we see White build up an excellent position on the queenside, only to be tempted by the siren call of a non-existent kingside attack.

Mindes (1061)–Gonzalas (1466), U.S. Amateur West 1993.
Queen's Gambit Declined.

1.d4 d5 2.c4 Nf6?!

A common error at the amateur level. Black is allowing White to trade his inferior c-pawn for the strong central d-pawn. Better is the immediate 2...e6 or 2...c6, when Black can retain a space gaining pawn on d5.

3.Nc3?!

Transposing back into the main lines of the Queen's Gambit Declined. White should have punished Black by 3.cxd5 Nxd5, after which White can always gain a full pawn center by e2-e4.

3...e6 4.a3?!

Fearing the pin by ...Bb4, White throws away a tempo without just cause. You can't let every little possibility by the enemy cause you to panic. If you see something that worries you, look at it closely and make sure that it's worth stopping—you may find that you are often preventing a bad move that the opponent never intended to play! Note that after the calm 4.Bg5 (4.Nf3 is also fine) 4...Bb4 5.e3 White need not fear the possible doubled pawns that come about after 5...Bxc3+ 6.bxc3 since he could always get rid of them by cxd5 followed by c3-c4. In this case Black has actually helped White—his capture on c3 brought the passive b2 pawn to a more dynamic central post.

4...Be7 5.Bg5

Having chased away the ghosts with a2-a3, White gets back to his own plans.

5...c6 6.Nf3 h6 7.Bh4 Nbd7 8.c5

Giving up some time (tempos) for lots of queenside space. More natural is 8.e3 but I will never criticize a move that aggressively fights for something (be it two Bishops, material, development, superior pawn structure, or in this case space)—it shows that his heart is in the right place. An insistence that every move you make creates some sort of gain will get you far in chess.

8...b6 9.b4 b5?

Wasting a move and destroying the tension that 8...b6 created. White's pawn moves (a3 and c5) allowed Black to take a lead in development and he should try to take advantage of this by ripping open the position. He could castle first before initiating a fight, but the immediate 9...e5! (destroying one of the defenders of c5) should turn out pretty well for Black: 10.dxe5 (the solid 10.e3 allows Black to make his own spatial gains in the center after 10...e4) 10...Ne4 11.Bxe7 Qxe7 with threats to win the pawns on e5 and c5.

By ignoring the one advantage he had (lead in development), Black finds himself in an inferior position.

10.e3 a5 11.Bd3 0-0 12.0-0 Re8

White has come out of the opening with a nice game: he has more space on the queenside and has possibilities to expand in the center with e3-e4, thereby stopping Black from doing the same thing with a later ...e6-e5.

In the actual game White was blind to the fact that his fortune was tied to his extra queenside space. Instead he

(103)

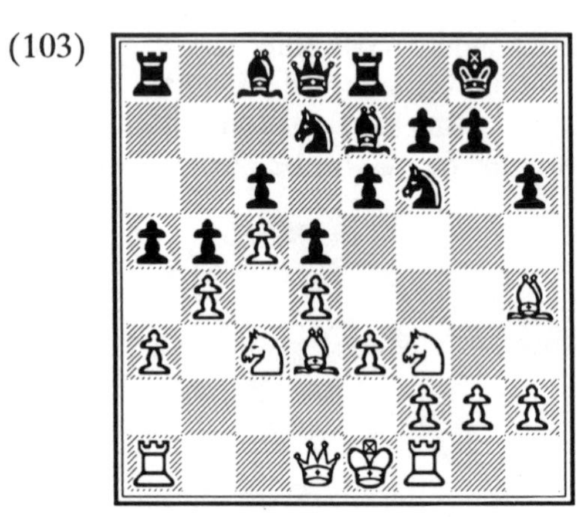

White to play.

decided that a kingside attack was in order. Why? My guess is that he likes to go after Kings and thought that this was as good a time to do it as any. Needless to say, this is not the way to play good chess!

13.Ne2?

White thinks that a Knight on g3 will help him create a kingside attack simply because he has an extra piece over on that side of the board. However, you should lead your pieces to squares where they have a future. Once the poor horse reaches g3 it will be badly posted since it can't go to e4, f5, or h5!

13...Bb7 14.Ng3??

Trapping his own Bishop on h4.

14...axb4 15.axb4 Rxa1 16.Qxa1

—and now Black can win a Bishop with 16...g5. In the end White did indeed hang his Bishop and he eventually lost the game.

Noting White's reluctance to play in the center or on the queenside, I began to wonder if my students would make the same mistakes—even though I had warned them of this type of error in the past. The next two games begin from the position after move twelve.

1600 vs. J.S.

(104)

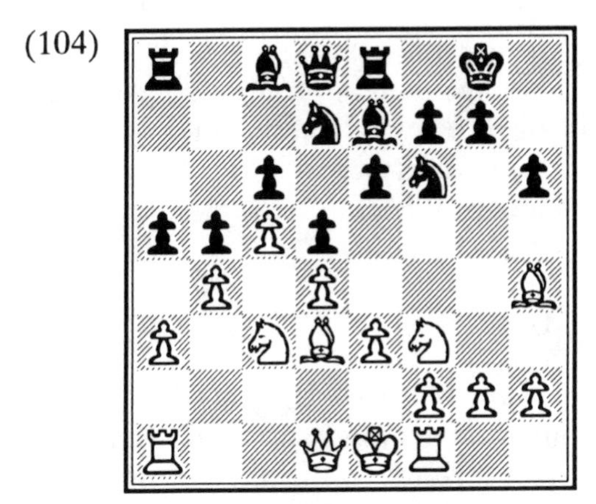

White to play.

1600: The first thing I have to do is find the candidate moves for White. They are 13.Ne5, 13.Bxf6, 13.Qc2, 13.Re1. Those are a few of them. Now I will see if we have even material. Yes, it's all even. Next I will look at King safety—both Kings appear to be safe. What are my weaknesses? White is solid, my dark-squared Bishop controls a good diagonal. On the queenside any trade opens the a-file and no weaknesses are created so I don't have to worry about that. Do I have any combination on the board? I don't see any for White. Any for Black? Nothing. His c6 pawn is weak but I don't see any way to get to it.

So my plan is to kick Black's Knights and make them retreat. Best is to move the Queen from the first rank so 13...axb4 14.axb4 Rxa1 15.Rxa1 gives me the a-file.

13.Qc2

JS: He played a good move but his reasoning was confused—to say the least! Never start by looking at the candidate moves—that's the last thing you do. My student, though, immediately began to list them (I had not seen him for two years, so it seems that he has forgotten what we had discussed in our old sessions). Next he jumped from one thing to another, never noticing that he possessed extra queenside space. Finally he makes the cryptic statement that he is going to kick Black's Knights (how?) and then he plays 13.Qc2.

At the risk of repeating myself, you start by listing all the imbalances. Then you ask which side of the board you (and your opponent!) are going to play on (you will only play where you have a favorable imbalance). You only look at candidate moves when you have assessed these other factors. See my third edition of *How To Reassess Your Chess* (completely rewritten and expanded) for a full explanation of this method of thinking.

13...Nh5 14.Bxe7 Qxe7

1600: I want to mate Black on the kingside. How do I get there? His h5 Knight is awkward so I don't want to chase it back into play. I have a Knight on c3 that's doing nothing so I should re-position it and make it more active. My pawn on e3 keeps his Knight on h5 out. I want to break in the center, though, and occupy d6. To do this I must get counterplay in the center. By playing e3-e4 I get play in the middle but give his Knight access to f4.

JS: My heart sank when he said that he wanted to mate on the kingside! What justification does he have for this, other than desire? Are there targets there? Is my King denuded? Is his whole army posted in that sector?

Interestingly, he then forgot about this idea and found the correct path. His comment about my Knight being offside and his not wanting to drive it back into play is excellent—attacking a piece is useless unless you improve your position by doing so or force his piece to an inferior square. I also loved his newfound idea to break in the center by e3-e4 and, hope of hopes, make use of the d6 square. Unfortunately, this is where his good intentions ran into that oh-so-common fear of ghosts—he didn't want to allow Black to answer e4 with ...Nf4. By concentrating on this unimportant Black possibility (who cares if Black takes two moves to trade Knight for Bishop; wouldn't White be able to make significant gains by then?), he got lured into the same error that we saw in the original example!

15.Ne2?

1600: This keeps him out of f4. My long-range plan is to play a Knight to d6.

JS: Horrible. One idea of playing e3-e4 is that he can answer ...dxe4 with Nxe4 when the dream of using d6 becomes a reality. With the Knight on e2, however, this is no longer possible. Another idea associated with e3-e4 is that he can follow up with a Rook to the e-file when White has considerable pressure in the center.

The immediate 15.e4 was called for, when Black could not counterattack with ...e6-e5 since d5 would fall. The Knight's absence from the center gives Black the time to free himself.

15...e5 16.e4

1600: I will counterattack.

JS: With Black suddenly showing signs of activity, White feels compelled to strike back. However, instead of being the one to dictate the tempo of the game, now White is reacting to Black.

16...Nhf6

JS: The Knight rushes back to the center where it defends d5 and attacks e4.

1600: I must watch out for 17.exd5 e4 with a fork. How do I exchange without allowing this fork?

JS: Decentralizing and time-wasting moves like 15.Ne2 usually lead to the opponent taking the initiative. Remember: you want to be the one who tells the other guy what to do. Passive moves have the opposite effect.

17.Ng3 axb4

JS: Black sees that an undefended White Rook on a1 might lead to problems for his opponent.

18.axb4 Rxa1 19.Rxa1 exd4

1600: Now I'm getting closer to his weakness on c6. Since my e4 pawn is attacked three times and guarded three times I have time to follow my plans. I can play Nf5, Nxd4, or exd5. I must watch out for back-rank mates on e1 after Nxd4 but everything seems safe.

20.Nxd4??

JS: You should always be aware of all your weak points and undefended pieces. In this case White must carefully watch his Rook on a1, his pawn on b4 (when a Black Knight comes to d5), and his pawn on e4. By not taking the opponent's possibilities seriously he allowed himself to be knocked out. Much better was 20.Nf5.

20...Qe5

1600: Pinning me and threatening my d4 Knight. The c6 pawn is poison now and I can't easily chase his Queen from its good square. On 21.Nf5 he has 21...dxe4 so I must defend my Knight.

21.Nge2?? dxe4

—Stopped the game.

Lessons From This Game:

1) Moving a piece away from the center (called a "decentralizing" move) should always be viewed with suspicion.

2) Only go after the enemy King if the position justifies it. A King hunt is *not* something you decide to do because you "feel like it."

3) Undefended pieces often lead to nasty tactical surprises. Make sure your pieces are well guarded.

One of the amateur's greatest weaknesses is his inability to grab the initiative. He wants to attack but he does not realize that the concept of attack must encompass the whole board. You should want to create a target (anywhere is fine) and then force your opponent to react to your threats against it.

In our next game White astutely notices the creation of a weakness and jumps all over it.

1400: Central space is even. There is some action on the queenside and I have more space there due to my pawn on c5. The squares and pawns on c6, d6, and b6 are weak but not easy for White to get to. White is safe on the kingside. White's pawns are pointing to the queenside. I would like to put my Bishop on the h2-b8 diagonal where it hits e5 and d6—it's not

1400 vs. J.S.

(105)

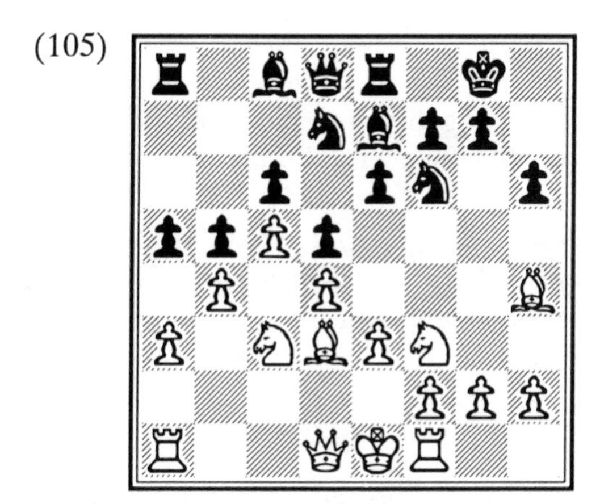

White to play.

doing much where it stands.

Now for a plan. I want to play either in the center or on the queenside. I like Bg3, which aims at both sectors, followed by Ne5.

JS: I'm extremely happy with his appraisal. He didn't even look at the kingside since there were no favorable imbalances in that sector. The only thing he didn't notice was Black's ultimate intention of advancing his pawn to e5. Don't forget to look for an active plan for your opponent as well as yourself!

13.Bg3

1400: I'm a bit better because Black is cramped due to my space gaining pawn on c5.

13...Bf8

JS: Trying to snag his Bishop with 13...Nh5 runs into 14.Ne5! Nxg3? (14...Nxe5 15.Bxe5) 15.Nxc6.

1400: Black is thinking of fianchettoing his King Bishop since it has no future on e7.

14.Ne5

JS: Played without thought. Why he chose this aggressive-looking move (which incorrectly permits the side with less space to trade pieces) over the logical 14.e4 remains a mystery.

14...Nxe5 15.Bxe5 Nd7

1400: Now it's looking bad for me. He will get the two Bishops if I stay on e5. However, if he takes me on e5 I get the d4 square.

JS: When he played 14.Ne5 he lost momentary control of the game. The mild panic that resulted from this is why he immediately began to think that something had gone wrong. Fortunately, he makes a nice recovery.

16.Ne2

JS: Strangely enough, all three of our test subjects have resorted to this ugly move!

16...Nxe5

JS: This and Black's following moves are very weak since they give the White Knight a beautiful central post and force him to improve his position. However, this student always had trouble attacking the enemy King (preferring quiet positional play) and I wanted to give him the opportunity to test his skills in that area.

17.dxe5 Qc7

1400: I must defend my pawn.

18.f4 Be7 19.Nd4

JS: White has built up a significant advantage in territory and also enjoys a great Knight on d4 versus a pathetic Bishop on c8.

19...f6

JS: So far I had made simple one-move threats or done nothing at all. Now I lash out and try to get counterplay in the center. Will he fold at the first sign of pressure or will he rise to the occasion?

1400: Black is trying to open lines for his two Bishops. He is weak on the light squares so I'm going to take advantage of that with Qh5.

20.Qh5!

JS: Bingo! All of a sudden my position takes a turn for the worse. He wants to blow me off the board and it's not clear if I can do anything about it. This switch from more space to an attack on the wing is quite natural—the side with more territory can move his pieces from one side to the other with great speed. Note, however, that White has only decided to go for a kingside attack after Black weakened the light squares around his King. In other words, this decision was not whimsical—he had a clear reason to attack my King!

20...Rf8

1400: I'm looking at how much damage Qg6 does. He can play ...f5 and shut off my Bishop. Since ...f5 makes Qg6 useless, I will bring up more pieces.

21.Rf3

JS: I like the idea of bringing more pieces into the attack. However, 21.Qg6 f5 22.g4! should be winning for White because 23.gxf5 will pick up some wood. Remember that mate is not the only goal of a kingside attack. A safe material advantage would be more than adequate.

21...Qd7

JS: Black's ugly contortions deserve a grim death.

22.Rg3

1400: Threatening Qxh6. I think I've got him!

22...f5

1400: He didn't like the mating possibilities that my Bishop gave me.

23.Qxh6

JS: See what the initiative does? By playing forcefully to take advantage of a weakness on the kingside (note the word "weakness"), a player with a 1400 rating has pushed someone around who is over a thousand points higher!

23...Rf7

JS: He is treating me like a dog! I waited expectantly for him to put me away.

1400: Now I want a way to finish him off. Rg6 aims at e6. I must be careful about breaking this pin, though.

24.Rg6?

JS: With an extra pawn and an attack he begins to get greedy for small gains. Instead of this move, which restricts the mobility of his pieces, he should do two things (if no immediate crush exists): 1) take away all possible counterplay—he is a pawn up and winning, so if he takes all my cheapo chances away he should easily score the point. 2) reorganize and then break through with the remainder of his forces.

Aside from 24.Bxf5! exf5 25.e6 which wins at once, White could play quietly and lock in the victory with 24.Rb1 (defending the b-pawn and stopping any nonsense down the a-file) followed by Qg6 and Rh3. The beauty of this line (if something like 24.Bxf5 did not exist) is that Black would be completely helpless and would likely resign.

Once again: If you have a long-range win (in this case White has a material advantage and an enduring attack) but don't have an immediate knockout, stop all enemy counterplay!

24...axb4

1400: Black is struggling for counterplay on the other side. Should I defend or ignore him and go for the kill? I'm still focusing on the e6 point. I just noticed that my intended 25.Nxe6 runs into 25...Qxe6! 26.Rxe6 gxh6. I will back off and get out of the pin.

25.Qh5

JS: Just giving up. Black has broken through on the queenside and now White must find a way to kill Black on the other wing. The move he played is simply too slow. 25.Bxf5! was still possible.

25...Bxc5

—Stopped the game since lines like 26.Nxe6 Bxe3+ 27.Kf1 Qxe6 28.Rxe6 Bxe6 are good for Black.

Lessons From This Game:

1) Only play where you have some sort of favorable imbalance. Simply wanting to attack on the kingside is not justification for doing so. However, if weaknesses appear there then by all means go after him with gusto!

2) Always try to force your ideas onto your opponent—get him to react to what you are doing. Of course, you must also make sure that what you are doing conforms to the needs of the position.

3) Never allow counterplay when you have a lock on the game.

Our final example in this chapter (some well-known opening moves annotated by a 1500 player) starts with a quiet positional opening. White is supposed to play on the queenside and in the center but somehow his amateur eyes still stare longingly at the Black King.

The first moves were: **1.d4 Nf6 2.c4 e6 3.Nc3 Bb4 4.e3 0-0 5.Bd3 d5 6.Nf3 b6 7.0-0 Bb7 8.a3 Bd6 9.cxd5 exd5 10.b4 a6** and now 1500 had to annotate the moves for both sides:

J.S. vs. 1500

(106)

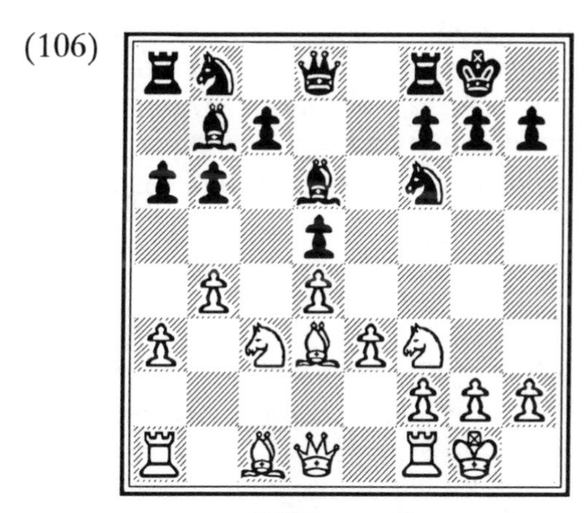

White to play.

1500: White wants to push his pawn on f2 to f4. To do this he must move his Knight to e1.

JS: Here I asked where White must play—which side of the board?

1500: Black's Bishops are aimed at White's kingside. So Black is attacking the King. I still like Ne1 followed by f4, though, with a kingside attack for White.

JS: Amazing! Look how the amateur player always wants to go after the King, no matter what the position calls for! He tells me that Black is attacking the King but he ignores this and says that he wants to do the same via Ne1 and f4 (which weakens e4 and e3 along an open file). Why so stubborn? Black's semi-open e-file is closer to the kingside than White's semi-open c-file. Where is White's space advantage? On the queenside, of course. Since you are supposed to play where your advantages are, this means that White should be setting his sights on the queenside.

11.Qb3

1500: Not the kind of move I would play. This pressures d5 but I don't like it since d5 is well defended . . . what's the point if something is already guarded?

JS: 11.Qb3 has several points. By attacking d5 White ties down two Black pieces (Knight on f6 and Bishop on b7) to its defense. The real purpose, though, is based on the semi-open c-file. White wants to place his Rooks on that file and bring pressure to bear on the Black pawn on c7. However, White sees that the Black Bishop on d6 not only eyes his kingside, but also defends the c7-pawn. White's plan is to trade off this fine Black piece for the bad Bishop on c1 via a4, Ba3, and b4-b5. This would trade off a poor piece for a good one, hurt Black's chances for a successful kingside attack, and leave the c-pawn more vulnerable to an assault by the White Rooks.

11...Qe7

1500: This pressures the center and centralizes a piece.

JS: It does those things but it also eyes b4 and makes a2-a4 and Ba3 more difficult to achieve.

12.Rb1

1500: Protects b4 so he can push a4 and a5.

JS: He does not see the real point to White's play but I did not expect him to; White is using an advanced idea that would probably be overlooked by most people under 2100. The main point of this exercise is to see if 1500 is able to concentrate on a queenside attack. Unfortunately, his wistful glances towards my King made it clear where his heart was.

At this point we ran out of time and stopped the game.

Lessons From This Game:

1) You must be able to play on all three sides of the board, depending on where your favorable imbalances are.

2) A person that does nothing but attacks the enemy King will end up a loser most of the time. Balance and a willingness to do whatever is called for is the key to success.

PART ELEVEN

Which Side of the Board Should You Play On?

The center of the chess board is the area you would like to control the most. Play there with as much energy as you can because the rewards are great for those that succeed in this quest. Why is the center important? Because your pieces can quickly reach any area of the board from the center. Pieces huddled on one wing are more or less committed to play in that area, leaving the other two parts of the board defenseless.

Of course, if the center is blocked by pawns, both armies are forced to seek employment elsewhere. This decision is not a matter of taste. You must use the "pawn pointing technique" (given elsewhere in this book) to tell you where to play.

So how does this tie in with a correct approach to understanding a position? That should be obvious! You can't find a good move if you don't know which side of the board you are supposed to play on. To do this you first take note of all the imbalances for both sides. Once this is done you try to find a plan based on those imbalances—you try to use those favorable aspects of your game as guidelines that will tell you where to seek extra space, where to attack weak enemy pawns, and where to create permanent homes for your pieces.

For example, the center is locked up. Your opponent has a weak, isolated pawn on the queenside and you also have a space advantage in that area. Your opponent is the one with the advantage in space on the kingside and most of his pieces are massed in that area. Where should you play? You may dream of running over to the kingside and trying to clobber his King but that is just an emotional reaction that has little to do with the reality of the board. You must conquer this illogical desire and quietly go after his weak pawn on the queenside. That's your side of the board, that's where you should play.

The Amateur's Mind

During my private chess lessons I constantly harp on certain key themes: Always pay attention to Bishop vs. Knight; Never play without a plan; Before playing a move, always ask yourself, "What wonderful thing does this move do for my position?"; and, of course, I remind them to follow one of the finest general rules in chess: *The best reaction to an attack on the wing is a counterattack in the center.*

When a person first comes to me they either don't know this rule or, if they had heard of it before, they never bothered to follow it. However, after a few sessions of me nagging them they usually begin to develop an awareness of such possibilities.

Of course, if "C", "B" and "A" players are able to use this rule then one would think that Grandmasters would never be victims of it.

The following game shows that this is simply not the case; players of all strengths leave themselves open to its effects. If you want to punish them, all you have to do is pull your arm back and punch them in the center!

A. Alekhine–G. Maroczy, Carlsbad 1923.
Queen's Gambit Declined.

1.d4 Nf6 2.c4 e6 3.Nf3 d5 4.Nc3 Be7 5.Bg5 0-0 6.e3 Ne4

In modern times Black throws in 6...h6 before deciding on 7...Ne4 or 7...b6.

7.Bxe7 Qxe7 8.Qb3 Nxc3 9.Qxc3 c6 10.Bd3 Nd7 11.0-0 f5?!

Creating a big hole on e5. If Black ever brings his Knight to e4 then White would get a superior minor piece by trading it for his Bishop and implanting his Knight on the permanent e5 square.

12.Rac1 g5?

(107)

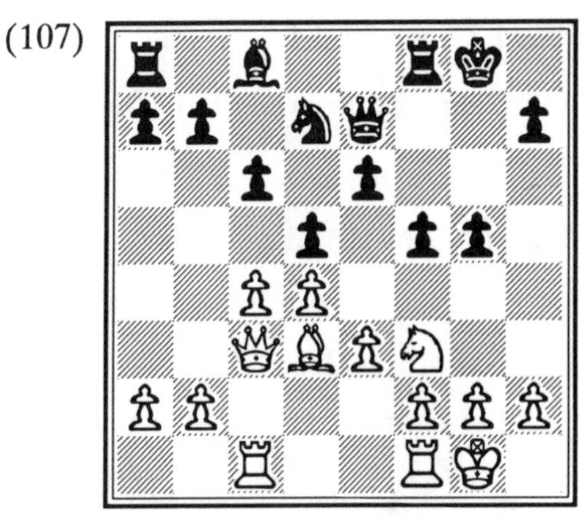

White to play.

Alekhine calls this inexplicable, though the amateur has no problem understanding it at all! Many players would think that Black is starting a strong kingside attack. However, the experienced master knows that this type of wing attack will always fail if the opponent can initiate a counterattack in the middle—in this case White can blow open the center with Nd2, f2-f3, and e3-e4. So why did an experienced Grandmaster like Maroczy make such a mistake? To answer that we would have to see what he drank before the game; demonic possession is another theory.

13.Nd2! Rf7?

Pointless.

14.f3

White continues his preparations to rip open the center.

14...e5 15.cxd5 cxd5 16.e4!

The center gets nuked and Black's open King and lack of development begin to become serious liabilities.

16...fxe4 17.fxe4 Rxf1+ 18.Rxf1 exd4 19.Qc7!

Pinning the Knight and tying up all of Black's pieces. Black is completely lost.

19...Kg7 20.Rf5! dxe4 21.Nxe4 Qb4

Giving up. The obvious 21...h6 would have held out longer.

22.Rxg5+ 1-0

I suspect that Maroczy was not playing his best chess during this game.

Let's go back to the position after 12...g5.

(108)

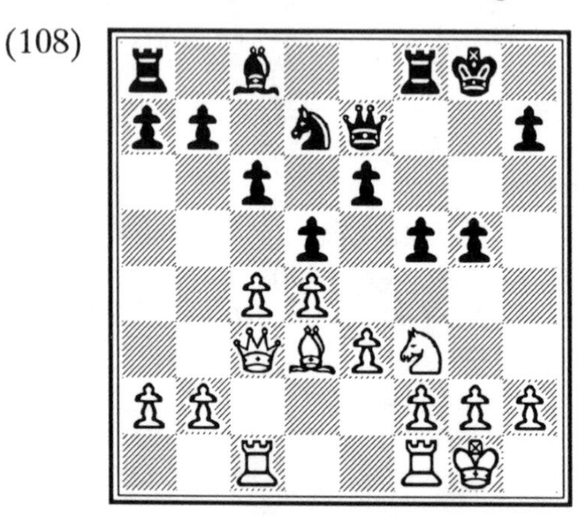

White to play.

In the next few examples I tested my students' ability to recognize when a central counterattack was called for by giving them the White side of the diagrammed position. If they showed a mastery of the necessary concepts they would be rewarded in the usual way: a new car, a date with some super model, a microscopic rendition of Elliott Winslow's signature, etc. However, if they failed to understand what was going on they would have to pay ten times the normal lesson fee (the idea of fines during a lesson has recently been expounded by IM John Grefe).

1000 vs. J.S.

1000: Black has a weak square on e5 which White could use for his Knight. If I could trade off my Bishop for his Knight I could use it but I don't know if that is possible. Black is starting a kingside attack which is justified since the center is locked—there are no open files. He will play ...g4 and chase my Knight to a poor square. I can trade Queens with Qa3 but I'm not sure if that does any good. I can take on d5 when ...cxd5 allows Qc7 with a pin on his Knight. If ...exd5 my Bishop gets more scope. I will play cxd5 and try to get play in the middle.

JS: This guy's rating is only 1000 yet he pointed out some profound things! He noted the possibility of gaining a superior minor piece if his Knight could stay on e5. He also remembered me telling him that a wing attack is only justified if the center is under your control or is closed. He was well aware that he should try to open the center up and so he tried 1.cxd5. I suppose the idea of Nd2 followed by f3 and e4 was too difficult since the Knight move to d2 looks like a retreat and it also goes away from the desired e5 post. Don't be afraid of retreating moves if they help achieve an important goal (in this case blasting open the center with e3-e4).

13.cxd5 exd5

1000: I would love to get his Knight or play e3-e4. Maybe that push would be possible after Rfe1.

JS: This earned a hefty fine. Words like "maybe" should not play a part in one's choice of move—you should <u>know</u> what your moves will lead to! For example, if he had tried 14.b2-b4 with the idea of opening the c-file with b4-b5 I would have been proud of him (it doesn't matter if it's the best plan or not, at least he is following a clear course of action and trying to do something positive by opening a file for his Queen and Rook) since that would have continued his reasoning behind 13.cxd5. Unfortunately, when I refused to open the c-file for him (via 13...cxd5) he simply gave up on the idea.

14.Rfe1 g4

1000: At this point I have to jump into e5.

JS: Now he is just reacting to my moves and is no longer trying to follow any kind of plan. Try to notice when the transition between thinking of your own ideas and reacting to the opponent takes place. In this game he got lazy on move two and never woke up.

15.Ne5 Nxe5 16.dxe5

1000: This is not working out well because I'm blocking my Queen.

JS: A typical post laziness mental process. The first stage is to get depressed and tell himself that he is doing badly.

16...Re8

1000: I'm losing a pawn! I should have played h2-h3 earlier and stopped his ...g4 push.

JS: The next stage is to panic and live in the past (I know because I've done it several hundred times in my career). Now he is thinking about all the things he could/should have done earlier in the game. Notice how even these dreams (h2-h3 to stop my ...g4 push) are defensive in nature.

Here we stopped the game.

Our next game once again starts from the previous diagram.

1700 vs. J.S.

(109)

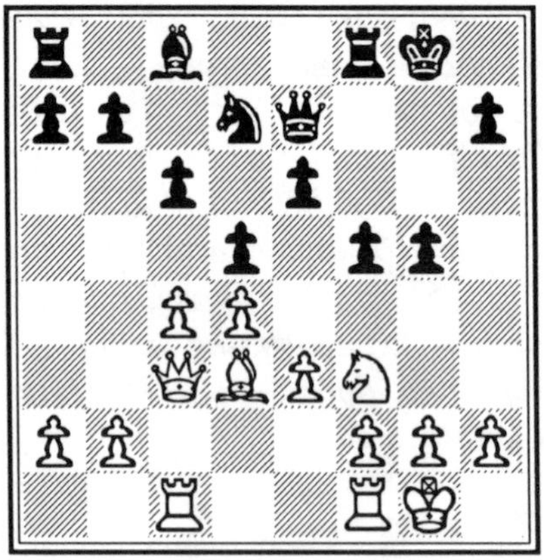

White to play.

1700: All of Black's weaknesses are covered. His King is safe since his Queen and Rook defend. Black has a kingside attack. Material is even. White must defend the e4 square—Black would love to stuff a piece there. Black has more space. Where would both sides like to place their pieces? Well, e4 and e5 are the squares. Black also has an unguarded Queen on e7. If White can push his pawn to e4 followed by Re1 then the Queen on e7 would be bothered. So what is White's best move? I think White is in trouble. Black has space and kingside pressure. Black threatens ...g4 and ...Rf6-h6. What can White do? How do I prevent mate on h2?

JS: Very interesting! He noted that the e4 and e5 squares were important but he failed to note that e5 is a permanent weakness while anything on e4 can be chased away by f2-f3 or even taken by the Bishop. All the positive things that he said about Black's position would be true if the center would stay closed. He mentioned the possibility of playing for e4 (opening the center) but he gave up on it immediately. After the game he told me that it would be too difficult to get e4 in. Listen! Serious chess means you have to solve difficult problems. If it takes you twenty or thirty minutes to find an answer then that is time well spent. If you can't solve the position at least you will have the satisfaction of knowing that you tried as hard as you could. If you are White here and see that White's only hope is to play for e3-e4, don't just give up on the idea. That's like giving up on yourself! <u>Insist</u> on finding a way to make positive things happen.

13.Ne5 Nxe5 14.dxe5

1700: Now his Rook can't go to f6.

JS: I suppose this is kind of clever in a way. I decided not to fine him yet.

14...Bd7 15.f4

1700: Trying to restrict his Bishop and equalize space on the kingside.

15...g4

1700: I will block his Queen's path to h4 via g2-g3.

16.g3?

JS: He is now in a completely defensive mentality. Who cares if my Queen goes to h4? A Queen by itself can't do much damage. He should have played on the queenside by b2-b4 or even c4-c5 (gaining more space). It is important to note that with the g-pawn on g2, Black's ...h7-h5-h4 advance has no sting since ...h4-h3 can be met by g2-g3 while ...g4-g3 is met by h2-h3. Now Black can advance his pawn to h4 and force open the h-file. White's fear led to the worsening of his own position.

16...h5

1700: I still like Black but White stands better now than he did before. White has a much better minor piece but Black still has chances on the kingside. Black wants to pile up on the h-file.

17.Rf2 h4

1700: I will bring my defenders around.

JS: He has been reacting to my possibilities from the very beginning and he is still doing it. No wonder that his position gets worse with every move.

18.Rg2 Rf7

1700: Expected. Now I run my King to safety.

19.Kf2 Rh7 20.Rh1 Kf7

1700: Black is still piling up on the h-file by ...Rah8. Black will exchange on g3 and White must be ready for that but I can't stop him from killing me on the h-file.

The game was stopped.

(110)

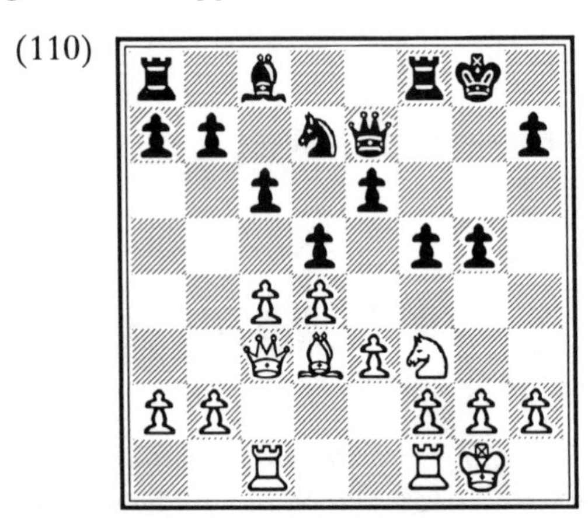

White to play.

Our next example is, like the others, played from the diagrammed position. Here we have two children (a six-year-old girl and an eight-year-old boy) playing as a team against me.

800 and 1100 vs. J.S.

800: Black wants to attack us, it's scary.

1100: I want to open files by cxd5, then I might move my Knight to e5.

13.cxd5 exd5

1100: That's the best recapture. I want to get to his King by Ne5 which might open the center and allow my pieces to get to him.

800: That's a good idea.

JS: I liked that 1100 saw that the Black King was getting a little open. Neither player is reacting to me yet; they are both still trying to create their own ideas.

14.Ne5 Nxe5 15.dxe5 Re8

Both: We have to guard our pawn.

16.f4 g4

1100: I will go Rce1 to attack in the center and bring my pieces over to the kingside.

800: I want to play g3.

JS: They argued for awhile. So far 1100's heart is in the right place—he wants to take control of the game but he does not know how to do it. His dreams of a central advance come too late, and queenside play via b2-b4-b5 was indicated. Unfortunately 800 wants to react to imaginary threats and begins their demise by playing a defensive game.

1100: 17.g3 just moves a pawn and does nothing. My move is better.

800: I want to block his pawn and stop ...Qh4.

1100: You have to concentrate on our plan and not worry about his.

JS: 800 won the argument and got her way because they agreed on 1100's ideas earlier. 1100's last comment was very wise—he deserves praise for it. 800 got punished for her defensive strategy—I took all the change in her pockets.

This and the previous game show us that you must make sure that a threat is real. Don't go out of your way to stop imaginary things.

17.g3 Be6

Both: We are not impressed with this move since your Bishop is blocked and bad.

JS: They are both aware of good and bad Bishops.

18.Rce1

JS: 1100 made this useless move since it was his turn to get his way. Is this getting his Rook into the game? No. Is this creating open files for the Rooks? No. You must create open files for your Rooks, so b2-b4 followed by Rcb1, Rfc1, and b4-b5 was called for.

18...h5

800: I hate it when people do scary moves. He's threatening ...h4.

1100: I want to move Qc2 to defend on the second rank and attack f5.

800: I'm really worried about ...h4 and want to play h4 myself.

JS: Having talked themselves into a state of panic, they both agreed.

19.h4

Both: Oh no! He can take *en passant*.

We ran out of time and stopped the game.

Lessons From These Games:

1) Find a chess teacher who won't fine you for your errors.

2) Don't fear retreating moves if they accomplish some sort of important goal. It is not unmanly to move a piece backwards!

3) Take note of the transition between positive thoughts involving active plans and negative thoughts revolving around reactions and defense.

4) Insist on making good things happen for your position. If it takes you a lot of time to find these ideas then consider this time well spent.

5) Before you take time out to stop a threat, make sure that his move is something you should really be afraid of. If it isn't then go ahead with your own ideas!

6) If someone tries to attack you on the wing, break open the center as quickly as possible.

In our next game we see the creation of a quiet position. Will the amateur demand kingside action or will he look to the other flank also?

1.d4 Nf6 2.c4 g6 3.Nc3 Bg7 4.e4 d6 5.Be2 0-0 6.Bg5 c5 7.d5 e6 8.Qd2 exd5 9.exd5 Re8 10.Nf3 Bg4 11.0-0 Nbd7 are the moves that led to the position in diagram #111.

2100 vs. J.S.
King's Indian Defense, Averbakh Variation

(111)

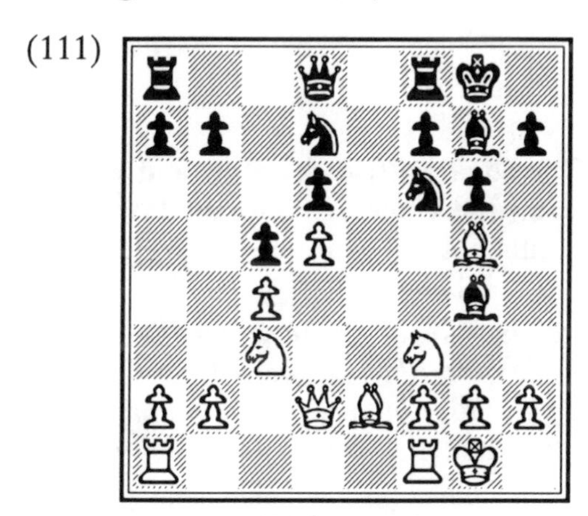

White to play.

2100: There is no way to direct an effective attack on d6.

What is a good strategic plan? Black's light-squared Bishop is not in a good position. It is not doing anything on g4. Black's dark-squared Bishop is strong, though. The Bishop on g5 is not doing anything other than pinning the Knight. One plan is to trade the g4 and e2 Bishops; my e2 Bishop is horrendous. My first plan of action is to create some sort of imbalance. 12.h3 Bxf3 leaves me with the two Bishops. He gets the e5 square but it's something to work with.

JS: He did not mention that White had more central space than Black. I did like his thought that, though the two Bishops is nothing to crow about in this position, at least it gave him something to work with. His willingness to create an imbalance and then try to make use of it in the future shows that 2100 has improved his understanding of the game.

12.h3 Bxf3 13.Bxf3 a6 14.a4

2100: To stop any sacrifices with ...b5 and threatens a5 with potential queenside play based on the extra territory there.

JS: I love it! He is killing counterplay and gaining space.

14...Qe7

2100: What does that do? I want to play Rfe1, when ...Ne5 is met by Be2 and Bf1 with a solid game and a pin along the e-file.

15.Rfe1 Qf8

2100: Yech! One idea is to defend d6 and chase off the g5-Bishop. However, the Queen is entombed on f8 so I don't like the maneuver much. I will continue to play for a queenside space advantage with a5.

JS: Nothing much is going on in the center (except a bunch of trades along the e-file) and Black's King is far too safe to attack. Due to this White plays to gain the upper hand on the queenside and also hopes to make use of his two Bishops in a later endgame.

16.a5 Rxe1+ 17.Rxe1 Re8

2100: Getting rid of the Rooks. What's that do? My imbalance consists of the two Bishops so I must open things up. If I trade Rooks his minor pieces will probably kill me due to the various weak squares. I'll try to get some play with Rb1 and b4.

JS: I don't know what he is talking about when he alludes to the weak squares in White's camp. However, his decision to play Rb1 and b4 is excellent. He has a space edge on the queenside and now he intends to increase it with the line-opening b2-b4.

18.Rb1!

2100: Black has central control. I have two Bishops but they are not doing much at the moment.

18...h6

2100: Since my plan is b2-b4, I want to hit c5 with everything I have. 19.Bf4 does nothing due to ...Ne5.

JS: Another excellent piece of reasoning. By playing Be3 he begins to eye a common target (c5) with several units. Don't just attack a point with one piece. Use everything you have!

19.Be3 Ne5 20.Be2 Nfd7

2100: Now I should go along with my plan by b2-b4. Winning a piece with 21.f4 is tempting, but it fails to 21...Nxc4! 22.Bxc4 Rxe3! 23.Qxe3 Bd4. I will continue on the queenside and at a later time push him back with f2-f4. It is important for me to realize that his Knight on e5 is not permanent—I <u>can</u> chase it away some day.

21.b4

We stopped the game here. White has the advantage because he recognized that his play would come on the queenside and he went for it with great energy.

Lessons From This Game:

1) Some imbalances, like the two Bishops, may not be too useful right away, but could easily become a force later in the game.

2) In closed or semi-closed positions you usually play in the

sector where you own the most space.

White's queenside strategy was very effective in this last game, but most amateurs have a tendency to reject queenside or central play—their eyes are only aimed at the King. This tunnel vision is not acceptable, though; you can't become good at chess unless you can make use of all three sectors of the board.

The position in the diagram was reached after the following moves: **1.d4 d5 2.c4 e6 3.Nc3 Nf6 4.Bg5 Be7 5.e3 0-0 6.Nf3 h6 7.Bh4 b6 8.cxd5 exd5 9.Be2 Bb7 10.Bxf6 Bxf6 11.Rc1 Nd7 12.b4 Re8**

1550 vs. J.S.
Queen's Gambit Declined, Tartakower Variation

(112)

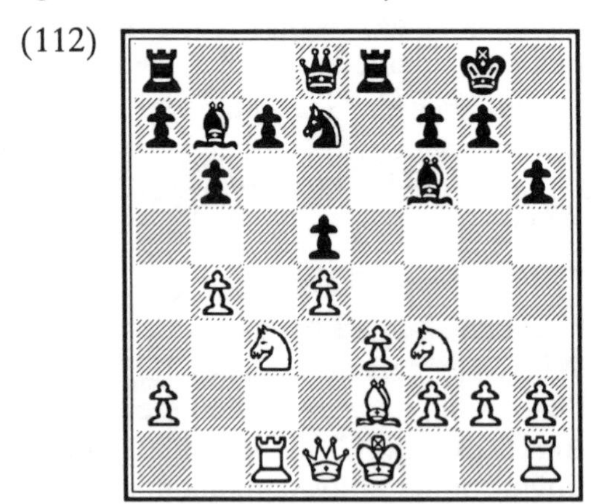

White to play.

1550: His light-squared Bishop is blocked in and his c-pawn is backward. I have good central control of the light squares. I could attack his d-pawn with Qb3 when ...c6 defends though it blocks in his Bishop. I'm not castled yet but my King is in no immediate danger, though it would be useful to get my other Rook into the game. The points of attack are d5 and c7. As much as I'm tempted to attack the d-pawn I think I'll castle and complete my development.

JS: So far, so good. He notices that c7 and d5 are the targets, though he did not mention that b2-b4 gained queenside space and prevented Black's liberating ...c7-c5 move.

13.0-0 a6

1550: This seems silly because it blocks his Bishop. It prepares b5, I guess, but I don't really know what this does. It doesn't really seem to do much of anything for him. Maybe he is trying to play c5 and I could not answer with b5. This must be what he has in mind. This is not such a terrible threat, so I should get back to my own plans. If 14.Qb3 c5 15.Nxd5 is possible. What are my other points of attack? Let's look at the kingside. There's nothing there; his Bishop on f6 is a little suspicious—without a Knight there I have some possibilities. His h7 square looks weak to me. 14.Qd3 eyes both h7 and a6. Let's go back to basics. What are the imbalances? He has two Bishops so I would like to trade a pair of Bishops, but how do I go about it? That's one thing that a6 does, it keeps me off of b5. How about Qc2 and Bd3 and e4? That would liberate his Bishop. How about Bd3 followed by Ne2 & Nf4. Does this do anything? Back to Qb3. How does he defend his pawn? He has ...Nf8 and ...c6. He won't want to stick his Knight back in the corner so 14...c6 15.Bd3. Maybe even Bd1 with the idea of Bc2 and Qd3. Yes! That would threaten a mate. Then Ne2-f4 follows his ..g6 defence with an attack.

JS: He had quite a think! Several important points were mentioned and he even asked about the imbalances. However, he is so caught up in creating immediate threats that he does not think of a slower plan based on a gradual buildup of queenside pressure by Qb3, Rc2 and Rac1 (eyeing c7). He could also pressure the d-pawn by Ne1 followed by Nd3-f4 and Bf3.

What is most interesting is that he knew that the queenside is where he is supposed to play, but he is desperately looking for any excuse to initiate play on the kingside.

14.Qb3 c6

1550: He did what I thought he would do. Is there any drawback to my Bd1 idea? Seems OK.

JS: He was tempted by the prospect of a kingside attack and he can't say no to the siren call. White should continue on the queenside or switch to a central break with Bd3, Rfe1, and e3-e4. This is now effective since Black's light-squared Bishop no longer influences the e4 square.

15.Bd1 Be7

1550: What is this? Oh, he is attacking b4. Is this a threat? No, I can ignore his threat for now and play either Bc2 or Ne2. My point of attack is c6 but only my Rook can attack it unless I can somehow get in Ne5. I could also double so I can afford to take some time. I think I'll go ahead with Ne2 and my attack. This also gives me options of Qd3 followed by Bb3.

JS: All of a sudden he decides that he has plenty of time (which he does) but he still goes ahead with his kingside hopes. The one thing he has done well during the last several moves is to always try and understand the point behind his opponent's move. This is a good habit that will save him in lots of games. If you know what the enemy is up to you will not have to suffer through unpleasant surprises. This doesn't mean that he actually understood what Black was really doing, but he gave it his best shot.

16.Ne2 Bd6

1550: I didn't anticipate that. It stops both Nf4 and Ne5. My Knight can go to g3 but where can it go from there? His Bishops are starting to look menacing. His pawns are potentially weak but at the moment they are all well defended. I'm losing track of my points of attack while I screw around with this mating attack. 17.Qd3 pressures his a-pawn and also threatens Ba4 with an attack on c6. Oops . . . If I play Qd3 my pawn hangs. Perhaps a3 is in order to free my Queen.

JS: Since Black's pawns point to the kingside, Black turns his Bishop's attentions to that side of the board. Since Black has stopped White's plans, poor 1550 starts to panic. To his credit, he defends his pawn and tries to keep everything safe.

17.a3 Qe7

1550: He is trying to play for a5 to free his Rook. He's slowly taking the initiative by finding my points of attack. How do I stop this threat? My Rooks are not linked. What if I go back to my original plan with Qd3. What does that open up for me? After Bc2 and Qd3 he will be forced to play ...g6. Then I can follow with Ng3 and Nh5. Can I just ignore his stuff?

JS: This whole kingside idea is bogus since Black can safely defend h7 with ...g6 or with ...Nf6 or ...Nf8. The student should take note of the White pieces. Are they all working for a central break with e3-e4? No. Are they working together to pressure the queenside? Two of them are, the rest are just sitting around doing nothing.

White went wrong by playing a bit on one side and a bit on the other. You must figure out where you want to play right away and make your whole army devote itself to the plan.

We stopped the game at this point.

Lessons From This Game:

1) Pick a side of the board and stake a claim! Go after it with gusto and don't allow the opponent or your secret desires to distract you.

2) The kingside is not the end-all and be-all of chess. Play in the center or on the queenside is just as effective as a kingside attack.

A direct kingside attacking set-up in an open position can be very dangerous, and the defender should start a central and/or queenside counterattack right away. When facing a kingside attack in an open position, speed is of the essence and you must play with a lot of energy or fall victim to the enemy's

(113)

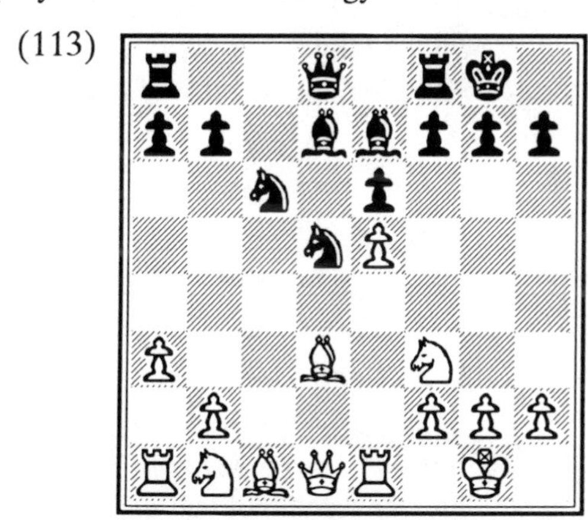

White to play.

attack.

The forced moves were **1.e4 c5 2.Nf3 e6 3.c3 Nf6 4.e5 Nd5 5.d4 cxd4 6.cxd4 d6 7.a3 Nc6 8.Bd3 Be7 9.0-0 0-0 10.Re1 dxe5 11.dxe5 Bd7**, after which the position in diagram #113 was reached.

2100 vs. J.S.
Sicilian Defense.

2100: A plan involving Qe2-e4 looks very strong.

JS: This is a dangerous idea and it fits very well into the placement of the other White forces: both his Bishops aim at the Black kingside and the pawn on e5 stakes a claim to kingside space.

12.Qe2 Na5

2100: Heading for the b3 square. I probably don't mind giving him my dark Bishop for his Knight. Since Nd2 fails to ...Nf4, I can look at letting him into b3 via ...Nb3 when Bxh7+ can be met by ...Kh8 and several of my pieces hang. So I can't rely on cheap tactics. I have to somehow get my Q-side pieces out. I'll stop his threat by a calm Bc2.

13.Bc2?

JS: This poor move shows that White is beginning to react to the Black counterplay—just what the second player had hoped for. White should have made a play for the initiative with 13.Qe4 when 13...g6 14.Bh6 Re8 15.Nbd2 takes care of everything in an economical way.

13...Rc8

2100: Now on b4 he has ...Nc4 but I don't know if this really does anything.

14.b4?

JS: White is still playing on the wrong side of the board. 14.b2-b4 must create new weaknesses on the c-file and forces the Black Knight to a nice square.

14...Nc4

2100: I want to play Nbd2 but that would leave my Bishop on c2 undefended. First I will defend it with tempo.

15.Qd3 g6 16.Bh6

2100: Taking advantage of the newly created dark-square holes.

16...Re8

2100: Black has two nice Knights but his kingside is badly weakened. If I don't play actively I can get mauled on the queenside. I would like to transfer my Queen to the kingside but I'm not sure how to do this. His Knights are strong and I would like to trade one of them. His d5 Knight is too strong so I will get rid of it with 17.Nc3 (Showed him 17...Nb2 which wins a piece so he took it back and placed the Knight on d2).

17.Nbd2 b5

2100: If I take his Knight his passer is dangerous. However, his c5 square is also weakened but I think I will ignore this and play for mate.

JS: He should have followed this "mate or die" philosophy much earlier in the game. If your game is geared for a kingside attack, you must attack or drown in the opponent's counterplay.

18.Ne4 Qc7

2100: How to stop his threats. Both 19...Nxe5 and 19..Nb2! are in the air.

Stopped the game.

Lessons From This Game:

1) If the board calls for a kingside attack then you *must* attack.

2) In an open position you must get your attack up and running as quickly as possible. If you do things too slowly, the opponent's counterplay will take over the initiative.

PART TWELVE

Developing Mental Toughness

It's time to develop an attitude! Since chess is largely a game of psychology, you must believe in yourself if you are going to have any hope of achieving good results; as soon as doubts enter into the equation the moves come more slowly, a tendency towards passivity raises its ugly head, and you find yourself entertaining destructive thoughts concerning the horrible things (often imaginary) your opponent is going to do to you.

To illustrate how strong a part attitude plays let's compare two of my students. Student number one is ten years old and knows very little about the game. He has no positional understanding at all, plays the openings very poorly, and thinks the endgame is an entirely different sport. With a style geared only for mating attacks, one would think he would do poorly but it turns out that he owns a 1900 rating and often beats players hundreds of points higher than himself! His success is made possible by an overwhelming desire to win every game. When he plays a move you know it has some mean intention behind it!

Student number two is fifty years old and possesses the positional understanding of an expert, a solid opening repertoire, and a fair knowledge of the endgame. Superior in almost every respect to student number one, he only has a rating of 1500. The reason? He lacks confidence and is too quick to give up on his plans in the face of imaginary threats.

The following suggestions should prove helpful to anyone who regularly makes mental errors during a chess game:

1) Always expect the opponent to see your threat and make the best reply. This forces you to look for moves that improve your position even if he is aware of your plans.

2) Play to win against anyone and everyone. Even if a draw suffices to give you a high placing in the final round of a tournament, playing to split the point is one of the best ways to lose a game. Play to win and make *him* beg *you* for the draw!

3) If you find a plan that conforms to the demands of the position, follow through with it. Don't allow the opponent to say "boo" and scare you from your proper path.

4) Play with confidence. Never allow yourself to believe that you are playing some sort of perfect chess machine (they don't exist). All human opponents make errors and have lapses. This means that *everyone* is beatable! Play without fear (after all, we are all going to lose lots of games, so there is nothing to be afraid of, is there?) and you will instill fear into your opponents.

5) If you find yourself in a lost position, tighten everything up and hang on like grim death—don't play one last cheap shot and resign. Play the move that you would hate to see if you were in his situation. Extending the game in this manner will make him work hard for the point and, if he gets tired or frustrated, may even lead to a mistake on his part and a success for you.

6) If your opponent is in time pressure, *never* try to move quickly and push him over on the clock. Take your time and concentrate on making the best moves. Moving fast places you in the same situation that he is in and gives you an excellent chance to make a major error.

The Amateur's Mind

The most common mental error in chess is that of supplication: you begin to get worried about your opponent's plans, stop implementing your own ideas and just react to his, and soon find yourself completely on the defensive. We have seen examples of this condition throughout this book. Here is another look at a disease that must be tamed before you can expect good results.

1378 vs. J.S.

1.c4 e5 2.Nc3 Nc6 3.g3 g6 4.Bg2 Bg7 5.d3 d6 6.Nf3 Nf6 7.0-0 0-0

(114)

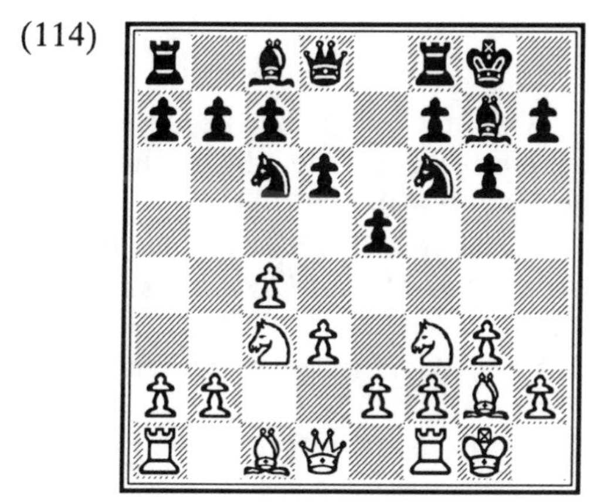

White to play.

1378: White's pawns are pointing towards the queenside, so according to Silman's pawn pointing theory I should be playing on that side of the board. What about Black? His pawns are aiming at my kingside; I don't like that at all! Black will probably play ...Ne8 followed by ...f7-f5 and try to mate me. I can't allow him to do that so I'll stop his plans with Bg5, pinning and immobilizing his Knight.

JS: White's correct plan is 8.Rb1 followed by the space gaining b4-b5. Unfortunately, after only seven moves White demonstrates a losing attitude by concentrating on Black's ideas to the exclusion of his own plans. It is very important to realize that White has already planted the seeds of his own defeat by refusing to take a more aggressive stance. This doesn't mean that you always have to attack; it means that every move you play should do something positive for your position. Keep the follow-

ing rule in mind: After deciding what move you want to play first write it down, look at all possible checks and captures, and ask: "What wonderful things is this move doing for my position?" If your move doesn't stand up to this question then don't play it!

Actually, White's 8.Bg5 is not bad; by getting rid of the Knight on f6 it fights for control of d5. Unfortunately, this is not why White played it. He was thinking about nothing more than stopping the enemy from attacking him—pure defense and nothing else. The best way to get an opponent to stop his aggressive intentions is to worry him with your own plans.

8.Bg5 h6

1378: Taking his Knight would be bad because he would just recapture, move the piece away and advance his pawn to f5. I need to retain this Bishop with a retreat.

JS: Still mesmerized by Black's kingside potential, White accepts a further loss of time. He still has not made one move to start a queenside attack. Best was 8.Bxf6, when the d5 square has been weakened and White is free to proceed with his own plans on the opposite wing. Don't just wish you had play somewhere! The great players insist on getting play—they make it happen.

9.Be3? Be6

1378: He might be getting ready to push his pawn to d5. I can move my f3 Knight and put more pressure on the d5 square.

JS: White is still in defensive mode—he's twitching to Black's tune. 10.Rb1 followed by 11.b4 is indicated. Actually, White would be happy if Black played for ...d6-d5 since that would lead to an open queenside file (the c-file) after cxd5.

10.Nd2? Ng4

1378: He's attacking my Bishop and I can't move it to safety. I suppose I should get things started on the queenside with 11.Rc1, when a later ...d5 allows me to create a semi-open file.

JS: More incorrect thinking. Rather than take matters into his own hands, White plays a move that may be good someday. I'm sorry, but this is not good enough. There is no room in chess for words such as "maybe", "someday", and "somehow"—either a move does something or it doesn't. Don't rely on your opponent to make your moves useful.

11.Rc1? f5

1378: I have to chase his Knight away.

JS: White has given up all hope of finding an active plan or even of thinking ahead. He is now simply reacting from move to move and has completed his slide to mental paralysis.

12.h3?

JS: This horrible move wastes more time and weakens the kingside. An aggressive move like 12.Nd5 (preventing ...f5-f4) would at least force Black to think a little bit.

12...Nxe3 13.fxe3 h5

1378: He threatens ...h5-h4 so I have to stop him.

JS: Poor White is so freaked out that he sees danger in every Black move. Why did Black play his 13th move? Chess is largely a game of targets (weak pawns are the most common type of target, but weakened squares and a vulnerable King may also fall into our category) and I often talk of "target consciousness" in my lessons. Two skills must be honed: 1) The ability to recognize and create targets; 2) The ability to attack them with as much energy as possible. Black's last move, ...h6-h5, was designed to allow the g7 Bishop to start an attack against White's newly weakened e3 pawn.

14.h4

JS: Attacking on different wings is a common part of chess and such a situation often creates a very violent struggle. The winner of these battles is usually the guy who can get the other player's attention off the side of the board where he should be playing. I liken this to grabbing the opponent's head and physically turning it in the direction you want it to face. Once you get him reacting to your threats (playing your game) he will no longer be thinking in terms of progressing with his own ideas and your victory will only be a matter of time.

14...Bh6

1378: Now he's attacking e3. I can only defend with the King and the Rook. If 15.Rf3 e4 16.dxe4 Ne5 is possible, so the King move is forced.

JS: Though 1378 was being trained in my system of thinking (as explained in How To Reassess Your Chess, third edition), he didn't make use of it at all in this game. As you can see from 1378's experience, living from move to move without ever looking at the imbalances or trying to assert mental mastery over the opponent will give you nothing but a miserable defensive chore and a likely loss.

15.Kf2?

JS: Strange—White got so worried about the weakness on e3 that he completely forgot about the danger to his King! 15.Nd5 would have held out a little longer, but White's game was already an unhappy mess.

15...f4

JS: Destroying the King's protection. Why have White's worst fears come true? Picture a car race. You have two ways to avoid defeat. You can either beat your opponent to the finish line or you can stand in front of his car and try to stop it. In this game White could not really stop Black from carrying out his plan of kingside pressure; he could only try to get his queenside play to make an impression first and hope that this would distract Black from his own agenda. Failing to do this, White played into Black's plans, created weaknesses in his own camp, and got run down by an opponent who was bigger and stronger on the kingside due to Black's advantage in space in that area. This is where reading the imbalances comes into play: if you can't list the imbalances you won't know which side of the board to play on.

At this point I stopped the game because the lesson's allotted time was coming to an end.

How was it that 1378, an aggressive player who works hard at the board, played so passively? The answer is that when you get involved in a frame of thought it's hard to extricate yourself from it (ever hear a song and have it play in your head for the rest of the day?); any person who starts thinking in a passive, fearful manner will find his/her attitude getting progressively worse. This disease can only be prevented by recognizing the problem and making a concerted effort to eradicate it.

I recommend the following simple study technique for those players who are affected by this "defensive/reactive" malady. Go through your losses and make a note at the point where you think you gave control to your opponent (note the distinction between the opponent taking control and you giving it away). When you have done this, look at the imbalances and try to find what the correct moves and ideas should have been. If you want to win you must *demand* a constructive continuation from yourself, so don't give up until you find something that satisfies you! What we are trying to do is create an attitude where you will not accept anything but a complete effort from yourself. The creation of proper mental habits will lead to a more satisfying tournament experience.

Another common mental error that amateurs make is the tendency to see threats where none exist. When you react to these imaginary threats you are often wasting time to prevent the opponent from making a bad move! Don't go out of your way to prevent something unless you are sure that it would really be a problem.

In the following example we see an amateur who is afraid of what Black does and also of what Black *might* do!

(115)

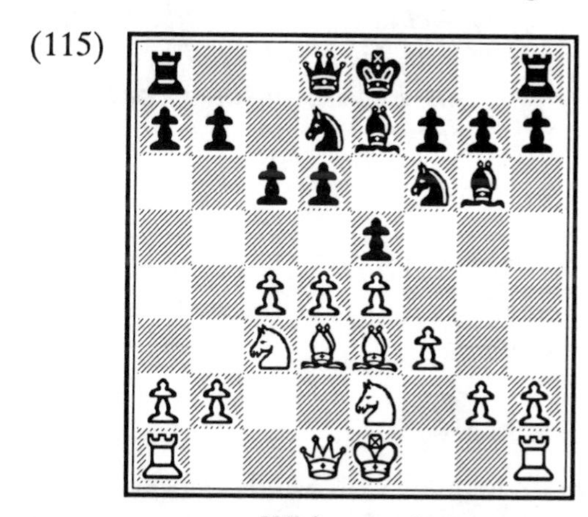

White to play.

1413 vs. J.S.
Old Indian Defense

The position in the diagram was reached after **1.d4 Nf6 2.c4 d6 3.Nc3 Bf5 4.f3 Nbd7 5.e4 Bg6 6.Be3 c6 7.Bd3 e5 8.Nge2 Be7**

1413: White has a space edge over the whole board; even in development. I think it's time to get my King out of the center.

JS: 1413 noted that he owned a space advantage but he did not even try to come up with an active plan. Of course, it is quite possible to devote all your attention to the extra space; make it even greater and the opponent might well be squeezed to death. Unfortunately, White made no real effort here.

9.0-0 0-0

1413: Black would like to trade pieces and relieve his cramp. I will play d5 to gain space in the center and if he takes I get an open c-file.

JS: Not bad, but he is basing his play on Black opening the c-file for him. You can't expect your opponent to tell you what to do.

10.d5 a5

1413: I will play a4 to control b5 and shut his queenside play down.

JS: What queenside play? Playing ...a7-a5 does not mean that you have queenside play. Actually, White could dictate matters on that side of the board with 11.a3 followed by 12.b4 with lots of territory. Instead of this logical, positive continuation, he begins to react to the opponent.

11.a4?

JS: Handing over the b4 and c5 squares for no reason whatsoever. The recommended 11.a3 followed by b4 leaves White in control of both these points.

11...h6

1413: Black wants to play ...Bh7 and ...g7-g5 and get more space on the kinside. I'm looking at the kingside and Ng3, which eyes f5.

12.Ng3 Nc5

1413: He wants to take the d3-Bishop and maybe play ...Na6-b4. I'll shut that down with Bxc5 and leave him with two inactive Bishops.

JS: Why would Black want to capture the bad piece on d3 with his fine c5 Knight? White's idea of playing for a superior minor piece deserves praise, but his reason for doing so was based on fear—fear of a threat (...Nxd3) that Black would never had done!

13.Bxc5 dxc5

1413: I'll continue with my queenside play and go for pressure on b7.

14.Qb3

JS: You only get real pressure on the enemy position if you can attack a point with several of your pieces. Remember that chess is a group effort; all your army should participate. 14.Qb3 is an obvious one-move threat that forces Black to move his Queen to a good square.

14...Qc7

1413: He connected his Rooks and protected b7 and e5. I will prepare for f4 by Nce2.

JS: Now he loses focus and forgets about his reasons for the capture on c5. Originally he wanted to leave Black with bad Bishops (actually, the Bishop on e7 is bad. The guy on g6 is good by definition but is obviously inactive) but now he goes for f3-f4, a move that opens the position and frees the e7-Bishop.

15.Nce2 Nd7

1413: Right now Black has the Bishop pair. His dark-squared Bishop is bad but my Bishop stinks. My g3 Knight is more active than his and I have more central space. It's pretty even over all. I will go ahead with the pawn push.

JS: He said some good things but what did all those factors have to do with him pushing his f-pawn? Nothing at all! Only play moves that highlight your positive imbalances.

16.f4?

1413: Trying to open up my Rooks.

JS: His 16.f4 did open the f-file for his Rooks but it also activated Black's dark-squared Bishop, gave Black play on the e-file, and allowed the Black Knight to take up residence on e5. You tell me who got the better deal.

16...exf4 17.Nxf4 Bd6 18.Nxg6 fxg6 19.Be2

1413: This allows my Queen access to the kingside and defends my Knight.

JS: White now has two connected passed pawns in the center but both of these pawns will be well blocked. Black has made serious gains in the form of nice posts for his pieces while White—after a brief but suicidal bit of activity—is still reacting to his opponent.

19...Bxg3

1413: It's ugly but I'll retake with the pawn.

20.hxg3 Ne5

1413: I don't want to trade Rooks because my Bishop stinks. His Knight would be far superior to my Bishop.

JS: He noticed the minor piece situation but it is now far too late!

21.Bf3 Rf6

1413: He will double up. I'll try the same thing, simply because I don't know what else to do.

JS: Still reacting, of course.

22.Rf2 Raf8 23.Raf1 g5

—and the game was stopped due to lack of time.

To avoid the unfortunate spiral into the abyss (be it on the board or in one's mind) that these amateurs experienced, I give these final recommendations:

1) Don't look at your opponent's rating before the game—this prevents you from freezing up and getting into a defensive "I want to draw" type of mindset. Once you convince yourself that the opponent is a chess god you might as well resign and take up knitting. Treat everyone you play with a touch of contempt! There is nothing a higher rated player hates to see more than an opponent who refuses to be respectful to a superior. A positive 'win at all costs' attitude will add at least 150 rating points to your stats!

2) Always have a plan and never forget that the only plan that matters is yours; the opponent's ideas should be treated as nothing more than minor annoyances—swat them away if they start to sting and then go back to what you were doing.

Now let's explore two other subjects: Giving up and depression. Sometimes things don't go the way we wanted to and we find that defeat appears to be looming. Depressed over this state of affairs, we make a few hopeless moves and accept our fate.

Don't let this happen to you! Fight back! Often we have more play than we supposed but we are trapped in a negative mind set and become blind to these promising possibilities. I remember one game in which I had been suffering for a long time. Finally I could not stand the abuse any more and so I resigned. Looking at me as if I were a vegetable, my opponent (a well-known Grandmaster) said, "What are you doing?"

"I'm giving up. It's lost."

"Lost? I was about to offer a draw. You have an immediate perpetual check!"

When I heard this I felt like a blindfold had been taken from my face. I immediatly saw the draw, ripe and tempting, but now out of my reach since I had wimpishly given up.

1857 vs. 1685

The position in diagram #116 shows this type of situation. My student (1685) felt only despair when he looked at this position, and a glance might tell us that this despair is justified. Black is two pawns down, he is not castled, his Knight is pinned

(116)

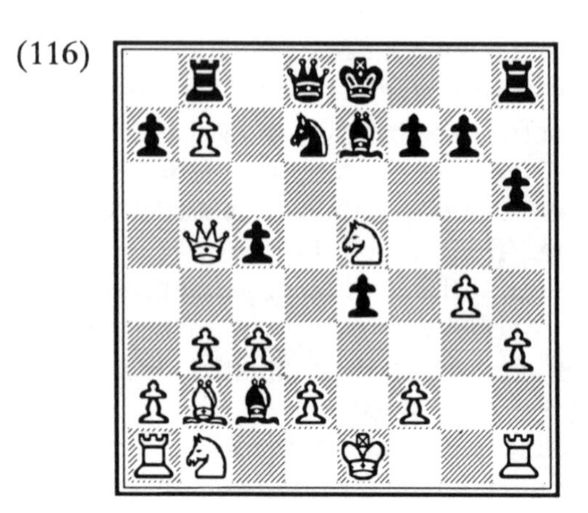

Black to play.

to his King, and Nc6 looms as a powerful threat. In the game Black saw the Queens were going to be traded (not something you normally want when you are down material) but since there was no apparent way out he opted for 1...Qc7?? which at least attacked the Knight and stopped Nc6. However, after 2.Qxd7+ Qxd7 3.Nxd7 Kxd7 4.Na3 followed by 5.0-0-0 White enjoyed good winning chances.

Such a poor attitude smacks of defeatism! Black only focused on the negative qualities of his position but he never bothered to ask what was right about his game. Though material down, he is ahead in development and has chances of an attack based on the weakened light squares on f3 and d3. If the Queens and Knights go off these attacking chances evaporate so you must find a way to retain your army and make use of the advantages you have.

1...Rxb7!!

This stops Nc6 and breaks the pin along the a4-e8 diagonal. It is true that Black loses some more material (not that much, though—just a Rook for Knight and pawn), but he is able to train his sights upon the weakened light squares in White's camp.

2.Qxb7 Nxe5

—and all of a sudden White is facing threats of ...Nf3+ and

...Nd3+. This turns the game around and leaves Black with a very powerful attack. Material doesn't matter—Black had already sacrificed material for the advantages just listed and throwing out some more ballast should not matter. The moral? Don't go along with the opponent's agenda! Don't allow yourself to be herded around like a sacrificial lamb! Look hard for the plusses in your position and insist on making use of them.

So far we have only discussed someone with a negative, defeatist attitude. What about overconfidence; is that a problem? Most definitely! When you fall into the trap of overconfidence you cease to concentrate properly. You *know* you are going to win and as a result you stop looking at the board. This lack of attention makes you miss ways to finish up the game quickly and leaves you open to tricks, traps, and time pressure blunders.

E. Caluag (1900) vs. S. Burtman (2150)
Los Angeles 1993

(117)

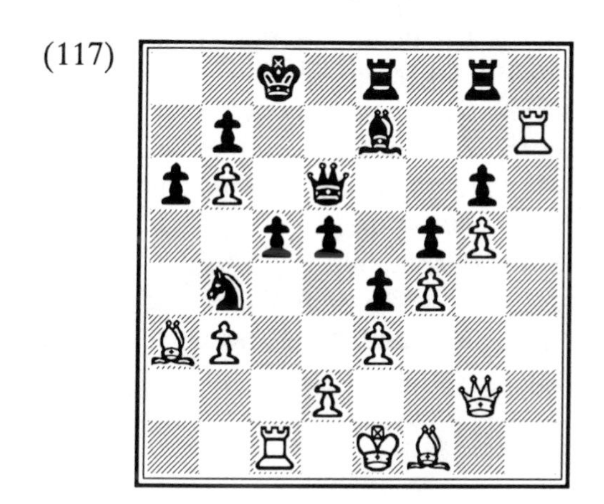

White to play.

Black was the higher rated player and had been in control of the game the whole way. Sharon's advantage in space and the lack of coordination of the enemy pieces had convinced her that the win of material (the b6-pawn) and a quick victory were within reach. A few moves earlier she had been right, but she had fallen asleep during her last few turns and lost all sense of danger. After all, what could the opponent possibly do to her here? The answer proved to be a rude shock.

1.Bxa6!

All of a sudden the White army is working together rather well! A safe advantage for Black has turned into an unpleasant tactical mess.

1...bxa6 2.Qe2 Be7 3.Qxa6+ Kd7 4.Qb5 Ke6 5.d4 Nb4??

After the initial shock, Black once again became confident of her win and once again tunes out the tactical possibilities in the position. Here White—who was playing in a desperate frame of mind—gave in to the will of his opponent and lost after 6.Bxb4?? cxb4, etc. However, White could have stolen a memorable point by 6.dxc5 Qxc5 7.Rxe7+! Qxe7 8.Bxb4 Qd7 9.Qc5 (threatening 10.Qd4) with material equality and a powerful attack.

It's funny, but both players were so stuck in their roles (Expert defeats Class 'A' player) that neither was aware of the fact that Black was on the brink of extinction. I am quite sure that if the roles had been reversed, Sharon would have seen 6.dxc5 followed by 7.Rxe7+ instantly. As Black, however, these lines were completely invisible to her simply because she had lulled herself to sleep—her overconfidence chopped hundreds of points off her strength.

It is very important to remember one thing: the game is not over until the opponent has resigned. Take pride in finishing the enemy off with gusto and <u>never</u> allow counterplay that might turn the battle around.